From Shtetl to Stardom: Jews and Hollywood

The Jewish Role in American Life

An Annual Review of the Casden Institute for the Study of the Jewish Role in American Life

From Shtetl to Stardom: Jews and Hollywood

The Jewish Role in American Life

An Annual Review of the Casden Institute for the Study of the Jewish Role in American Life

Volume 14

Steven J. Ross, *Editor*
Michael Renov and Vincent Brook, *Guest Editors*
Lisa Ansell, *Associate Editor*

Published by the Purdue University Press for the USC Casden Institute for the Study of the Jewish Role in American Life

© 2017
University of Southern California
Casden Institute for the
Study of the Jewish Role in American Life.
All rights reserved.

First printing in paperback, 2024.

Production Editor, Marilyn Lundberg

Cover photo supplied by Thomas Wolf, www.foto.tw.de, as found on Wikimedia Commons. Front cover vector art supplied by aarows/iStock/Thinkstock.

978-1-55753-763-8 (hardcover)
978-1-61249-909-3 (paperback)
978-1-61249-478-4 (epdf)
978-1-61249-479-1 (epub)
978-1-55753-788-1 (KU)

Published by Purdue University Press
West Lafayette, Indiana
www.thepress.purdue.edu
pupress@purdue.edu

Printed in the United States of America.

For subscription information,
call 1-800-247-6553

Contents

FOREWORD vii

EDITORIAL INTRODUCTION ix
Michael Renov and Vincent Brook, Guest Editors

PART 1: HISTORIES

CHAPTER 1 3
Vincent Brook
Still an Empire of Their Own: How Jews
Remain Atop a Reinvented Hollywood

CHAPTER 2 23
Lawrence Baron and Joel Rosenberg, with a Coda by Vincent Brook
The Ben Urwand Controversy: Exploring the Hollywood-Hitler Relationship

PART 2: CASE STUDIES

CHAPTER 3 49
Shaina Hammerman
Dirty Jews: Amy Schumer and Other Vulgar Jewesses

CHAPTER 4 73
Joshua Louis Moss
"The Woman Thing and the Jew Thing": Transsexuality,
Transcomedy, and the Legacy of Subversive Jewishness in *Transparent*

CHAPTER 5 99
Howard A. Rodman
Eastern-European Fatalism in Minnesota:
The Mournful Destinies of *A Serious Man*

CHAPTER 6 109
Jeffrey Shandler
"If Jewish People Wrote All the Songs": The Anti-Folklore of Allan Sherman

PART 3: UP-CLOSE AND PERSONAL

CHAPTER 7 127
David Isaacs
Comedy and Corned Beef: The Genesis of the Sitcom Writing Room

CHAPTER 8 137
Ross Melnick
The Faemmle Business: Laemmle Theaters, Los Angeles, and the
Moviegoing Experience—An Interview with Bob and Greg Laemmle

CHAPTER 9 157
Michael Renov
An Outsider's View of Sixties America: Matthew Weiner
Talks with Michael Renov about the Jews of *Mad Men*

ABOUT THE CONTRIBUTORS 185

ABOUT THE USC CASDEN INSTITUTE 189

Foreword

For all its fame, the history of Jewish Hollywood remains underwritten. Who could have imagined that the strange brew of movies made by Jews and censored by Catholics for a largely Protestant audience would change the world and have such a profound impact on the Jewish people? This issue of the Casden Annual, *From Shtetl to Stardom: Jews and Hollywood*, sheds fascinating new light on the roles—literally and figuratively—Jews and Judaism have played on the big and small screens, behind the scenes, and in running Hollywood.

Despite the fact that most studios during the Golden Age of Hollywood were run by Jews, many actors and actresses—whether by choice or because of studio pressure—hid their Jewish identity well into the twentieth century. During the 1930s and early 1940s, Nazis and fascist Silver Shirts in Los Angeles, and even several US Senators, delighted in writing articles and giving speeches exposing the real names of many of the nation's most famous Jewish film stars: Emmanuel Goldenberg was Edward G. Robinson, Betty Joan Perske was Lauren Bacall, Asa Yoelson was Al Jolson, and Frederich Meshilem Meier Weisenfreund was Paul Muni.

As the volume's Introduction notes, even after World War II and the revelation of the full extent of the Holocaust, many Jews inside and outside Hollywood continued to downplay their Jewishness. But, as several of the volume essays point out, Jews would eventually emerge from the shadows and make their ethnic identity very much part of their screen identity. From Woody Allen to Jerry Seinfeld to Jon Stewart to Amy Schumer, a new generation of performers celebrated what their elders avoided for decades, what Jon Stewart might call their "Jewy Jewsteiness."

Vincent Brook and Michael Renov, the volume's co-editors, have brought together a series of original, informative and provocative looks at the transformation of the film and television industries from their early days to the present. They divide their mosaic of evolving Judaism into three parts: Histories, Case Studies, and Up-Close and Personal. Taken together, these nine essays offer us fresh and exciting new looks at the ways in which Jews have shaped the nature of American entertainment.

Steven J. Ross, *Myron and Marian Casden Director*

Editorial Introduction

by Michael Renov and Vincent Brook, Guest Editors

Jews' outsized contribution to American entertainment precedes their rise to prominence in the Hollywood movie studios. Spurred by their mass migration from Eastern Europe and Russia in the late 1800s, just as mass culture was emerging, immigrant and second-generation Jewish business owners, producers, and artists had already established themselves at the forefront of live theater and popular music by the time motion pictures caught on in the first decade of the twentieth century. Not until the paradigm shift in film production from the East Coast to Los Angeles in the 1910s, however, and cinema's ascendance from lowbrow fare to cultural phenomenon and big business, did Jewish "control" of Hollywood become an open secret.

Once the "Jewish question" was broached, the movie moguls (the term "moguls" itself of antisemitic origin) reacted defensively, diverting attention from their newly mounted catbird seat while also making concessions to it. The avoidance included altering stereotypical Jewish stars' names and appearances and eschewing, especially with the spike of American antisemitism in the 1930s, Jewish characters and themes; the concessions included appointing non-Jews to head in-house public relations and content-policing agencies.[1] The insecurity and defensiveness extended to organized Jewry, which from painful past experience, reasoned that flaunting Hollywood's Jewishness, behind or on the screen, much less griping about antisemitic attitudes towards the industry or Jews in general, would only make matters worse. Even with their overall increased entry into the US mainstream after World War II and the lessons of the Holocaust, Jews inside and outside Hollywood continued to downplay Jewish industry influence, which now extended to the new medium of television as well.

In the wake of the identity politics movements of the 1960s and '70s, which Jews joined with renewed vigor after Israel's victory in the 1967 Six-Day War, Jewish intellectuals began to tip-toe toward open acknowledgment of their co-religionists' seminal place in popular culture. A few journal articles in the mid-1970s, by Howard Suber on Jewish characters in television, and by Tom Tugend on the early Hollywood moguls, were the first short-form pieces to crack the code of silence. They were followed a decade later by the first full-length books on the subject: Sarah Blacher Cohen's anthology *From Hester Street to Hollywood: The Jewish-American Stage and Screen* (1983), Patricia Erens' *The Jew in American Cinema* (1984), and Lester D. Friedman's *The Jew in American Film* (1987). All these early "exposés," however (except for Tugend's four-page article), focused on Jewish representation *on screen*, leaving fuzzy the elephant in the room: the astonishing number of Jews (given their mere two percent of the US population) *behind the scenes*, creatively and most crucially, in ownership and executive positions. With the publication in 1989 of Neal Gabler's *An Empire of Their Own: How the Jews Invented Hollywood*, the genie was finally out of the bottle—a refreshing end to the taboo for many Jews, renewed cause for alarm for others.

After all, here was a Jew unabashedly admitting, and documenting, what the anti-Semites had claimed all along. Moreover, in ascribing "imperial" designs to Hollywood's Founding Fathers and crediting them with peddling an American Dream of their own concoction, Gabler seemed to be playing into the Jew-haters' conspiracy-mongering hands. What he was actually doing, of course, was beating the bigots at their own game. Following the lead of identity political groups that had begun strategically turning pejorative labels into badges of honor—gay, black, even eventually Heeb—Gabler was owning, and proudly proclaiming, the profound imprint Jews, via Hollywood, had made on American society.

Dissension in Jewish ranks remained, however. In 1993, David Desser and Lester Friedman followed Gabler's opus with an exploration of contemporary American Jewish directors. In a survey of over 170 presumed Jewish filmmakers (a remarkable number in itself), several of those contacted deemed the project "divisive because it separated Jews from the rest of American society."[2] One accused the authors of providing "great ammunition for anti-Semites," and a particularly annoyed respondent "expressed hope that he would not have to look forward to studies of American-Jewish physicists, harpists, pizza-makers, bookies, and pederasts" (34, 35).

The grousing of Hollywood insiders notwithstanding, the tide had clearly turned in Gabler's favor in the public discourse and cultural practice. Steven

Carr picked up where *An Empire of Their Own* left off in his 1994 doctoral dissertation (published in book form in 2001): *The Hollywood Question: America and the Belief in Jewish Control of Motion Pictures before 1941.* Jewish Forward editor J. J. Goldberg, in *Jewish Power: Inside the American Jewish Establishment* (1996), upped the ante by confronting the corollary question of Jewish influence in US society as a whole. By the new millennium, Jews were "coming out" all over the place, and with barely a fuss. New waves of Jewish-inflected film, literature, and art were heralded; a major klezmer revival was underway; "bagels had become as commonplace as pizza, kabbalah as cool as crystals"; and over forty episodic TV programs with explicitly identified Jewish main characters hit the airwaves in the 1990s (compared to less than ten in the previous forty years), including the most popular and defining series of the decade, *Seinfeld* (1989–98) (Brook, *You Should See Yourself* 1).

Despite or because of the "New Jew" phenomenon, all was still not well in the New Hollywood (or New Babylon, depending on your viewpoint). With the subsidence of the old "Hollywood question," a new one, now posed by Jews themselves, arose. The double-edged sword of assimilation, exacerbated by intermarriage, had long troubled traditionally minded Jews. As rapidly rising national intermarriage rates approached the fifty percent "threshold of no return" in 2000, according to the National Jewish Population Survey, some hard-liners went so far as to deem the ubiquitous depiction of interfaith romance and marriage in US films and TV shows as not only a reflection of, but contributor to, a "Silent Holocaust" (Brook, *Something Ain't Kosher Here* 126).[3]

For Jews of all stripes, while it was certainly welcome to "see yourself" more frequently and multi-dimensionally portrayed on screens large and small, the "tenuous, largely inferred, and increasingly 'virtual' nature of Jewish" representation also could be viewed as both reflecting and reinforcing a similar trend in American society (Brook, *Something Ain't Kosher Here* 1). With little sign of a reversal of the trend as the 2000s progressed, the dilemma became: now that Jews had been fully absorbed into the American mainstream, now that a Jewish presidential candidate had less to worry about than a Mormon, "now that we're like everybody else," as Jonathan and Judith Pearl asked already in 1999, "who are we?" (Pearl and Pearl 231).

This neo-Hollywood question, among others, is what *From Shtetl to Stardom* explores. And while the exploration is not unique—as the various Works Cited sections attest—the book's methodology arguably is. Rather than take a primarily historical, theoretical, biographical, or insider approach, as have most other studies of Jews and entertainment, ours combines these differing approaches in overlapping and innovative ways.

The historical torch is carried by two essays: Vincent Brook's "Still an Empire of Their Own: How Jews Remain atop a Reinvented Hollywood," and Lawrence Baron and Joel Rosenberg's "The Ben Urwand Controversy: Exploring the Hollywood-Hitler relationship." Brook's piece, as the title's nod to Gabler's ur-text indicates, examines the historical legacy and contemporary nature of power relations in Hollywood. Taking into account radical transformations in the studio system, the burgeoning influence of talent agencies, and the recent corporate ascendance of a handful of multi-media giants, the essay frames its discussion around recurring external charges and insider jokes about the fact and fallacy of Jewish industry control.

The Baron/Rosenberg chapter intersects with history on multiple levels. The two essays reproduce, in manuscript form, the authors' oral panel presentations at the Western Jewish Studies Conference in Tucson, Arizona, in spring 2014. The panel was structured as a debate on a highly controversial book by Ben Urwand, published the year before, which took a stridently revisionist view of the Hollywood moguls' relations with Nazi Germany. Another, more sober study of the subject by Thomas Doherty, fortuitously published a few months before Urwand's, offered a lively foil for the controversy, and the panel discussion. A coda by Brook, on information uncovered by scholars Laura Rosenzweig and Steven Ross subsequent to Urwand's and Doherty's publications, adds a twist both to the past events and to the brouhaha ignited by Urwand's book.

Four essays offer case studies of noted Jewish performers, films, and TV shows. Taking the most theoretical approach of the book's essays, Joshua Louis Moss's "'The Woman Thing and the Jew Thing': Transgression, Transcomedy, and Subversive Jewishness in *Transparent*" applies diaspora theory derived from Franz Fanon and Hamid Naficy and what Moss terms "transcomedy" to probe how Jewishness functions in Jill Soloway's groundbreaking dramedy on a father's late-life coming out as a transgender woman to his three adult children. Soloway herself has provided support for Moss's approach by having stressed the centrality of Jewishness to the show and emphasizing the critical importance of the Jewish diaspora to the show's explorations of gender fluidity.

Shaina Hammerman's "Dirty Jews: Amy Schumer and Other Vulgar Jewesses" highlights Amy Schumer, Lena Dunham, Sarah Silverman and other current Jewish female comedians to argue "that performing Jewishness in contemporary America requires a kind of transgendering." Viewed in the

Introduction

context of an earlier cohort of so-called "unkosher comediennes" (Sophie Tucker, Belle Barthes, Totie Fields, Joan Rivers, and Bette Midler, among others), the postfeminist Jewish comics, Hammerman argues, continue to struggle with "a sexist system that compares them only to other women and continues to assert that women cannot possibly be as funny as men (or in the same way)."

Jeffrey Shandler's "'If Jewish People Wrote All the Songs': The Anti-Folklore of Allan Sherman" similarly blends history and theory in resurrecting and re-examining the work of one-time television writer Allan Sherman, a song-writer and recording artist in the 1960s, highly popular for a series of folk-song parodies, most famously "Hello Muddah, Hello Faddah." Shandler posits that beyond satirizing hit folk songs of the day and by association the folk song craze writ large, Sherman's spoofs and performance mode (his live-recorded albums benefit from intimate audience response and parody other singers' audience interactions as well as their songs) "are revealing artifacts of middle-class American Jews at the time" while also raising "provocative questions about what might constitute 'original' American Jewish folkways."

Howard Rodman's "Eastern European Fatalism in Minnesota: The Mournful Destinies of *A Serious Man*" reviews the Coen brothers' most autobiographical and Jewish 2009 film as a partial corrective to what Rodman calls Jews' overall relegation to a "sub-staple" in American cinema. Exceptions duly noted, Rodman decries the generally tenuous or stereotypical nature of Jewish media representation. He applauds *A Serious Man* for purveying a multi-dimensional Jewishness and "a Judaism older, less kind, . . . and far more compelling" than has been the rule among Jewish writers and directors, whose characters, when they're recognizably Jewish at all, tend to vacillate between "the secular dyad of schlubby guy/greedy gal."

The book's final portion takes a more personal tack, offering three "hands-on," insider angles on Jews and Hollywood. David Isaacs' "Comedy and Corned Beef: The Genesis of the Sitcom Writing Room" is part memoir in its guided tour down the memory lane of Isaacs' forty years as one of the "Shtetl Jews" who pioneered television comedy. Beyond his blow-by-blow description of the wild and zany and, yes, often un-PC tenor of the Sitcom Room—"Civility and political correctness are checked out at the door"—he also offers pearls of comedic wisdom about today's more diverse (read: less exclusively Jewish) makeup of comedy writers who continue to foster the "irreverence and a touch of anarchy" of the best comedy writing.

Ross Melnick's interview with Laemmle Theatre owners Bob and Greg Laemmle, "The Faemmle Business: Laemmle Theatres, Los Angeles, and the

Movie-Going Experience," places the current owners of one of LA's last remaining art house/indie theater complexes in the context of their theaters' founding father, Max Laemmle, and his partner-brother Kurt. German Jewish immigrants lured to the US by their cousin, legendary Universal Studios' founder Carl Laemmle, Max and Kurt started the business in the 1930s and pioneered the city's art house scene in the 1950s. Bob and Greg have carried on the Laemmle legacy, maintaining the theaters' family-run business structure and dedication to foreign and independent cinema.

Michael Renov's dialogue with Matthew Weiner, "Reinventing the 1960s: The Jews of *Mad Men*," explores the ways in which Weiner's award-winning television series recreated the style, psyche, and ethos of the 1960s while more subtly framing the possibilities and limitations of Jews within the hierarchical world of the New York ad agency. Given the spotlight on the series' high-flying, ever-so-gentile central characters, most notably Don Draper, Weiner's claims for the significance of the Jewish outsider—notably Rachel Menken, the attractive female client, but also the psychologist consultant, the insult comic, and the second generation Holocaust survivor copywriter—may surprise. *Mad Men* demonstrates that television writing, like its more pedigreed literary forebears, is capable of unfolding sagas, developing complex characters, and narrating nuanced histories that reward second viewings—viewings from which a (Jewish) subtext may emerge as central.

The eclectic mix of topics and approaches found in *From Shtetl to Stardom: Jews and Hollywood* more than upholds the old saw, "Two Jews, three opinions." By blazing new trails and opening up avenues of further exploration, the book also offers a uniquely multifaceted, multi-mediated, and up-to-the-minute account of the remarkable role Jews have played, over the centuries and ongoing, in American popular culture.

Notes

1. Presbyterian deacon and Postmaster General Will Hays was picked in 1922 to head the Motion Picture Producers and Distributors of America (MPPDA), now the Motion Picture Association of America (MPAA); and a Catholic insider, Joe Breen, was chosen in 1934 to direct the Production Code Administration (PCA), an arm of the MPPDA. The PCA, disbanded in 1966 and replaced in 1968 by the Classification and Ratings Administration (CARA), was never headed by a Jew. The MPAA would not see a Jew at the top until Congressman Dan Glickman replaced Jack Valenti in 2004, though Glickman's replacement in 2011 was another non-Jew, former senator Christopher Dodd.
2. Desser and Friedman's sole reliance on Jewish-sounding last names in their survey's selection process naturally led to a mismatch in a few of the one hundred or so directors who responded out of the 170-plus who were contacted (34). The overall number was likely balanced, however, by Jewish filmmakers with non-Jewish-sounding surnames who were left out of the selection process.
3. By 2013, according to the Pew Research Center, the Jewish intermarriage rate of fifty-eight percent had left the "no return" threshold far behind.

Works Cited

"A Portrait of Jewish Americans." *Pew Research Center: Religion and Public Life*, 1 Oct. 2013, www.pewforum.org/2013/10/01/jewish-american-beliefs-attitudes-culture-survey/. Accessed 6 Sept. 2016.

Brook, Vincent. "Introduction." *You Should See Yourself: Jewish Identity in Postmodern American Culture*. Edited by Vincent Brook, Rutgers Univ., 2006, pp. 1–15.

———. *Something Ain't Kosher Here: The Rise of the "Jewish" Sitcom*. Rutgers Univ., 2003.

Carr, Steven. *The Hollywood Question: America and the Belief in Jewish Control of Motion Pictures before 1941*. Dissertation, University of Texas, Austin, 1994.

———. *Hollywood and Anti-Semitism: A Cultural History up to World War II*. Cambridge Univ., 2001.

Cohen, Sarah Blacher. *From Hester Street to Hollywood: The Jewish-American Stage and Screen*. Indiana Univ., 1983.

Desser, David, and Lester D. Friedman. *American-Jewish Filmmakers: Traditions and Trends*. Univ. of Illinois, 1993.

Erens, Patricia. *The Jew in American Cinema*. Indiana Univ., 1984.

Friedman, Lester D. *The Jew in American Film*. Citadel, 1987.

Gabler, Neal. *An Empire of Their Own: How the Jews Invented Hollywood*. Crown, 1989.

Goldberg, J. J. *Jewish Power: Inside the American Jewish Establishment*. Addison-Wesley, 1996.

"Jewish Intermarriage Statistics," *InterfaithFamily*, Spring 2011, www.interfaithfamily.com/news_and_opinion/synagogues_and_the_jewish_community/Jewish_Intermarriage_Statistics.shtml. Accessed 6 Sept. 2016.

Pearl, Jonathan, and Judith Pearl. *The Chosen Image: Television's Portrayal of Jewish Themes and Characters*. McFarland, 1999.

Seinfeld. Created by Larry David and Jerry Seinfeld, performances by Jerry Seinfeld et al. West-Shapiro and Castle Rock Entertainment, 1989–98.

Suber, Howard. "Hollywood's Closet Jews." *Davka*, Fall 1975, pp. 12–14.

———. "Television's Interchangeable Ethnics: 'Funny, They Don't Look Jewish.'" *Television Quarterly*, volume 12, issue 4, Winter 1975, pp. 49–56.

Tugend, Tom. "The Hollywood Jews." *Davka*, Fall 1975, pp. 4–8.

PART 1: HISTORIES

CHAPTER 1

Still an Empire of Their Own: How Jews Remain Atop a Reinvented Hollywood

by Vincent Brook

Co-host Steve Martin's opening joke at the 2010 Academy Awards ceremony, as attested by its uproarious audience reception and YouTube preservation, stands out not only as that event's entertainment high point. It also marks a turning point in Jewish-Hollywood relations. As part of the standard tongue-in-cheek introduction of celebrity nominees seated in the front rows, Martin turned to German actor Christoph Waltz and continued his spiel. "And in *Inglourious Basterds*, Christoph Waltz played a Nazi obsessed with finding Jews. Well, Christoph . . ." Martin paused, then slowly spread out his arms to embrace the audience—which exploded with laughter, followed by a second explosion when Martin added, with arms still spread wide, ". . . the Mother Lode!" ("A Jew-y Moment at the 2010 Oscars").

Martin's jab at Jewish uber-representation in Hollywood was nothing new. Indeed, getting the joke demanded prior knowledge of Jews' numerical predominance in the industry, and at the highest levels, compared to their meager proportion (circa two percent) of the US population. What was groundbreaking was Martin's light-hearted treatment of the phenomenon (by a gentile, no less), its buoyant reception by his (Jewish and non-Jewish) peers, and the lack of controversy it generated among critics, organized Jewry, or (as far as has been reported) the bulk of the telecast's billion-plus viewers. What the joke provided instead was immense comic relief, which, as with the best humor, stemmed from its touching a cultural nerve whose tendrils, in this case, extended beyond the present moment to Hollywood's early-twentieth-century origins as the world's movie capital.

Adding to the joke's potency was its functioning on multiple levels. The site-specific aspect was a bonus, allowing the jokester to show rather than tell and to give tangible substance (the Oscar night audience) to an abstract concept (the "Jewish industry"). That Waltz's SS character was the butt of the joke and Jews, for a change, got the last laugh, added poetic justice that both resonated with *Inglourious Basterds*' Jewish revenge fantasy and carried historical weight. Hitler's Führership had triggered a massive influx to Hollywood of Jewish film personnel. Their replenishment of the industry's creative ranks (from directors, actors, and writers to cinematographers, editors, set designers, and composers) bolstered an executive structure already top-heavy with an earlier generation of Jewish émigrés (Brook, *Driven to Darkness*)—and which, a few generations removed, the 2010 Oscar night audience mirrored. Antisemitism, in other words, lay at the crux of Martin's one-liner. And while a full understanding of the backstory wasn't essential to slaying the Academy audience, it is required for appreciating the joke's broader cultural significance.

JUST DESSERTS

Without antisemitism, of the European and American variety, Jews never would have "invented Hollywood" in the first place (Gabler). The masses of largely eastern European Jews who set sail for the United States in the late-nineteenth and early-twentieth centuries, just as the movies were taking root, were driven to American shores by the latest violent eruptions of Jew-hatred in their erstwhile homelands. Here they met less virulent but mounting antisemitism, fueled by their largely lower-class immigration, which blocked their rise in more established industries and shunted them into what was then a lowly, if not wholly disreputable, motion picture business. Centuries of Old World antisemitism, meanwhile, which had barred Jews in Europe from owning land and joining guilds, forcing them instead into *Luftmensch* (airman) occupations such as salesman, agent and broker, primed their New World descendants for the similarly rag-tag, fly-by-night, seat-of-the-pants operation "the flickers" initially represented.[1]

Jews, in other words, were at the right place, at the right time, with the right skill set. And American anti-Semites who soon began railing against Jewish "control" of Hollywood had only their ilk to blame. Of course, minus its conspiratorial overtones, the control canard was not without statistical support. Already during the Nickelodeon era (1905–15), Jews had secured a foothold in the exhibition side of the movies as theater owners and managers. When New York Mayor George McClellan closed all the city's nickelodeons in 1908, allegedly in response to public concern over the "exhibition of depravity," and local theater owner Jacob Weinberg was arrested, the Jewish immigrant community perceived the actions as a form of pogrom (Hoberman and Shandler, "Nickelodeon Nation" 16; May 43–44). Nothing could stall the movie juggernaut, however, nor Jews' involvement in all facets of it. By the 1920s, in addition to continued predominance on the exhibition side (Klein), Jews helmed all the major studios that would become household names, define Hollywood's golden age, and still exist today: Paramount (Adolph Zukor and Jesse Lasky), MGM (Marcus Loew, Nicholas Schenck, and Louis B. Mayer), Fox (William Fox), Warner Brothers (Harry and Jack Warner), Universal (Carl Laemmle), Columbia (Harry Cohn), and United Artists (Joseph Schenck).[2]

Rather than showered with praise for their model American entrepreneurship, however, no sooner had the moguls transformed a once scoffed-at business into a lucrative and core cultural enterprise, than the Jewish control canard took center stage (Brook, *Driven to Darkness* 73). The term mogul itself, derived from the word "Mongol" and coined specifically for the immigrant studio bosses, referred pejoratively to their "alleged Asiatic [read: alien] provenance and appearance, perceived boorish [read: uncivilized] behavior, and admittedly aggressive [read: unscrupulous] business practices" (68). The moguls' selection in 1922 of Will Hays, current Postmaster General and a Presbyterian deacon, to head Hollywood's newly formed public relations arm, the Motion Picture Producers and Distributors of America (now Motion Picture Association of America), sought only partly to stave off criticism over a spate of sex-and-drug-related movie-star scandals. It also clearly aimed to counter "increasingly anti-Semitic attacks on the film business, not only from fringe groups but also from respected religious and business leaders" (73).

Auto magnate Henry Ford, whose *Dearborn Independent* newspaper in 1921 reprinted as fact the long-discredited *Protocols of the Elders of Zion* (concocted by Czarist agents in 1905 and purporting to document a Jewish conspiracy for world domination), singled out the movies for special opprobrium. Hollywood, Ford wrote, was "exclusively under the control of the Jewish manipulators of the public mind," whose producers, because of their "Oriental view [that] is essentially different from the Anglo-Saxon . . . don't know how filthy their stuff is—it is so natural to them" (Ford 51–52). Episcopalian minister William Sheafe Chase, head of the church's International Reform Bureau, similarly charged "the few producers who control the motion picture who are all Hebrews" with using "a marvelous power for good or evil in the world . . . for selfish commercial and unpatriotic purposes, even that it has been prostituted to corrupt government, to demoralize youth, and break down Christian religion" (Chase 53).

"Filthy stuff," of course, proved a far better fit than Jew-hatred with the Roaring '20s. With Deacon Hays projecting gentility and toning down some of the movies' and movie stars' excesses, Hollywood and its Jewish elite not only managed to weather the first big antisemitic storm, but on-screen a brief period of defiant self-representation ensued. Explicitly identified Jewish characters and themes were frequently and sympathetically portrayed throughout the decade, peaking with Warner Brothers' Al Jolson vehicle *The Jazz Singer* (1927). In foregrounding the conflict of tradition and modernity that the immigrant moguls themselves experienced, however, *The Jazz Singer* also foreshadowed troubles to come—from anti-Semites and Jews themselves.

"TOO JEWISH"

The Great Depression, the Nazi takeover in Germany, and burgeoning fascism at home refueled a Judeo-phobia that spread beyond the confines of Hollywood but again saw in the movie capital a made-to-order target. With the concurrent rise in radical leftist politics, Hollywood Jews found themselves "demonized at both political extremes"—as cynical capitalists, on the one hand, atheistic Communists, on the other—often in the same breath (Hoberman and Shandler, "Hollywood's Jewish Question" 61). Antisemitic grumbling was one thing, but calls for government censorship and theater boycotts that threatened the bottom-line forced the industry's hand. Going Presbyterian Will Hays one better, the moguls brought in Catholics Daniel Lord and Martin Quigley to write a puritanical Production Code for film content, and another Catholic, Joseph Breen, to head the Production Code Administration charged with enforcing it.

Once the PCA was in place and business restructuring caused by the Depression ceded financial control to Wall Street, anyone scratching the surface of purportedly Jewish-run Hollywood in the 1930s would have found the studios largely beholden to WASP investors, such as the Rockefellers, and policed by the Pope. Nothing short of a Stalinist purge would have satisfied die-hard anti-Semites, and in these increasingly fearful times, showing a non-Jewish face mattered more than ever—behind and on the screen. "Too Jewish," a pejorative apocryphally attributed to Harry Cohn in the 1920s to justify de-Judaizing actors' names and appearances, in the 1930s led the hyperdefensive moguls to extend the practice to Jewish characters and subject matter as well (Desser and Friedman 1). In the process, the studios made strange bedfellows not only with Breen—himself an anti-Semite who called the moguls (in private correspondence) "the scum of the earth" (Hoberman and Schandler, "Hollywood's Jewish Question" 58). Organized Jewry as well, concerned with further inflaming anti-Jewish animus, jumped on the de-Judaizing bandwagon, which now also required shelving or bowdlerizing anti-Nazi films. Other factors informed the self-censorship, and the moguls' actions behind the scenes were a different story (see the Ben Urwand Controversy chapter for the fine points). But the Hollywood majors throughout the 1930s, a period Henry Popkin later termed the "Great Retreat" in Jewish cultural representation, tended to deracinate Jewish characters or eliminate them entirely, and to downplay or ignore the Nazi threat.

World War II took care of Hitler, but the Cold War, in thrusting antisemitism's Communist pole to the forefront, triggered another peril for Hollywood's Jews. The fact that six of the so-called Hollywood Ten (alleged Communist film personnel subpoenaed by the House Committee on Un-American Activities, or HUAC, in 1947) were Jews reinforced the perceived link between Heebs and Commies and their joint hold on the movie industry (Navasky).[3] HUAC's reigning bigot, Mississippi Congressman John Rankin, had no trouble connecting the dots. By listing the stage and birth names of only the Jewish movie stars who had come to Washington in support of the Ten (e.g., Edward G. Robinson, né Emmanuel Goldenberg; Paul Muni, né Muni Weisenfreund), Rankin both "affirmed" the Jew/Communist connection and "proved" their joint conspiratorial intent via the actors' "hidden" identities.[4]

Lest they too be tarred as Reds, Pinkos, or Fellow Travelers, the moguls not only publicly denounced the Ten before HUAC, but in the Waldorf Statement, issued shortly after the first hearings, promised to rid the industry of its Communist members. The resulting blacklist spread to the radio and upstart television industries as well, which, though then under separate ownership from the movie studios, were, if anything, even more Jewishly "infested."

The Big Three radio/TV networks—CBC, NBC, and ABC—were all headed by Jews (William Paley, David Sarnoff, and Leonard Goldenson, respectively), thereby expanding, for anti-Semites, the parameters of Jewish media control and requiring, of equally defensive TV moguls, adapting the "too Jewish" rule to their fragile new medium as well.[5]

Network execs even tried to de-Judaize the popular radio show turned TV sitcom *The Goldbergs* (1949–56) by moving the titular family in mid-run from a kosher enclave in New York City to the white-bread suburbs. "They had a fit about the show being Jewish," co-producer Cherney Berg, son of creator-star Gertrude Berg, recalls. "They wanted the Goldbergs to be the O'Malleys and it just couldn't be done" (Brook, *Something Ain't Kosher Here* 22). A decades-long Great Retreat on TV, similar to what the movies experienced in the 1930s, ensued. Mimicking Ivy League college admission quotas for Jews (in place since the 1910s), TV producers began adopting quotas for Jewish characters. A certain "ghetto mentality" prevailed, according to Simon Wincelberg, a prominent TV writer of the time. "They rationed you: one Jewish character a year" (Michael Elkin 25). De-Judaizing reached an extreme in *The Dick Van Dyke Show* (1961–66). The show was originally conceived by Carl Reiner as an autobiographical riff on his acting and writing stint on *Your Show of Shows* (1951–54), which starred the Jewish Sid Caesar and boasted an all-Jewish writing staff that included Reiner, Woody Allen, Mel Brooks, Larry Gelbart, Mel Tolkin, and Neil and Danny Simon. Reiner, however, was forced to cede the lead-writer role to quintessential WASP Dick Van Dyke and to give his Sid Caesar-based character the Irish-sounding name Alan Brady (Marc 80–82).

"COMING OUT JEWISH"[6]

Though the "too Jewish" syndrome continued to dominate episodic TV into the 1990s, it began to loosen its grip on Hollywood movies in the late-1960s: partly due to radical changes in American society, partly to the contrasting balance sheets of the two industries. US television's penetration soared from less than one percent of households in 1948 to over ninety percent in 1960. Domestic movie attendance over the same span plummeted from a peak of ninety million a week in 1946 to twenty million (of a substantially larger population) in the early 1960s. Beholden to their burgeoning mass audience and under scrutiny by the Federal Communication Commission (FCC), television content paled (literally and figuratively) to that of the movies. Desperate for any audience at all, free of the FCC, and by the countercultural mid-1960s unchained to the Production Code as well, the movies began pulling out the stops—sexually, politically, and demographically.

The explosion of Jewish film representation, though clearly indebted to the overall identity politics movements, was boosted for Jews specifically by their increasing entry into the American mainstream and by Israel's astonishing victory in the Six-Day War. This event, which, according to American Jewish Congress leader Jacqueline Levine, "made us all stand a little taller in 1967," went a long way to allowing organized Jewry, if not quite to revel in, at least to countenance the movies' Jewish representational renaissance (Goldberg 134). Surpassing their 1920s forerunners, a new A-list of Jewish actors such as Woody Allen, Richard Benjamin, Elliott Gould, Dustin Hoffman, Charles Grodin, Carol Kane, George Segal, Barbra Streisand, and Gene Wilder could now be seen and heard playing openly Jewish types, and with Jewish names, noses, hair, and nasal accents intact—Carl Reiner's included (Erens 256).

Jews' greater visibility on screen, in mainstream society, and, via Israel, on the world stage, was certainly an advance from the defensiveness and suppression of yore. But it also highlighted what Sander Gilman calls Jews' "double bind." Attempts at hiding their Jewish identity, as John Rankin insinuated, only "[compounded] the connotations of conspiratorial subterfuge." But dropping the mask, as Jews themselves warned, carried even greater peril, in its reinforcing perception of the Chosen People's "undue" influence (Gilman 19). As the perceived Jewish threat tended to increase with the level of social unrest, it was no surprise that the upheaval of the late 1960s and early 1970s witnessed the first major antisemitic reaction since the McCarthy era. Even African Americans, long-time Jewish allies (and vice versa) based on the two groups' once-shared oppressed minority status, now began scapegoating their more upwardly mobile brethren.[7] Though not as hyperbolically as Henry Ford or William Sheafe Chase, black leader Jesse Jackson revived claims of Jewish media and government control, the latter charge having first surfaced during Franklin Roosevelt's purported "Jew Deal" (Dinnerstein 218). Jackson undercut his federal cabal case by falsely identifying Nixon aides John Erlichman and Robert Haldeman as Jews, but Nixon himself lent the presidential seal to the media control myth, and then some, declaring in an interview that "the Jews in the U.S. control the entire information and propaganda machine, the large newspapers, motion pictures, radio and television, and the big companies" (233). Taking a cue from his commander in chief, Joint Chiefs chairman

General George S. Brown brought the conspiracy full circle, alleging not only that Jews owned all the banks and newspapers (they actually owned 3.1 and 8 percent, respectively) but that their influence in Congress was "so strong you wouldn't believe" (233).

THE MORE THINGS CHANGE...

Had they stuck to the entertainment industry, neo-anti-Semites would have been on more solid ground. Besides heading the TV networks and most of the major movie studios, another Jewish cog in the media machine—talent agencies—had become ever more prominent in the post-World War period. Tom Kemper's *Hidden Talent: The Emergence of Hollywood Agents* (2010) has revised upwards agency influence already in the classical Hollywood period (1920s to 1940s). Although "the basic functions and practices of talent agents did not change" in the post-classical period (1950s to present), the clout of increasingly corporatized agencies, similar to the trajectories of the movie and TV business over this span, rose as that of the studios receded, achieving parity with if not surpassing them altogether by the 1970s (248).

Two Jewish "super-agents," Irving "Swifty" Lazar and Sue Mengers, made mogul-like inroads in the postclassical period through their personal stables of A-list clients. But the true paradigm shift in the industry's power relations was orchestrated chiefly by one agency, MCA (Music Corporation of America), and one figure, CEO Lew Wasserman. A latecomer to the movie business but a pioneer in television, Wasserman established the "points system" for big-name stars, granting them a percentage of a film's profits in addition to burgeoning up-front salaries, and, most importantly, perfected the "package system" of leveraging above-the-line talent (stars, producers, directors, and writers), thereby compounding the agencies' return on interest from multiple clients. With talent no longer contractually bound for long stretches, as in the classical era, to a single studio, the industry dynamic was irrevocably altered, with above-the-liners and their agency underwriters now literally calling the shots.

And not only in the movies—indeed, it was MCA's and the William Morris Agency's (WMA) initial foothold in television, through their original New York offices' greater proximity to the major networks and advertising agencies, that helped these firms leap-frog, when not buying outright, their Los Angeles-based agency rivals (Kemper 247). Ultimately, through their broad talent pools, a corporate structure more suited to a rapidly changing industry, and diversified "holdings in real estate, production companies, and other businesses," MCA, WMA, and other emergent agencies became, in effect, the new studios, and Beverly Hills, whence most of the top agency offices soon gravitated, the new Hollywood (248).[8]

Whatever their geographical headquarters—and "Hollywood," of course, had always been more generic signifier than jurisdiction—the agencies' makeup was as Jewish as ever. With its acquisition of Universal Studios in 1962, Wasserman's MCA, from anti-trust concerns, was forced to dissolve its agency arm. Its (mainly Jewish) former agents would go on to form newly prominent firms such as the Agency for the Performing Arts (APA) and United Talent Agency. And there was no lack of other heirs apparent. WMA, the granddaddy of them all and the ur-Jewish agency by virtue of its 1898 founding and eponymous immigrant founder (né Zelman Moses), started out representing vaudeville performers and only became a major player in Hollywood, like MCA, in the late 1940s (Kemper 234, 241). By the 1970s, under longtime head Abe Lastfogel and movie chief Mike Zimring (both Jewish), WMA was prominent enough to spawn another agency powerhouse via the defection of five of its top agents: Michael Ovitz, Michael Rosenfeld, Ron Meyer (future head of Universal), William Haber, and Rowland Perkins (the only non-Jew). The newly formed (in 1975) Creative Artists Agency (CAA) soon catapulted to the top of the heap, with CEO Ovitz further demonstrating agency supersession of the studios by replacing Wasserman as Hollywood's "most powerful man" (Brady 122).[9]

Ovitz and CAA were by no means the only new Jewish players. Taking a cue from WMA and MCA, which had bought their way into the business by acquiring classical-era agencies, Jeff Berg formed International Creative Management (ICM) in 1975 through a merging of Creative Management Agency and International Famous Agency. Bitten by the CAA bug, four ICM agents—Ari Emanuel, Rick Rosen, Tom Strickler, and David Greenblatt, all Jews—fired for secretly planning to form their own agency, did just that, starting Endeavor Talent Agency in 1995. The incestuousness came full circle in 2009 when Endeavor, under partners Emanuel and Patrick Whitesell (also Jewish, despite the name), merged with WMA to form William Morris Endeavor (WME). By the second decade of the new millennium, seven agencies, mirroring the eight major studios of the classical era, ruled the New Hollywood roost: CAA, WME, United Talent, APA, Paradigm, ICM, and the Gersh Agency—headed or majority-partnered by Jews—all except for APA's James H. Gosnell, Jr. (who sure looks Jewish!).

Hollywood finally gave agencies their due in the hit HBO cable series *Entourage* (2004–11) and same-titled Warner Bros. movie (2015). Inspired by the real-life experiences of Mark Wahlberg, both the small- and big-screen versions prominently feature Walhlberg's stand-in's agent Ari Gold, based on Wahlberg's actual agent Ari Emanuel (played by the Jewish Jeremy Piven and unabashedly—some would say embarrassingly—portrayed as such on the show). Overdue acknowledgment notwithstanding, while the balance of New Hollywood power may have shifted from the studios to the agencies, by the new millennium the entire industry had undergone such a mega-corporate makeover as to render their usurpation moot. Spurred by globalization, merger mania, and Internet-based technological convergence, not only the major movie studios and television networks (broadcast and cable) but the entire media machine including music companies, newspapers, magazines, book publishers and theme parks were gobbled up by six multinational multimedia giants: Disney (ABC, Marvel, Pixar, etc.), Viacom (Paramount, CBS, Showtime, etc.), News Corp. (Twentieth Century Fox, Fox TV, etc.), Time-Warner (Warner Bros., HBO, etc.), Comcast (NBC, Universal, etc.), and Sony (Columbia, TV production, etc.).[10]

SAME FOLKS, DIFFERENT STROKES

Though the industry's internal dynamics may have altered dramatically, Jewish numerical predominance at the highest levels, and thus fodder for the Jewish control canard, has not. Thus while overt antisemitic reaction generally subsided from its Nixon-era stirrings to the 1990s, Jews, from long experience, remained wary. Sounding like a broken record from the 1930s, Jewish NBC President Brandon Tartikoff explained in 1985 that TV's aversion to portraying Jews and Judaism was because "so many Jews are behind the camera," and as Eric Goldman, director of the Jewish Media Office, elaborated, they "don't want to draw attention to themselves" (Michael Elkin 25). Tartikoff even played the "too Jewish" card on *Seinfeld* (1989–98), initially nixing the show because the eponymous star's name, stand-up comic profession, and New York City residence amounted to ethnic overkill (Kronke and Gautier C13).

Seinfeld, of course, not only went on to become the biggest hit of the 1990s but helped spark an unprecedented surge in episodic series featuring explicitly identified Jewish main characters: from *The Nanny, Mad About You*, and *Friends* to *The Larry Sanders Show, Dharma and Greg,* and *Will and Grace* (Brook, *Something Ain't Kosher Here*). What role the increased exposure played in the ensuing backlash is open to question, but Tartakoff and Goldman's neo-defensiveness was vindicated in the mid-1990s, from two unlikely sources. In 1994, William Cash, in an article for the British magazine *Spectator,* ironically helped perpetuate the Jewish control myth by claiming that "a self-perpetuating Jewish cabal had created an exclusive Power Elite in Hollywood" (Games 12). Avowed philo-Semite Marlon Brando counterintuitively stirred the pot in a 1996 *Larry King Live* interview, complaining that Jews who "run" and "own" the entertainment industry "should have greater sensitivity about the issue of people who are suffering because they've [also been] exploited." Exhibiting questionable sensitivity (and historical accuracy) himself, Brando added, "We have seen the nigger, we have seen the greaseball, we have seen the slit-eyed Jap . . . but we never saw the kike, because they knew perfectly well that's where you draw the wagons around" (Tugend 13).

Brando tearfully apologized for his remarks at a Los Angeles news conference a few days later, and subsequently tried to make amends by praising Yiddish theater to the skies. His *mea culpa*s were a sign that attacks on the "Jewish" media had become politically incorrect, but their obituary was far from being written. In the early 2000s, the salvos actually increased—in number, virulence, and, in some cases, originality. *New Republic* columnist Greg Easterbrook fell back on the old clichés in 2003, blaming boorish Jewish movie moguls who "worship money above all else" for a spate of Hollywood gore-fests (Blake Elkin 21, 37). The Parents Television Council took the tired "Christian" line in 2004, decrying the anti-religiosity of the "Jewish" television industry (Smith E1, E6). William Donahue of the Catholic League for Civil Rights began his 2004 diatribe conventionally: "Hollywood is controlled by secular Jews who hate Christianity in general and Catholicism in particular." Then he boldly trod where previous bigots had only tiptoed: "It's not a secret, OK? . . . Hollywood likes anal sex" (Rutten E1, E26–27).

Strikes below the belt from the religious right, as perverse as they might be, also were somewhat predicable from a group that felt its straight WASP (and Catholic) privilege under siege in the multicultural age. More unusual and more revealing, not in their messages but in the reactions to them, were the antisemitic rantings from within the belly of the beast. Two years after reviving the Christ-killing canard in his self-directed and produced film *The Passion of the Christ* (2004), Mel Gibson became the latest Jewish-control freak when TMZ (a celebrity news website) leaked his remarks to a police officer following a pull-over for drunk driving in Malibu. After seeming to counter the notion of a Jewish-run Hollywood by telling the officer that "he owns Malibu and will spend all his money to 'get even' with me," Gibson took the Jewish control canard to new extremes by spewing, "F*****g Jews! Jews are responsible for all the wars in the world. . . . Are you a Jew?" (TMZ staff).

Gibson, like Brando, publicly apologized for the outburst. And in another indication that anti-Jewish broadsides were no longer kosher, the actor-director's post-tirade career, which had reached new heights with *The Passion*'s blockbuster success, sank to a new low, with the Malibu incident itself becoming an industry marker for unacceptable antisemitic behavior. When Charlie Sheen, then co-star of the hit sitcom *Two and a Half Men* (2003–15), in 2011 called showrunner Chuck Lorre a "stupid little man and a pussy punk," *Business Insider*'s Ujala Sehgal blogged, "The only thing missing from Sheen's rant was some Mel Gibson-style antisemitism. Then he came back with some Mel Gibson-style antisemitism." Aping John Rankin's Jewish-outing routine before HUAC, Sheen called Lorre (né Charles Levine), in interviews and in a letter to TMZ, "Chaim Levine."[11] Sheen, given his already notorious bad-boy rep, didn't suffer quite the ostracism Gibson did. Though his first attempt to flout his Trump-like outrageousness in a one-man stage show, "Violent Torpedo of Truth, Defeat Is Not an Option," bombed, his second, in the sitcom *Anger Management* (2012–14), based on the 2003 film of the same name, lasted for two seasons on the FX cable channel.

THE MOTHER LODE

The controversy over the lack of black nominees for the 2016 Academy Awards was not the only reason the show's emcee Chris Rock chose not to revisit the Jewish media control myth for his standup material. His own race also played into the omission. Though the black antisemitism that surfaced in the late 1960s and early '70s was by then old news, a more virulent form that emerged in the 1980s and '90s, and had not fully subsided, remained a sensitive topic. The twist to the new strain, and cause for its longer shelf life, was its academic imprimatur. According to Leonard Jeffries, a City College of New York professor and "a leading voice in the new black scholarship," Jews had not merely to answer for being "cynical manipulators of the civil rights movement" and "demonizers of blacks through their control of Hollywood"; their tormenting of the black race allegedly went back centuries: as "architects of the Atlantic slave trade" and "apologists for the Southern plantation system" (Goldberg 327–28). Though thoroughly discredited by other researchers, Jeffries's "historically based" charges gave new life, "legitimacy," and, most ominously, an effective recruiting tool for Black Muslim leader Louis Farrakhan's long-running anti-Jewish campaign. Besides avidly promulgating the slave trade and plantation myths, Farrakhan and his followers honored Henry Ford by selling copies of the *Protocols of the Learned Elders of Zion* (329). Partly to avoid being painted with the Jeffries/Farrakhan brush, both Jesse Jackson and NAACP head Kweisi Mfume steered clear of the Jewish control canard while decrying the dearth of African American representation in network television during the so-called "Lily White" controversy[12] of the late 1990s (Brook, *Something Ain't Kosher Here* 172).

Rock would have been on firm ground *factually* had he taken a swipe at the persistently sizeable Jewish presence in Hollywood, especially in positions of power. Jewish predominance in the agency business has already been glossed. As for the upper echelons of the half-dozen media giants, these also mirrored to a remarkable degree the demographics of yore. Though deposed around Oscar time, due to declining health, from his decades-long throne at Viacom, Sumner Redstone's hand-picked successor, Philippe Dauman, maintained the Jewishness of the reign.[13] The corporation's main media subsidiaries, Paramount and CBS, have long had Jews at the top: Brad Gray and Leslie Moonves, respectively. Although Warner Brothers studios' longtime Jewish co-bosses Barry Meyer and Ron Horn recently stepped down, parent company Time-Warner regained Jewish leadership in 2013 under CEO Robert Marcus. Disney, which went Jewish for the first time in the 1980s under chieftain Michael Eisner, has remained firmly under Jewish management since Eisner passed the baton to Robert Iger, with the main movie and TV branches Jewish-helmed as well: Alan Horn of Walt Disney studios, Kevin Feige of the recently acquired Marvel studios, and Alan Sherwood of ABC. Comcast, which recently acquired Universal and NBC from GE, is run by Jewish Brian Roberts, with Jews Adam Fogelson and Jimmy Horowitz in charge of Universal and Robert Greenblatt of NBC. News Corp.'s top dog Rupert Murdoch, though not raised or identifying as Jewish, was born to a Jewish mother, while the unequivocally Jewish Stacey Snyder co-chairs 20th Century Fox studios. And even the Japanese company Sony's movie and TV operations featured Jewish heads: Michael Lytton and Tom Rothman for movies and Steve Mosko for TV.[14]

Along with the undeniable persistence of Jewish executive predominance, a quick web search reveals that the media control canard, with antisemitic overtones intact, also maintains a hold on the public imagination. That a more balanced counter-narrative has usurped its antipode in cultural cachet, however, was reaffirmed at the 2016 Golden Globes ceremony, held a month prior to the Oscars. British comic Ricky Gervais, unconstrained by race, had been handed the perfect foil for a Steve Martin-like jape in Mel Gibson, whom he was set to introduce as a presenter. Christoph Waltz, after all, had only played a Nazi; Gibson had actually spouted Hitlerian views, which Gervais duly dredged up in his set-up, recalling how he had scolded Gibson for the Malibu incident upon introducing him at the Globes ceremony a few years back. That experience, he bemoaned with his best hang-dog expression, made his introducing Gibson now rather awkward. "And I blame NBC for this terrible situation," he groused at the show's producing network, then added, to Mother Lode-like laughter, "Mel Gibson blames—you know who he blames!" ("Ricky Gervais Mel Gibson Golden Globes 2016").

Notes

1. Jews, along with southern Europeans, were not designated as "white" in the US census until the 1940s (Brodkin). The term "flickers" derived from the flickering of light caused by an initially inadequately rapid projection rate, which was soon corrected. "Flicks" remained a slang synonym for the movies into the 1960s, and has been revived in the digital age by the movie streaming/production company Netflix.
2. Fox Films was founded by Jewish immigrant William Fox in the 1910s. When it became 20th Century Fox in the 1930s, with non-Jew Darryl Zanuck as head of production, its chairman, Joseph Schenck, was still Jewish. Schenck had also served as president of United Artists (UA), founded in 1919 by Mary Pickford, Douglas Fairbanks, Charlie Chaplin, and D. W. Griffith. In the 1950s, UA was taken over by two Jewish lawyers, Arthur Krim and Robert Benjamin. Jewish involvement in the lone defunct golden age studio, RKO, is the most complex. The studio was formed by a Jew, David Sarnoff, head of Radio Corporation of America (RCA), and Jews David Selznick, Pandro Berman, Charles Koerner, and Dore Schary variously served as heads of production in the 1930s and 1940s. Company ownership, however, shifted to the Rockefeller family in the mid-1930s and to Howard Hughes in the late 1940s.
3. The Hollywood Ten's six Jews were screenwriters Alvah Bessie, Lester Cole, John Howard Lawson, Albert Maltz, and Samuel Ornitz, and director Herbert Biberman. Non-Jews included producer Adrian Scott, director Edward Dmytryk, and screenwriters Ring Lardner, Jr., and Dalton Trumbo.
4. The actors and other film personnel who publicly supported the Ten were part of an ad hoc group called the Committee for the First Amendment.
5. Paley and Sarnoff had founded the CBS and NBC radio networks as well.
6. The section heading is the title of a book by Jon Stratton.
7. Jews had helped form the National Association of Colored People (NAACP) in 1909 and played a disproportionate role, among whites, in the civil rights movement.
8. International Creative Management (ICM), as the newly formed ICM Partners, moved its offices from Beverly Hills to nearby Century City in 2006, and Creative Artists Agency (CAA) followed suit the same year.
9. That the studios, despite their relative loss of power, still lorded it over the agencies in glamour and prestige was demonstrated when Ovitz left CAA at its peak in 1995 to become Disney President—a short-lived move that ended disastrously for all concerned. After a tumultuous tenure under CEO Michael Eisner, Ovitz was unceremoniously (if lucratively) sacked in 1997. His severance package (a come-on for his taking the job in the first place) was valued at $38 million in cash and $100 million in stock.

10. Viacom and CBS split into separate companies in 2006, but both remained under the corporate umbrella of Viacom-founder Sumner Redstone's controlled National Amusements, Inc.
11. Sheen's attempted antisemitic disclaimer, that his mother, Janet Templeton, was Jewish, was quickly debunked (Bloom).
12. The controversy was dubbed "Lilly White" because, counter to recent incremental progress in casting characters of color in network TV shows, the proposed slate for the 1999 season had backtracked. An unprecedented united front among black, Latino, Asian/Pacific Islander, and American Indian media-monitoring groups led to immediate casting concessions by the networks and, more importantly, a promise to hold annual meetings with the groups. The groups also began issuing annual diversity report cards, giving networks letter grades in casting and the hiring of other creative personnel.
13. As of mid-2016, a power struggle between Dauman and the Redstones (the mentally feeble Sumner and his daughter, Shari Redstone), left Viacom's ultimate, though likely still Jewish, leadership in limbo.
14. Mosko left Sony in June 2016 and was replaced by an executive team that includes Jews Jamie Erlicht and Andy Kaplan (and obvious non-Jew Keith Le Goy!). For confirmation and the latest changes, see the various companies' and related websites.

Still an Empire of Their Own: How Jews Remain Atop a Reinvented Hollywood 19

Works Cited

"A Jew-y Moment at the 2010 Oscars." *YouTube*, uploaded by Jewlicious, 10 Mar. 2010, www.youtube.com/watch?v=zHE8CrZYgyA.

Anger Management. Directed by Peter Segal, performances by Jack Nicholson, Adam Sandler, and Marisa Tomei. Sony, 2003.

Anger Management. Performance by Charlie Sheen. Mohawk Productions, Revolution Studios, and Estevez Sheen Productions, 2012–14.

Bloom, Nate. "Sorry, Charlie: We Have More than Enough *meshuganas*." *Jewish World Review*, 16 Mar. 2011, www.jewishworldreview.com/0311/sheen_is_jewish.php3#.VzYx9ZXmqAI. Accessed 15 Aug. 2016.

Brady, Celia. "Rolling Heads." *Spy: A New York Monthly*, Mar. 1988, pp. 122–23.

Brodkin, Karen. *How the Jews Became White Folks . . . and What That Says about Race in America*. Rutgers Univ., 1998.

Brook, Vincent. *Driven to Darkness: Jewish Émigré Directors and the Rise of Film Noir*. Rutgers Univ., 2009.

———. *Something Ain't Kosher Here: The Rise of the "Jewish" Sitcom*. Rutgers Univ., 2003.

Chase, William Sheafe. "Catechism of Motion Pictures." Hoberman and Schandler, pp. 53.

Desser, David, and Lester D. Friedman. *American-Jewish Filmmakers: Traditions and Trends*. Univ. of Illinois, 1993.

Dharma and Greg. Created by Chuck Lorre and Dottie Dartland Zicklin. 20th Century Fox Television, 4 to 6 Foot Productions, and Chuck Lorre Productions, 1997–2002.

The Dick Van Dyke Show. Created by Carl Reiner, performances by Dick Van Dyke, Mary Tyler Moore, Rose Marie and Morey Amsterdam. Calvada Productions, 1961–66.

Dinnerstein, Leonard. *Anti-Semitism in America*. Oxford Univ., 1994.

Easterbrook, Gregg. "Take Out the Gore and 'Kill Bill' Is an Episode of 'Mighty Morphin Power Rangers.'" *New Republic*, 23 Oct. 2003, www.tnr.com/Easterbrook.html?pid=844. Not accessible.

Elkin, Blake. "Brando's Geshrei for Yiddish Theater." *Jewish Journal of Greater Los Angeles*, 12 Aug. 1999.

Elkin, Michael. "Jews on TV: From 'The Goldbergs' to 'Hill Street's' Cops." *Jewish Exponent*, 25 June 1985.

Entourage. Created by Doug Ellin, performances by Kevin Connolly, Adrian Grenier, and Kevin Dillon. HBO and Leverage Management, 2004–11.

Entourage. Directed by Doug Ellin, performances by Adrian Grenier, Kevin Connolly, and Jerry Ferrara. Warner Bros., 2015.

Erens, Patricia. *The Jew in American Cinema*. Indiana Univ., 1984.

Ford, Henry. "The Jewish Aspect of the 'Movie' Problem" and "Jewish Supremacy in the Motion Picture World." *Dearborn Independent*, 12 and 19 Feb. 1921. Hoberman and Schandler, pp. 51–52.

Friends. Created by David Crane and Marta Kauffman. Warner Bros. Television, and Bright/Kauffman/Crane Productions, 1994–2004.

Gabler, Neal. *An Empire of Their Own: How the Jews Invented Hollywood.* Anchor Books, 1989.

Games, Stephen. "'Spectator' Fallout." *Jewish Journal of Greater Los Angeles,* 2–8 Dec. 1994.

Gemünden, Gerd. *German Exile Cinema: 1933–1951.* Columbia Univ., 2014.

Gilman, Sander. *The Jew's Body.* Routledge, 1991.

Goldberg, J. J. *Jewish Power: Inside the American Jewish Establishment.* Addison-Wesley, 1996.

The Goldbergs. Created by Gertrude Berg. NBC, 1949–56.

Hoberman, J., and Jeffrey Schandler, editors. *Entertaining America: Jews, Movies, and Broadcasting.* Jewish Museum, 2003.

———. "Hollywood's Jewish Question." Hoberman and Schandler, pp. 47–75.

———. "Nickelodeon Nation." Hoberman and Schandler, pp. 15–25.

Inglourious Basterds. Directed by Quentin Tarantino, performances by Brad Pitt, Diane Kruger, and Eli Roth. Universal, 2009.

The Jazz Singer. Directed by Alan Crosland, performance by Al Jolson. Warner Bros., 1927.

Kemper, Tom. *Hidden Talent: The Emergence of Hollywood Agents.* Univ. of California, 2010.

Klein, Dennis B. "The Movies: Notes on the Ethnic Origins of an American Obsession." *Jews and American Popular Culture, Volume. 1: Movies, Radio and Television,* edited by Paul Buhle, Praeger, 2007, pp. 1–11.

Kronke, David, and Robert Gautier. "There's Nothing to It." *Los Angeles Times,* 29 Jan. 1995, p. C13.

The Larry Sanders Show. Created by Dennis Klein and Garry Shandling. Brillstein-Grey Entertainment, Columbia Pictures Television and HBO, 1992–98.

Mad About You. Created by Danny Jacobson and Paul Reiser, performances by Paul Reiser, Helen Hunt and John Pankow. In Front Productions, Nuance Productions and TriStar Television, 1992–99.

Marc, David. *Comic Visions: Television Comedy and American Culture.* Univ. of Pennsylvania, 1997.

May, Larry. *Screening the Past: The Birth of Mass Culture and the Motion Picture Industry.* Univ. of Chicago, 1980.

The Nanny. Created by Fran Drescher et al., performances by Fran Drescher, Charles Shaughnessy and Daniel Davis. CBS, Highschool Sweethearts and Sternin & Fraser Ink, 1993–99.

Navasky, Victor S. *Naming Names.* Penguin, 1981.

The Passion of the Christ. Directed by Mel Gibson, performances by Jim Caviezel, Monica Bellucci, and Maia Morgenstern. Icon, 2004.

Popkin, Henry. "The Vanishing American Jew in Our Popular Culture." *Commentary,* July 1952, pp. 46–55.

"Ricky Gervais Mel Gibson Golden Globes 2016." *YouTube*, uploaded by Inglés de cine, 10 Jan. 2016, www.youtube.com/watch?v=_Ty-z_3M1Z0.

Rutten, Tim. "Yule Tidings of a Culture War." *Los Angeles Times*, 18 Dec. 2004, pp. E1, E26–27.

Sehgal, Ujala. "Here Are Charlie Sheen's Insane, Anti-Semitic Rants that (FINALLY) Forced CBS to Pull 'Two And A Half Men.'" *Business Insider*, 25 July 2011, www.businessinsider.com/charlie-sheen-two-half-men-chuck-lorre-video-2011-2. Accessed 15 Aug. 2016.

Seinfeld. Created by Larry David and Jerry Seinfeld, performances by Jerry Seinfeld et al. West-Shapiro and Castle Rock Entertainment, 1989–98.

Smith, Lynn. "Advocacy Group Says TV Has Little Respect for Religion." *Los Angeles Times*, 7 Dec. 2004, pp. E1, E6.

Stratton, Jon. *Coming Out Jewish*. Routledge, 2000.

TMZ staff. "Gibson's Anti-Semitic Tirade: Alleged Cover Up." *TMZ*, 28 July 2006, www.tmz.com/2006/07/28/gibsons-anti-semitic-tirade-alleged-cover-up/. Accessed 15 Aug. 2016.

Tugend, Tom. "Jewish Leaders Denounce Brando's Attack on Hollywood Jews." *Jewish Journal of Greater Los Angeles*, 12–18 Apr. 1996, p. 13.

Two and a Half Men. Created by Lee Aronsohn and Chuck Lorre, performance by Charlie Sheen. Chuck Lorre Productions, Tannenbaum Co., and Warner Bros. Television, 2003–15.

Will and Grace. Created by David Kohan and Max Mutchnick, performances by Eric McCormack, Debra Messing, and Megan Mullally. KoMut Entertainment, Three Sisters Entertainment, and NBC Studios, 1998–2006.

Your Show of Shows. Created by Sylvester L. Weaver, Jr., performances by Sid Caesar, Imogene Coca and Carl Reiner. Max Liebman Productions, 1951–54.

CHAPTER 2

The Ben Urwand Controversy: Exploring the Hollywood-Hitler Relationship

INTRODUCTION

Few film history books, and none from a Jewish angle, provoked more controversy in recent years than Ben Urwand's *Collaboration: Hollywood's Pact with Hitler*, published in late 2013. The book's incendiary nature, flaunted in its title, would have created a critical firestorm in any case. But the fortuitous publication earlier that same year of Thomas Doherty's *Hollywood and Hitler, 1933–1939*, a more sober account of the major Hollywood studios' engagement with the Nazi regime, stoked a fierce debate on the issue. Besides the flurry of radio interviews and reviews in academic journals, the popular press, and on-line, several conference panels were held on the topic. This chapter capsulizes the Urwand controversy by reprising two papers, presented at the Western Jewish Studies Conference in Tucson, Arizona, on May 4, 2014, which take opposing views on the controversy. A coda briefly discusses two other books in the works at the time, by Laura Rosenzweig and Steven Ross, which tended to counter, or at least, significantly qualify, Urwand's broadside, adding another tantalizing dimension to the brouhaha.

Caution or Collaboration?
The Doherty-Urwand Controversy[1]

by Lawrence Baron

In their books published in 2013, Thomas Doherty and Ben Urwand concur that the major Hollywood studios avoided direct criticism of Hitler and his anti-Semitic policies, abandoned scripts that would antagonize Germany, and eliminated Jewish characters in their films between 1934 and 1939. Urwand attributes Hollywood's acquiescence to German pressure primarily to the Nazi consul Georg Gyssling, dispatched by Berlin to monitor the film industry, and to the studio owners' fear of losing revenue from the German market. Although Doherty does not dispute that the studios capitulated to Germany's demands to keep doing business there, he places as much blame on the inhibiting roles of the Production Code Administration (PCA), the Motion Picture Producers and Distributors of America (MPPDA), the United States government, and studio owners and Jewish organizations justifiably worried that blatantly anti-Nazi films would be construed as violations of American neutrality and as evidence for American anti-Semites, isolationists, and nativists that the Jewish movie moguls exploited their creations to promote an interventionist and pro-Jewish agenda.

The two scholars vehemently disagree over whether the self-censorship engaged in by Hollywood during this period constituted a formal policy of "collaboration" with the Nazi authorities, as Urwand claims, or a continuation of Hollywood's standard practice of editing films and scripts to gain the approval of the PCA and local and state censorship boards in the United States and to placate domestic interest groups and foreign governments, as Doherty posits. Urwand categorically declares, "Over the course of the investigation, one word kept reappearing in both the American and German records: 'collaboration' (*Zusammenarbeit*). And gradually it became clear that this word accurately described the particular arrangement between the Hollywood studios and the German government in the 1930s" (8). Urwand acknowledges that other American corporations did business with Nazi Germany throughout the 1930s, but deems the studios' pursuit of profit uniquely reprehensible because they acted as "purveyors of ideas and culture," who could have alerted the world to the danger that Hitler posed to Europe and its Jews (8–9).

Doherty objected to Urwand's "slanderous and ahistorical" use of the term collaboration: "Collaboration is how you describe the Vichy government during the Nazi occupation of France or Vidkun Quisling, the Norwegian double-crosser whose name became synonymous with treason. To call a Hollywood mogul a collaborator is to assert that he worked consciously and purposely, out of cowardice or greed, under the guidance of Nazi overlords" ("Does 'Collaboration' Overstate"). Moreover, he decried Urwand's characterization of Hollywood's interactions with Nazi Germany as a "pact" implying a moral equivalence to the notorious Munich and Molotov-Ribbentrop pacts. Instead, Doherty contended that the studio owners acted more like the democracies of Western Europe and the United States by appeasing Hitler, erroneously assuming that he would moderate his anti-Semitic and expansionist policies ("Does 'Collaboration' Overstate").

The first test case for how the studios would adapt to Gyssling's myopic vision of what cinematic fare was appropriate for German audiences involved Warner Brothers' *Captured!* (1933). In June the studio invited him to preview the film and solicit his feedback. He demanded extensive changes in this film about the treatment of British POWs by their German captors during World War One. Despite Gyssling's protest against the unflattering portrayal of the German guards, Warner Brothers released the movie in the United States without any cuts. Extrapolating from letters Gyssling wrote to other studios around the same time, Urwand presumes he threatened to revoke the studio's license to distribute films in Germany if it did not comply with his demands. Instead, Warner Brothers turned to Frederick Herron, the head of the MPPDA's foreign division, who resented Gyssling's fanaticism and interference. Herron screened a reedited version of *Captured!*, but one that did not contain all the changes Gyssling had stipulated, to a more moderate German consul in New York who conditionally approved of it if minor revisions were made. Urwand speculates that Gyssling was so enraged by Warner Brothers' circumventing his authority that he instigated the Propaganda Ministry to expel the studio from Germany (55–58). Since Warner Brothers did redact *Captured!*, Urwand includes it among the studios which "collaborated" with the Nazis. Yet elsewhere he states that Gyssling "kicked Warner Brothers out of Germany for not making changes to *Captured!*" (178). Based on its handling of the film, Doherty, on the other hand, regards Warner Brothers as "the first of the majors to withdraw on principle" because it refused to accept Gyssling's ultimatum ("Does 'Collaboration' Overstate").

Nevertheless, the precedent of altering or discarding scripts that offended the Nazis rapidly became the standard approach of the other major studios to avert the loss of revenue from Germany.[2] This was epitomized by the failed attempt to produce Herman Mankiewicz's anti-Nazi script *The Mad Dog of Europe* (1933), which inveighed against Hitler's persecution of German Jews. Both Doherty and Urwand enumerate several causes for the film industry's passivity including its reluctance to jeopardize the German market for American films, the federal government's commitment to foreign trade and neutrality, and the Anti-Defamation League's (ADL) circumspect preference that Gentiles and organizations not associated with Jews in the public's mind carry the anti-Nazi banner. For Urwand, however, Gyssling's threat to bar American films from Germany, even if one was overtly hostile to Hitler's regime, constituted the "first and foremost" (68) factor in suppressing *The Mad Dog of Europe* and defining "the limits of American movies for the remainder of the decade" (75), even though he admits that "the evidence is inconclusive" (68) in this particular case.

While Urwand considers Will Hays of the MPPDA and Joseph Breen of the PCA the pawns of Gyssing in preventing *The Mad Dog of Europe* from being made, Doherty views them as the drivers of the policy. Frederick Beetson, the Secretary-Treasurer of the MPDDA, told Al Rosen, the feisty Hollywood agent determined to produce the first cinematic indictment of Nazi rule, that he should desist rather than endanger the German market for American films. After Rosen vainly sued the MPPDA for undermining his effort to film *The Mad Dog of Europe*, he submitted a proposal for it to the PCA. PCA chief Joseph Breen issued an "unofficial judgment" of Rosen's proposal and similar ones that might follow. Therein he declared, "The purpose of the screen primarily *is to entertain* and not to *propagandize*." He raised the specter that such films might provoke a pro-German and anti-Semitic backlash. The latter charge echoed the concerns of the ADL: "Because of the large number of Jews active in the motion picture industry in this country, the charge is certain to be made that the Jews, as a class, are behind an anti-Hitler picture and using the entertainment screen for their own personal propaganda purposes." Doherty reminds his readers that "around Hollywood, in dealing with the Breen office, an official prohibition and an 'unofficial judgment' was a distinction without a difference" (*Hollywood and Hitler* 58–59).

The other half of the studios' pact with the Nazis, Urwand argues, was their voluntary removal of Jewish characters from their films. When Twentieth Century's Darryl Zanuck announced his intent to make a movie about the origins of the Rothschild banking dynasty, the Anti-Defamation League (ADL) and its Los Angeles Jewish Community Committee (LAJCC) tried to dissuade him.[3] Zanuck signed the esteemed British actor George Arliss to play the dual role of the family's patriarch Mayer and his son Nathan to assure that *The House of Rothschild* (1934) would be a prestige picture. He felt the film drew obvious parallels between the ghettoization and persecution Jews endured in premodern Germany and their plight under Nazism. Two scenes featured ostensibly anti-Semitic caricatures. In the first Mayer hides his ledgers from a tax collector. In the second he summons his sons to his deathbed and instructs them to found branches in major European cities to guarantee that loans to the national governments there will not be stolen in transit. But Mayer excuses his subterfuge because the tax-collector extorts higher taxes from him as a Jew than from Gentiles and counsels his sons that their wealth will mean nothing until Jews achieve equality and respect. Furthermore, Nathan's loan to England enables it to defeat Napoleon.

The ADL anticipated that the film would reinforce stereotypes of Jewish money-lenders, thereby fueling economic resentments against Jews during the Great Depression and Hitler's first year in power. The organization asked Will Hays of the MPPDA to intercede with Zanuck who countered by sending positive feedback from an audience which attended a preview of *The House of Rothschild*, an endorsement from the National Council of Jewish Women, and a complimentary letter from the editor of the *B'nai B'rith Messenger*. The film garnered critical acclaim and box-office success. Many reviewers discerned the similarities between the precarious status of German Jews in the film and under Nazi rule; others appreciated how the Rothschild family triumphed over adversity. Nevertheless, the LAJCC formed a film committee comprised of its representatives and studio owners who agreed to be more prudent in their portrayals of Jewish characters. Appointed the head of the PCA in 1934, Joseph Breen translated the film committee's recommendation into a practice of rejecting scripts with sympathetic and unsympathetic Jewish characters to preempt perceptions that Hollywood either championed Jewish causes or perpetuated anti-Semitic stereotypes. Parenthetically, the purge of Jewish characters was never complete, with twenty-four Hollywood films featuring them between 1934 and 1939 compared to sixty-three in the prior six years (Erens 428–33).[4]

Urwand, however, condemns the Rothschild movie for containing "ideas so compatible with Nazi ideology that it was incorporated into the most extreme Nazi propaganda film of all time" (94), *The Eternal Jew* (1940). This infamous pseudo-documentary illustrated that even Hollywood did not conceal the deceitful machinations of the Rothschild bankers by inserting clips from the aforementioned scenes of Mayer. Of course, *The Eternal Jew* omitted Mayer's mitigating explanations for his conduct. Urward asserts that the depiction of Mayer was so noxious that *The Eternal Jew* was "unthinkable" without it (91–92). It never dawns on him how deeply engrained conspiracy theories about the Rothschilds and pernicious images of Jews were already rampant in Nazi ideology in particular and in Western culture in general.

Urwand also apparently neglected to consult Judith Doneson's pioneering study of American Holocaust cinema and her more balanced assessment of *The House of Rothschild*. She highlighted the mixed messages imparted by the film. Surveys of American public opinion in the 1930s indicated that most Americans admired the business acumen and industriousness of Jews while disapproving of their clannishness, duplicity, and materialism. Doneson concluded, "In the earliest of these [anti-Nazi films], we find the European stereotype, distinctly Jewish, and a warning about the dangers inherent in political anti-Semitism" (54). Doherty, on the other hand, lauds the film as one of the handful of early "allegories by default on Nazi anti-Semitism" to be released in the United States and views it as "pro-Jewish" (*Hollywood and Hitler* 46, 47).

Urwand cites MGM's cancellation of an adaptation of Sinclair Lewis novel *It Can't Happen Here* (1935) as another egregious example of the studio's deference to German censorship. The book envisioned how a fascist takeover of the United States could occur and how repressive it would be. MGM head Louis B. Mayer proceeded under the impression that the film's American setting would not upset Germany, but ultimately heeded warnings from Breen and Hays to scrap the project. In lieu of any archival proof Urwand surmises that Breen and Hays were acutely aware that Gyssling would oppose a film on this topic and sought to preempt a confrontation over it with Nazi Germany (156–77). The whole episode begs the question why MGM would have expended so much money and time on a manifestly anti-fascist project if it had been party to a pact obligating it to prevent such endeavors from ever coming to fruition.

Doherty mentions *It Can't Happen Here* in conjunction with MGM's contemporaneous treatment of its production of Franz Werfel's popular novel about the Armenian genocide, *The Forty Days of Musa Dagh* (1933). Turkey threatened to boycott American films and persuaded its ally France to do so as well if MGM transformed the book into a film. In both cases the studio spent hundreds of thousands of dollars on screenwriters to draft and sanitize scripts to render them innocuous to the protesting countries, but to no avail, prompting Mayer to drop the projects. Doherty does not deny that Breen, Hayes, and Mayer put profits before principle, but he detects, as did *The Hollywood Reporter* at the time, that they were growing weary of the "'Hitler fist' pummeling the industry" as efforts to placate Berlin yielded diminishing returns (*Hollywood and Hitler* 209–10).

Warner Brothers emerged as the first studio to tackle anti-fascist and anti-racist themes in its films. In 1937 it produced *The Life of Emile Zola*. This biopic of the great French writer lionized him for defending Alfred Dreyfus from being unjustly convicted and imprisoned for stealing French military secrets on behalf of Germany. Urwand notes that Gyssling phoned an associate producer at the studio to express his government's consternation over a film dealing with anti-Semitism and German militarism. He speculates that Gyssling's call prompted Jack Warner to delete the few verbal references to Dreyfus's Jewish background in the final script and retract the sole visual cue about it. While the dialogue about Dreyfus's religious affiliation was cut, the image of a French general pointing to a registry entry identifying Dreyfus as a Jew was left in the film. Urwand is outraged that this brief visual "turned out to be one of the few explicit references to a Jew in American cinema for the remainder of the 1930s" (159–60).

Conversely, Doherty places *The Life of Emile Zola* within the context of Warner Brothers' anti-Nazi activities, which encompassed its support of the Hollywood Anti-Nazi League (*Hollywood and Hitler* 313–14), broadcasting the League's programs on the studio's radio station KFWB (106–10), and releasing a series of "allegorical anti-Nazi feature films like *Black Legion* (1936) (against homegrown racist vigilantism), *The Life of Emile Zola* (1937) (against anti-Semitism), and *They Won't Forget* (1937) (against mob rule and lynch law)" (338). These movies dramatized infamous outbursts of anti-Semitism like the Dreyfus Affair, the lynching of Leo Frank, which served as the basis for *They Won't Forget*, and the recent murder trial of members of the nativist Black Legion which terrorized African Americans, immigrants, Jews, and New Deal officials in Detroit. To be sure, Warner Brothers jettisoned the Jewish origins of one of the League's victims to evade PCA censure for violating both its prohibition of derogatory references to ethnic and religious groups and its minimization of Jewish characters and issues in Hollywood productions. Yet anybody who kept abreast of the headlines or recalled the events of the Dreyfus Affair and the Frank lynching either firsthand or from public commemorations held in the 1930s could recognize the anti-Semitism motivating the antagonists in these motion pictures and could perceive the similarities to Hitler's anti-Jewish obsessions.

Following the formula it employed in *Black Legion*, Warner Brothers' *Confessions of a Nazi Spy* (1939) drew on revelations emanating from the 1938 trial of a German-American spy ring which procured American military secrets and passed them on to Berlin. The FBI agent in charge of a successful investigation and prosecution serialized the story and then published it as a book. Warner Brothers snapped up the film rights. Upon hearing of the project, Gyssling sent a letter to Breen to nip it in the bud. Warner Brothers refused and leaked the letter to the trade press to generate publicity for the forthcoming motion picture. Having lost patience with Gyssling's relentless demands, Breen approved of the movie with the rationale: "The activities of this nation [Germany] and its citizenry, as set forth in this script, seem to be supported by the testimony at the trial and evidence adduced by the United States Attorney and federal operations" (*Hollywood and Hitler* 337). Cognizant of security threats posed by the German American Bund and other fascist groups in Los Angeles, Warner Brothers cloaked the shooting of the film in secrecy.

Confessions of a Nazi Spy fosters a semblance of documentary authenticity by intercutting commentary by an authoritative narrator with clips from newsreels. It castigates Nazi despotism and racism as fundamentally un-American, but veers away from explicitly naming Jewry as the force behind the international conspiracy Germany is combatting. This narrative tactic not only hewed to PCA guidelines, but also allayed suspicions that the studio subliminally cultivated sympathy for Jews and communism. Only a year earlier, the House Committee for the Investigation of Un-American Activities had convened hearings about Soviet infiltration of Hollywood.

While *Confessions of a Nazi Spy* strikes us as tepid and vague in retrospect, Doherty reminds us that when it was screened in American theatres in 1939, it was perceived as "a high profile provocation from a major studio: the Code seal and the Warner Bros. shield flashed a bright green light signaling that anti-Nazism, if based on credible evidence, was now a fit subject for Hollywood cinema" (*Hollywood and Hitler* 337). Even Urwand concedes that the movie "pulled no punches, depicting all Nazis—whether spies or members of the German American Bund—as radical fanatics who took their orders directly from Berlin." Nevertheless, he belittles it as "an obvious B-picture with exaggerated German characters, a cheesy narrator, and a simpleminded script" that failed to "broach important subjects such as the persecution of the Jews" (208). He seems oblivious to the probability that many viewers deciphered the euphemisms the Nazi agents use when they vilify their foe in terms their real counterparts reserved for Jews.

Doherty neither apologizes for Hollywood's crass commercialism and political timidity in response to the threat Hitler posed to Europe and its Jews nor withholds praise from Warner Brothers, *The March of Time* newsreels, and the Hollywood Anti-Nazi League for exhibiting more courage and foresight in sounding the alarm about what was transpiring in Germany. While Urwand has discovered much new material on Gyssling's mission to intimidate the studio owners, the MPDDA, and the PCA from making movies that would cast a positive light on Jews or a negative one on Nazi Germany, he falls prey to tunnel vision. He is so intent on demonstrating that the studios consciously collaborated with Germany that he stretches his evidence beyond what it actually substantiates and minimizes adherence to the PCA guidelines, Breen's rigid application of them, the insecurities of Jewish organizations, and the federal government's policies of maintaining business and diplomatic relations with Germany as other factors affecting Hollywood's reluctance to withdraw from the German market by waging a cinematic war on Hitler. The accusatory and revelatory tone of Urwand's book is scintillating, but, in the end, it produces a smokescreen and not a smoking gun.

Notes

1. This presentation summarizes a lengthier review article by the author, listed below under Works Cited. [Ed.]
2. Only Paramount, MGM, and Twentieth Century Fox, among the major Hollywood studios, retained operations in Germany throughout the 1930s.
3. Twentieth Century, which was formed in 1933, merged with Fox Films in 1935 to become Twentieth Century Fox.
4. These statistics are based on the filmography of Jewish movies compiled by Patricia Erens and count only films produced by the Big Five and Little Three Hollywood studios and film companies they acquired between 1928 and 1939.

Works Cited

Baron, Lawrence. "Tarnishing Tinseltown: Hollywood's Responses to Nazi Germany." *Journal of Jewish Identities*, issue 6, no. 2, July 2013, pp. 59–78.

Black Legion. Directed by Archie Mayo, performances by Humphrey Bogart, Ann Sheridan, and Dick Foran. Warner Bros., 1936.

Captured! Directed by Roy Del Ruth, performances by Leslie Howard, Douglas Fairbanks Jr., and Paul Lukas. Warner Bros., 1933.

Confessions of a Nazi Spy. Directed by Anatole Litvak, performances by Edward G. Robinson, George Sanders and Francis Lederer. Warner Bros., 1939.

Doherty, Thomas. "Does 'The Collaboration' Overstate Hollywood's Cooperation with Hitler?" *The Hollywood Reporter* 31 July 2013, www.hollywoodreporter.com/news/does-collaboration-overstate-hollywoods-cooperation-595678. Accessed 24 Aug. 2016.

———. *Hollywood and Hitler, 1933–1939.* Columbia Univ., 2013.

Doneson, Judith E. *The Holocaust in American Film.* Jewish Publication Society, 1987.

Erens, Patricia. *The Jew in American Cinema.* Indiana Univ., 1984.

The Eternal Jew. Directed by George Roland, performances by Louis "Leibele" Waldman, Celina Breene, and Ruben Wendorf. Jewish Talking Picture Company, 1940.

The House of Rothschild. Directed by Alfred L. Werker, performances by George Arliss, Boris Karloff, and Loretta Young. 20th Century Pictures, 1934.

Lewis, Sinclair. *It Can't Happen Here.* Doubleday, Doran, 1935.

The Life of Emile Zola. Directed by William Dieterle, performances by Paul Muni, Gale Sondergaard, and Joseph Schildkraut. Warner Bros., 1937.

Mankiewicz, Herman. *The Mad Dog of Europe.* 1933.

They Won't Forget. Directed by Mervyn LeRoy [uncredited], performances by Claude Rains, Gloria Dickson, and Edward Norris. Warner Bros., 1937.

Urwand, Ben. *The Collaboration: Hollywood's Pact with Hitler.* Bellknap of Harvard Univ., 2013.

Werfel, Franz. *The Forty Days of Musa Dagh.* Viking, 1933.

Hollywood and Nazi Germany: Reflections on What Might Have Been[1]

By Joel Rosenberg

I think we three[2] are basically in agreement on at least two things: one is that Ben Urwand's study is riddled with exaggerations, especially in his provocative use of the word "collaboration." The other is that, as both Doherty and Urwand argue, the major Hollywood studio heads did in fact manifest failures of moral and civic courage in squelching or censoring Hollywood films critical of fascism, totalitarianism, Nazi Germany, or anti-Semitism. We also might agree that this resulted in references to Jews and Jewish experience being excised from most American films made in the 1930s following Hitler's accession, a situation with potentially grave historical consequences.

It is by no means a new idea that the efforts of Hollywood studios to preserve the lucrative German market for American cinema, where American films were very much in demand, led them to bend over backward to accommodate almost every demand by Nazi censors over the content and crediting of Hollywood films (Rosenberg, "Jewish Experience on Film," 19–20). Hollywood bowed as well to the American Catholic and Protestant communities on the moral content of films, and to the Jewish community on films feared likely to arouse domestic anti-Semitism. Such censorship, often for ideologically contrasting motives, had, at any rate, two main historical consequences for relations abroad: Films even implicitly critical of Germany, National Socialism, or Nazi anti-Semitism and violence were strictly forbidden at a time when focusing public concern on the systematic destruction of democracy in Germany and its neighboring nations might have done some good; and second, perhaps equally important, portrayals of Jews in American films (a thriving custom up until the rise of Hitler) almost completely vanished, to the detriment of their claim on the public imagination and thus their visibility as a people now in the grip of a profound humanitarian plight. In Urwand's appealing formulation, tales of Jewish ways had been "part of the American curriculum" (76), but were so no longer.

Urwand's book almost coincided with the earlier release of Thomas Doherty's study, *Hollywood and Hitler: 1933–1939*. Doherty, an accomplished historian working at the top of his craft, provides, in many ways, a better-rounded and historically more variegated account of his subject. His interest is in the broader social tableau that made up Hollywood culture in those years, and he thus provides whole chapters on subjects Urwand treats only in passing, if at all, including the Hollywood Anti-Nazi League, the screen representation of the Spanish Civil War, the important subject of screen newsreels of both high and low quality, and the courageous role of Warner Brothers in the anti-Nazi cause, a studio which Groucho Marx, without cigar or bouncing eyebrows, dubbed "the only studio with any guts" (*Hollywood and Hitler* 311).

Urwand's study, by contrast, is more focused on week-by-week, and sometimes day-by-day, negotiations over individual films. But he pursues his subject with an obsessive energy that is, in its way, quite impressive, and advances an argument seemingly more radical than Doherty's: that Hollywood's cooperation with Hitler amounted to nothing less than full-scale "collaboration," a volatile and provocative concept that can mean equally well a business, artistic, or political relation. If Urwand's thesis is correct, such a relationship was the moral equivalent of other forms of political collaboration between Germany and surrounding nations in those years. It is precisely this issue that has already provoked a sharp retort from Doherty: "I consider Urwand's charges slanderous and ahistorical—slanderous because they smear an industry that struggled to alert America to the menace brewing in Germany and ahistorical because they read the past through the eyes of the present" ("Does 'Collaboration' Overstate").

We shall return to this assessment in its proper place; but, for now, suffice it to say that Urwand quite problematically raises the question of whether equivalences can be drawn between the activity of the Hollywood studio moguls and the full-state cooperation with Germany by Pierre Laval, who headed the pro-Nazi Vichy regime in France, or that of Norway's Vidkun Quisling, whose surname has become synonymous with a collaborationist individual or head of state. I find Urwand's contention less troubling than does Doherty because it will at least promote thinking about the nexus of cooperation between any Western power (or business) and Germany in that era, and, more pertinently, about degrees of conceptual separation between Nazi and non-Nazi, between totalitarian and democratic culture, between fascist Europe and the democratic nations that surrounded it, including the politically imperiled democracies of Central and Eastern Europe. (I explore these issues more fully in my recently completed book, presently in manuscript: *The Era of Catastrophe—A Judeo-Cinematic Trajectory: Five Studies in Mass Media and Mass Destruction*.)

It is hard to assess whether an American film in this period suffered more from being butchered into incoherence by censors and studio executives or from being squelched altogether. Sometimes a canceled film is as much a cultural product as one stripped of its principal message step-by-step. One of the most interesting cases of a canceled film was the effort to provide a screen version of literary Nobelist Sinclair Lewis's 1935 novel *It Can't Happen Here*, which imagined the possibility of fascism in America. Lewis's search for this subject coincided with the meteoric career of Huey Long, a Louisiana governor from 1928 to 1932, and senator until 1935. Long's tactics as a politician resembled fascism, albeit in a more homespun way. He ruthlessly took away jobs from those who opposed him, and treated legislation as a mere formality. By 1935, the year Long was assassinated, Lewis was inspired by his example (and probably by his own 1920s sojourn in Mussolini's Italy) to write *It Can't Happen Here*, which Urwand calls "the most important anti-fascist work to appear in the United States in the 1930s" (161). It recounted the rise of a fictional Democratic senator named Buzz Windrip, who is shown stealing the 1936 presidential nomination from Franklin D. Roosevelt. Windrip recruited uniformed followers to terrorize opponents, took over the press, and created an official salute. The studio engaged accomplished screenwriter Sidney Howard. Both he and Lewis were pleased with the result. Had this work reached the cameras, America would have had, as Urwand later describes it, "Hollywood's first great anti-fascist picture" (177). Then it went to the censors.

Any role of Georg Gyssling or Nazi Germany in suppressing the film was never documented. And Joseph Breen, head of the Production Code Administration (PCA), found nothing objectionable according to his main jurisdiction, moral standards. But certain Jewish community leaders, most notably a Reform rabbi named William H. Fineschriber, wrote letters to heads of MGM with the following complaint: "[W]e ought not to thrust the Jew and his problems too much into the limelight . . . now is the time for us [Jews] to be silent" (Urwand 173).

Letters from Fineshriber and others finally forced Will Hays to pressure MGM into canceling the production. Sinclair Lewis's full-throated protest to this is memorable:

> "The world is full today of Fascist propaganda. The Germans are making one pro-Fascist film after another, designed to show that Fascism is superior to liberal democracy. . . . But Mr. Hays actually says that a film cannot be made showing the horrors of fascism and extolling the advantages of liberal democracy because Hitler and Mussolini might ban other [American] films. . . . Democracy is certainly on the defensive when two European dictators, without opening their mouths or knowing anything about the issue, can shut down an American film. . . . I wrote 'It Can't Happen Here', but I begin to think it certainly can." (Urwand 174–75)

Urwand's summary of the matter deserves to be quoted here as well: "[T]he most powerful men in Hollywood had decided in a closed meeting that they could not film a purely imaginary portrait of fascism in America. . . . Lewis [as quoted above] was saying that while his book was hypothetical at best, the decision to cancel the movie had actually happened. The authorities had chosen not to screen a warning about the fragility of the democratic system of government to the American people" (176).

Whatever other ways Urwand's book might be taken as overstating Hollywood's relationship to European fascism as one of "collaboration," this assessment is, I think, basically correct. In whatever other ways Hollywood's pliability was purely a business decision, fascism's tactic of intimidation had long led to anticipatory self-censorship in Hollywood, and it severely limited what could be said onscreen, thus cramping the public mood and forestalling much-needed debate and self-examination among the American populace. "Business-as-usual" is intimately tied to larger historical, political, and cultural forces whose history goes back centuries. None of these larger considerations can fit easily into Urwand's decidedly limited purview. But, one way or another, popular culture had let Americans down, and Urwand is right to suggest it. Cinema, in a sense, remained in a bubble. As the graveyard of promising projects and butchered first-drafts, Hollywood, even amidst this otherwise glorious age of American cinema, was a culture we should comprehend by its failures as much as its triumphs. This was less a matter of challenging or offensive words and ideas: it was a problem that went to the heart of thought itself, to a culture's candid assessment of its own situation. Americans were arguably being deprived of a roughly five-year head start on coming to terms with fascism.

Whether such a start would have made a difference is unclear. But one cannot help asking about the difference in national self-understanding that such a head start might have meant.

To return to Doherty's dispute with Urwand: in fairness to the latter, Doherty's charge that this book "smear[s] an industry that struggled to alert America to the menace brewing in Germany" ("Does 'Collaboration' Overstate") is questionable even by Doherty's own book's account—that is, both authors show an industry where this struggle was engaged only with varying degrees of sincerity and fervor, and far more at middle echelons than at the highest. Courageous authors, screenwriters, directors, and performers (many of them involved in the truly heroic activism of the Hollywood Anti-Nazi League) carried the brunt of it, took the greatest risks, and were often neutralized from the top. I am not inclined to reject outright, as does Doherty, "read[ing] the past through the eyes of the present." But I do agree that false coherences can easily be drawn. Doherty's words here (but for one reservation I shall raise shortly) are eminently well-considered:

> In the 1930s, the Nazis were not yet the Nazis of our history, our imagination. They had not yet started World War II, they had not yet implemented the Holocaust and they had not yet become what they are now: a universal emblem for absolute evil. From our perspective, the rise of Nazism looks like a linear trajectory, a series of accelerating events terminating inevitably at the gates of Auschwitz. . . . Most Americans, including the Hollywood moguls, had no inkling of the horrors to come, no understanding that dealing with the new regime in Germany was not business as usual. . . . I saw [in my research] some greed and cupidity, to be sure, but mainly I saw confusion, wishful thinking, and disbelief. How did a nation Hollywood had long considered sane and rational become so pathological? Was this a permanent affliction or would the fever break? ("Does 'Collaboration' Overstate")

I view skeptically only three words from this assessment: "had no inkling." There were inklings aplenty during the period covered by both authors, even before *Kristallnacht*. Fascism, including Nazism, had been around since the century's teens; genocidal violence and ethnic cleansing, at least since World War I and indeed far longer. Anti-Semitism was a phenomenon with deep roots going back centuries; the radical anti-Semitism of Hitler a murderous fantasy amply advertised by Hitler himself. Political anti-Semitism and the beginnings of fascism go back more or less to the era of the Dreyfus case in France (Arendt esp. 89–120, 267–302). Totalitarian control of culture existed at least since the rise of Fascist Italy and the Soviet Union, and cutthroat battles for shaping mass media raged throughout the same period. Mass media and mass violence are twin siblings born of the modern era, and while the Hollywood moguls were not historians or deep thinkers, they surely sensed the stakes were high. And so, "had no inkling" rings a bit hollow, at least to me. It is these muddled boundaries and improvised responses, and, above all, the ever-present hum of commerce, that makes the situation a shared one among all parties. The intricate interconnectedness of all these factors is what makes the period (or rather the whole era of catastrophe dating back to 1914) so worth studying.

All this, for me, encourages a conclusion that, I would like to think, accords with both authors' approaches but which neither author might be inclined to accept wholeheartedly: that the realities of the era of catastrophe from 1914 to 1945 were the collective product of both fascist and democratic nations and must be seen as a continuous and systemic unity. This situation needs to be understood without resentment or indignation, though also without perceptual mercy toward any quarter—East or West; democratic or fascist; communist, socialist, or capitalist—yet also (if we are to progress beyond its hold on us) with forgiveness, lucid and self-critical awareness, and persistent memory. Such an approach does not obliterate the absolute evils of fascism and genocide: on the contrary, it strives to keep them in sharp focus. It honors the memory of Holocaust victims but recognizes the universal potential for genocide's contagion (already realized again and again, arguably countless times, *since* 1945). It requires firm standards of human rights and international justice. It recognizes the reality of war crimes, and does not relativize evil by declaring (as evildoers often do) that good and evil are only determined by the victors.

Urwand's book suffers from a surfeit of crucial "turning points" that seem to blend into one another after a while, and he seems a bit too fond of saying that had this or that movie been allowed to proceed to production, or survived butcherings by censors, or attacks by Gyssling, or the pressures of Jewish civic groups, or the failures of nerve by studio heads, or the Breen office, or the Hays Office, then Hollywood would have had a cinema creation addressing the menace of Nazism in a more timely and forceful way. There is a hidden utopianism in such assessments, one that repeatedly holds "what might have been" over Hollywood culture the way one might suspend a mountain over it. And yet, as I suggested earlier, we deprive ourselves of something valuable by refusing to ask what might have been. The answer, to be sure, might be silence, or confusion, or fruitless speculation, but to ask it is to think about the inner resources of a society and about its capacity to change. Urwand, in retelling a film story, as he occasionally does, begins a journey that has a chance to lead deeper into the public dialogue these films, at their hypothetically most timely and most incisive, were supposed to have provoked. But the inquiry entails more than plot summaries—it requires close reading, and ambitious and adventurous interpretation. "What might have been" should not be measured in terms of its effect on a foreign adversary but its effect on the body-politic at home. The result is not a better anti-Nazi movie *then*, but better resources for dealing with barbarism *since* then, including now. The dialogue those suppressed or ideologically sanitized movies might have created must be measured by what is on our lips today.

Notes

1. This presentation summarizes a longer review article by the author, "The Good, the Bad, and the Fatal," listed below under Works Cited. [Ed.]
2. The third person Rosenberg is referring to here is Vincent Brook, who participated in the panel along with Lawrence Baron, but whose full presentation is not included here because it was felt its anti-Urwand take, on top of Baron's, would unduly upset the balance of the debate. Brook has supplied a brief Coda below. [Ed.]

Works Cited

Arendt, Hannah. *The Origins of Totalitarianism*. Meridian/World, 1951, 1958.

Doherty, Thomas. "Does 'The Collaboration' Overstate Hollywood's Cooperation with Hitler?" *The Hollywood Reporter* 31 July 2013, www.hollywoodreporter.com/news/does-collaboration-overstate-hollywoods-cooperation-595678. Accessed 24 Aug. 2016.

———. *Hollywood and Hitler, 1933–1939*. Columbia Univ., 2013.

Lewis, Sinclair. *It Can't Happen Here*. Doubleday, Doran, 1935.

Rosenberg, Joel. *The Era of Catastrophe—A Judeo-Cinematic Trajectory: Five Studies in Mass Media and Mass Destruction*. Unpublished manuscript.

———. "The Good, the Bad, and the Fatal: Ben Urwand on the Hollywood Moguls and Hitler." *Jewish Film and New Media*, vol. 1, issue 2 (2013), Article 5, digitalcommons.wayne.edu/jewishfilm/vol1/iss2/5/. Accessed 24 Aug. 2016.

———. "Jewish Experience in Film: An American Overview." *American Jewish Year Book*, vol. 96, edited by David Singer and Ruth R. Seldin. American Jewish Committee, 1996, pp. 3–50.

Urwand, Ben. *The Collaboration: Hollywood's Pact with Hitler*. Bellknap of Harvard Univ., 2013.

Coda to the Doherty-Urwand Panel[1]

by Vincent Brook

Neither Urwand's nor Doherty's book can be held accountable for significant additional information that came to the fore around the time the controversy surrounding the books unfolded. But the material, housed at California State University, Northridge (CSUN), casts Hollywood's response to the Nazi threat in an entirely new light. First rediscovered by San Francisco State University lecturer Laura Rosenzweig for her doctoral dissertation, the material now forms the basis for separate forthcoming books by Rosenzweig and Steven Ross. As Rosenzweig outlines in a Winter 2014 *Jewish Review of Books* article and Ross recounted to me in conversation, a broad outline of the CSUN disclosures is the following:

With Hitler's ascension to power in 1933, the then still comparatively small and fragmented Nazi movement in the US quickly organized into a national organization called the Friends of the New Germany (or FNG). Precursor to the German American Bund (formed in 1935), the FNG's mission was to spread Nazism throughout the country in preparation for "*der Tag*"—the day when the Hitler Revolution in America would begin. In Los Angeles, specifically, the FNG, already in March 1933, opened the Aryan Bookstore downtown, and in the spring and summer held public rallies, sponsored weekly lectures, and reached out to the American Legion and other veterans groups to attract new members.

The rise of the FNG would have prodded Los Angeles attorney Leon Lewis—the former, and first national secretary of the Anti-Defamation League—to action in any case. The FNG's effort to recruit American veterans, however, not only especially vexed the veteran Lewis, but, ironically, also offered him a surefire way to infiltrate the group through his contacts with non-Jewish, anti-fascist veterans.

The magnitude of the conspiracy that Lewis's anti-Nazi spies, led by Neil Ness, uncovered was stunning and renders as child's play Georg Gyssling's shenanigans in Hollywood. Around the time the German consul purportedly was gaining concessions on American film content, the FNG was meeting secretly with Nazi Party officials aboard ships in the Port of Los Angeles. Besides involving the smuggling of large amounts of money and Berlin-produced Nazi literature, the meetings "planned bombings, lynchings, and assassinations of Jewish business and civic leaders"—including the studio heads and their non-Jewish "allies" like Charlie Chaplin and James Cagney. Other plots included "recruiting American soldiers, acquiring military secrets, blowing up aviation, munitions, and port facilities" (Kafka B9).

Though not nearly as important as helping thwart the bomb plots, Lewis's spy ring also managed to restore some of Hollywood's moral stature. For it was none other than the studio heads, including MGM's Louis B. Mayer, who ended up financing Lewis's counter-espionage campaign. Lewis had bankrolled the early stages of his operation largely on his own. To secure additional funding, he first approached LA's "old money" Jews: bankers, developers, merchants, judges, and doctors. Their contributions were so meager, however, as to lead Lewis to call Los Angeles "the toughest city in the country to raise money for any purpose" (Rosenzweig 3). Lewis turned next to the Hollywood Jews.

In March 1934, he organized a dinner for studio bigwigs at Hillcrest Country Club, founded by LA's Jewish elite as an alternative to the gentile clubs from which they had been excluded. Among the honchos in attendance were MGM's Mayer and Irving Thalberg, Paramount's Emanuel Cohen, Warner Brothers' Jack Warner, RKO's Pandro Berman, Columbia's Sam Briskin, and executives from Universal, Fox, and Twentieth Century (the latter two studios not yet having merged into Twentieth Century Fox). Big-time producers David O. Selznick, Harry Rapf, and Sam Jaffe were among the dignitaries, as were A-list directors Ernest Lubitsch and George Cukor. Prominent local Jewish community leaders Rabbi Edgar Magnin, Judge Lester Roth, and banker Marco Hellman also were on hand—but, according to Rosenzweig, "the movie men were the decision-makers in the room" (Rosenzweig 4).

And who would be the most vocal of the movie-men in support of Lewis's efforts but Ben Urwand bugaboo Louis B. Mayer. "I for one am not going to take [the Nazi activities] lying down," Mayer said. "Two things are required, namely money and intelligent direction . . . it [is] the duty of the men present to help" (Rosenzweig 4). A committee was promptly formed, composed of one man from each studio, along with the Jewish community leaders.

An additional tidbit that Ross provided, and which may have further spurred studio support, was Lewis's disclosure that the FNG had managed to infiltrate the Hollywood studios as well, and was actively working to remove Jewish personnel from below-the-line ranks. This was possibly to purge the "Jewish-controlled" studios from the bottom up or to lay the groundwork for the above-mentioned film industry bombings and assassinations.

Fresh from his fund-raising success with the studios, Lewis sought to secure political support from Washington. As for his accomplishments there, Rosenzweig and Ross appear to differ. Ross, in our conversation, complained that Congress and the FBI, more concerned with domestic Communist subversion, tended to downplay the fascist threat and generally ignored Lewis's call for help. Rosenzweig, however, writes that Lewis not only was encouraged by a congressional committee formed in 1934 to investigate Nazi activity but was appointed West Coast counsel to the committee. The information Lewis's studio-supported operation collected from 1933–41, Rosenzweig concludes, "was used in several federal investigations and prosecutions," including those of Los Angeles Bund leader Herman Schwinn and Silver Shirts leader William Dudley Pelley. Lewis would continue to direct the so-called "Hollywood spies" through the end of World War II (6).

The Cal-State Northridge archival disclosures by no means fully exonerate the studio heads, the Breen office, or the Jewish community for the failure of Hollywood movies to more forthrightly confront the Nazi threat during the 1930s. Leon Lewis's studio-abetted spy operation does demonstrate, however, that, at the very least—contra Ben Urwand—Hollywood-Nazi "collaboration" cut both ways.

Note

1. Portions of the Coda material were included in Brook's panel presentation and in an on-line book review by the author, listed below under Works Cited. [Ed.]

Works Cited

Brook, Vincent. "Collaboration Without Corroboration Is Tyranny—A Tale of Two Takes on Hollywood's Dealings with Nazi Germany." Review of *The Collaboration: Hollywood's Pact with Hitler* by Ben Urwand and *Hollywood and Hitler: 1933–1939* by Thomas Doherty. *Mediascape* 28 Oct. 2013, www.tft.ucla.edu/mediascape/blog/?p=2157. Accessed 24 Aug. 2016.

Kafka, Alexander. "When Hollywood Held Hands with Hitler." *Chronicle of Higher Education,* 2 Aug. 2015, pp. B4–5, 7–9.

Rosenzweig, Laura. "Hollywood's Anti-Nazi Spies." *Jewish Review of Books*, Winter 2014, jewishreviewofbooks.com/articles/582/hollywoods-anti-nazi-spies. Accessed 24 Aug. 2016.

Ross, Steven. Interview with Vincent Brook. Los Angeles, Feb. 2014.

PART 2: CASE STUDIES

CHAPTER 3

Dirty Jews: Amy Schumer and Other Vulgar Jewesses

by Shaina Hammerman

Jewish humor, boiling as it is with angst and self-deprecation, is almost masculine by definition.

—Christopher Hitchens

Amy Schumer's image dominated West Hollywood's Sunset Strip in the weeks before the debut of her October 2015 HBO comedy special. Gazing seductively from a skyscraper-sized billboard, Schumer sips a glass of whiskey and holds a cigar between her fingers. She wears a grey three-piece suit with a tie; next to her face, the text reads, "She's a lady." The ironic blend of the text and her masculine attire and accoutrement is comically overdetermined. But anyone who knows Schumer's work—and by 2015 she had become ubiquitous on the big and small screens—understands that the humor behind the "She's a lady" text points not just to her appearance on the billboard but to her overt sexuality, her pleasure in talking about pleasure, and her openness in joking about bodily functions. These characteristics come together with the billboard image to make Schumer appear most *un*-ladylike. At the tail-end of her year of many accomplishments, which included an Emmy for her comedy sketch series *Inside Amy Schumer*, a Golden Globe nomination for her performance in *Trainwreck* (a film she also wrote), her gig as host of the MTV Movie Awards, and her appearance as the opening act for Madonna's "Rebel Heart Tour," Schumer's apparent refusal to behave like a "lady" may be the key to her success as a writer, actress, and stand-up comic. But Schumer has also won acclaim from fans as more than just an entertainer; she has emerged as a feminist icon.

As a woman in the public eye, Schumer's looks are fodder for much discussion: Is she too fat to be beautiful? Too beautiful to be funny? Schumer's comic brilliance surfaces when she pre-empts these types of sexist critiques on her show, skewering both her own looks and those who think that the way they look at her should matter. The most poignant example of this preemptive maneuvering came when Schumer's series meticulously recreated the classic jury-trial drama, "12 Angry Men." On trial in this parody was Schumer's attractiveness—whether she was "hot enough" to appear on television. Replete with a high-profile cast that included Paul Giamatti and Jeff Goldblum, the men delve into impassioned debate about everything from whether the use of sex toys is an indication of a woman's attractiveness, to whether women can be funny, to whether sexual attraction is subjective. The parody calls out every kind of hypocrisy and sexism, based at least in part on actual comments Schumer has received from critics or anonymous online commenters. The sketch demonstrates that Schumer knows exactly what she looks like, exactly how much it matters to some (quite a bit), and exactly how much she cares (she's ambivalent).

Schumer's performance (both how she looks and how she acts) is at once sexy, classy, ugly, and raunchy. Or, to quote an Instagram post she shared featuring a nude photograph of her taken by Annie Liebowitz, Schumer is "Beautiful, gross, strong, thin, fat, pretty, ugly, sexy, disgusting, flawless, woman" (amyschumer). One adjective Schumer leaves off this descriptive list is "Jewish," a fact that she and many of her fans elect to ignore or maintain in the realm of the parenthetical. Schumer is not alone in her parenthetical Jewishness, or, as she once described herself, in being "Jewish-ish" (SwaysUniverse).

A cohort of similarly "Jewish-ish" comedians have achieved substantial success in the past decade alone. Lena Dunham, Ilana Glazer and Abbi Jacobson, Jenny Slate, and Rachel Bloom, and before them, Sarah Silverman, have brought a fresh blend of self-proclaimed feminist, raunchy humor to the forefront of American comic consciousness. Even as some of these women may deny the significance of their Jewishness either to their comic personae or in their personal lives, their Jewishness—and its parenthetical quality—has deep roots in the history of American comedy, a history that itself cannot be extracted from Jewishness. Jewish male comedians from the earliest days of Vaudeville to the present have regularly and overtly referenced their Jewishness as a kind of hilarious vulnerability. From Henny Youngman to Woody Allen to Jerry Seinfeld to Jon Stewart to Seth Rogen, Jewishness and its attendant anxieties in a gentile world offered an unending stream of punchlines. Jewish women comedians, from what Sarah Blacher Cohen called the "unkosher comediennes" of the twentieth century (Sophie Tucker, Belle Barth, Totie Fields, and Joan Rivers) to Amy Schumer and her cohort, reference their bodies and sexuality and keep the Jewish jokes to a minimum. When they do reference their Jewishness, it lacks the anxiety-laden humor of their male colleagues. Jewish men make Jewish jokes. Jewish women make women jokes.

Looked at one way, Schumer and her cohort can be justifiably viewed as part of a revolution in feminist performance in their embracing of women's sexuality and pleasure without euphemism, in talking openly about how they feel about their bodies, and in calling out the misogyny that often targets them directly. Looked at another way, these comics also clearly stem from a long line of vulgar Jewish comediennes. While their jokes lend toward the recent "bare it all" trend in American popular culture, their bawdy comedy is both particularly Jewish and not particularly new. This essay is a meditation on these two ways of looking at the Schumer phenomenon, the parenthetical and the traditional, arguing that the specificities of Jewishness in America make both readings of her and her cohorts' performances possible. What is it about the particularities of being Jewish women that allows for audiences to make this kind of choice: A choice that does not appear to apply to performances by Jewish male comics?

JEWS AND (JEWS)

I adapt the notion of the "parenthetical Jew" from Naomi Seidman who uncovered a handful of queer and feminist theorists who quite literally put their own Jewishness into parentheses in their writings. These thinkers struggle to lay claim to their Jewishness, or at least to foreground it, preferring instead to identify their queerness, their gender identities, or their activist agendas as the driving factors of their subject positions. Recalling a history of American-Jewish political activism on behalf of "other Others" as part of the Jewish investment in American multiculturalism, Seidman lays bare the parenthetical Jewishness of these activists and begins to theorize how their downplayed Jewish identities actually formed a key component of their ability and desire to stand up for other marginalized groups.

Writing nearly twenty years ago, Seidman described her multiculturalist moment and the suspicion that followed parenthetical Jews who stood up for causes not quite their own.

> In a culture that equates the battle for representation and rights with political progressivism, the Jew who resists a straightforward identity politics in exchange for participation in the struggle of "someone else" opens herself up to the charges of assimilationism, self-hatred, and parasitism. (Seidman 266)

In other words, even as these (Jews) fight for progressive causes, their failure to identify as Jews first and foremost becomes an invitation for derision from seeming political allies. "In an environment that celebrates marginality," Seidman continues, "the Jewish politics of the vicarious is a marginal position that has yet to find its champion." In Seidman's equation, parenthetical Jewishness, like the reviled category of the fag-hag, amounted to its own kind of marginalization, one that had yet to achieve the chic underdog status of other marginalized identities within American multiculturalist tendencies.

The feminism of Schumer, Dunham, and the other comedians I explore here may not carry the sophisticated theoretical underpinnings of Eve Kosofsky Sedgwick or Judith Butler, nor do they elide their Jewishness as completely as these scholars. But their Jewishness operates in similar ways. In fact, Schumer, Dunham, Bloom, Jacobson, and Glazer may be the very champions Seidman missed in the late 1990s. Part of the reason these women have obtained their caché owes precisely to the ways they keep their Jewishness strategically within parentheses. They neither deny it nor completely ignore it. Instead, as the following examples demonstrate, they engage with it purposefully without ever allowing it to eclipse the other components of their humor or personae.

Consider, for example, the *Broad City* stars who release a series of web shorts between seasons of their half-hour-long Comedy Central show. In the first episode of Season 3 of "Hack into Broad City," Abbi and Ilana (Jacobson and Glazer's fictionalized onscreen personae) are attempting to fast for Yom Kippur. The women chat with each other on Skype as they lie in bed, each with a large sandwich next to her computer. "I don't get Yom Kippur, it sucks!" bemoans Ilana. Abbi responds; "it's like, how is me waiting until the sun sets to eat this bacon, egg, and cheese gonna cancel out the time I laughed in that hot dude's face about his weird-shaped nipples mid-coitus? It's not!" Abbi's joke is predicated on the well-known Jewish practice of fasting for Yom Kippur; but the real gag, and the key joke for the entire three-minute webisode is Abbi and

Ilana's self-centered immaturity and their questionable ethics. The two go on to list "all the bad shit we've done this year." To be sure, they are "bad Jews," to which Abbi's brazen reference to her bacon sandwich attests. But more than "bad Jews," they are "bad girls"—their list of "bad shit" includes stealing a neighbor's magazines and giving tourists the wrong directions. They are petty and selfish, but honest and loveable; their list of sins includes behaviors only slightly more extreme and absurd than the average person's white lie. They conclude by deceiving themselves into believing that the most righteous (Jewish?) thing they could do is eat their sandwiches right then and there, hours before the sun sets. While Yom Kippur sets the precedent for their hunger and their confessional behavior in the episode, Jewishness is not the punchline. Instead, the joke is about two twenty-something friends, stoner millenials, whose actions and conversations are designed to feel warm and recognizable at the same time as they are made to feel outrageous and hilarious.

The elephant in the room when it comes to any discussion of Jews and humor is the question that causes so many scholars to throw up their hands in frustration—what makes comedy so Jewish? One self-described "shiksa" interviewer posed this question directly to Schumer: "Why are all the best comedians always Jewish? . . . It just seems like . . . there's always been a Jewish dominance in comedy. . . . Is it something about the ethnic identity that lends itself to so much hilarity?" (Richardson 2011). Schumer tries at first to deny that "all the best comedians are Jewish," but cannot avoid the preponderance of successful Jewish comics. "I guess it's the sense of self-importance and entitlement and being unapologetic, . . ." she ventures. Schumer goes on to describe her personal experiences with antisemitism growing up, the way she was regularly "apologizing for being Jewish." She continues, "for me . . . I'm pretty good with the crowd and I can handle hecklers, so I think that comes from me having to be defensive."

Jewish male comedians cannot be described in the same way. Their approach to Jewishness is neither unapologetic nor parenthetical. Take, for example, an anecdote from Jewish actor and comedian Jason Segel.

> Segel recalled explaining his bar mitzvah to his Christian classmates as a pivotal moment that pushed him away from his peers and toward acting. "This is when you become funny. . . . Little 13-year-old Jason Segel standing there like, 'On Saturday I become a man,'" he said, imitating his adolescent voice breaking. "It's literally a direct cut to getting punched in the face." (Tobin 2015)

For Schumer, negative Jewish experiences fostered the self-assuredness at the root of her comic persona. For Segel, negative Jewish experiences *are in and of themselves* the joke. Both find a way to credit their Jewishness for their comedy.

Schumer's depiction of Jewishness as embodied in performances of self-importance, entitlement, and being unapologetic describes performances by Dunham, Abbi and Ilana, and Silverman. Her depiction also captures the comedic stylings of the earlier generations of "unkosher comediennes" beginning with Sophie Tucker, "the pioneer flaunter of taboos, who made illicit laughter more comfortable" (Blacher Cohen 106). Like the Jewish women performers who followed, Tucker's body was a focal point of her act. Nearly a century before Schumer's rise to fame, Tucker's comedy acknowledged how the audience saw her body, exaggerated any qualities that ran counter to conventional standards of beauty, and then joked about her insatiable desire for sex. Like their comedic progeny in the 2010s, Tucker and her cohort—especially Belle Barth and Totie Fields—never apologized for their bodies (they played up being "fat") or their Jewishness (using Yiddish to drive home punchlines). Their comedy confidently made demands of Jewish men to fulfill both their sexual and financial needs. In one song, Tucker takes on the character of a pregnant, unmarried woman:

> Mistah Siegel, Mistah Siegel, in my *boich is schoen a kiegel*
> (In my belly is already a noodle pudding.)
> Mistah Siegel, make it legal for me. (Blacher Cohen 108)

This character can handle her circumstances and knew what she was getting into when, "Something happened, accidently." Instead of a polite request, she self-assuredly demands the man fulfill his responsibility for this "accident" by marrying her.

Decades before the sexual revolution of the 1960s, Tucker, Barth, and Fields already relied on Yiddish-inflected body humor to expose women's sexual desires. As their careers progressed, they continued to push the comic envelope. In the 1970s, Fields controversially joked about rape in a way that "would infuriate today's feminists" (Blacher Cohen 113). "I'm so tired of being everybody's buddy," she joked, "Just once to read in a newspaper, Totie Fields raped in an alley." The joke is on Fields' extreme lustful desperation, but it also destabilizes the latent power structures that make women into victims—how can you victimize a woman who wants so badly to be ravaged? When the joke is performed, its Jewishness comes through clearly in Fields' phrasing, "just once to read." Hers is the radical precursor to Sarah Silverman's (in)famous one-liner: "I was raped by a doctor. So bittersweet for a Jewish girl." Here, Silverman's persona likewise refuses to play the victim in her joke. She undermines the expected desires of Jewish women (namely, the JAP stereotype) to "land" a doctor, by imagining that doctor as a violent sex offender, even as she exposes, as Fields did, her taboo desire to be desired by that kind of man. These women are not only unapologetically libidinous; they are also unapologetically offensive. "Who's going to complain about rape jokes? Rape victims?" Silverman muses. "They barely even report rape."[1] While Jewishness plays a role in Silverman's punchline, the joke is on American rape culture, not on Jewish women. Just as Schumer and Dunham call out unreasonable standards of beauty by skewering their own bodies, Silverman calls out the culture of silence among rape victims by skewering her own joke. She dares her audience to be offended, forcing those who enable silence to examine their complicity in rape culture.

ENGENDERING LAUGHTER

Jewish men's comedy in America—known to most simply as "comedy"—may be rooted partly in an Eastern European past, but there is no methodological need to reach that far back.[2] Jews dominated American comedy circuits first by performing mostly for each other in Yiddish Vaudeville and as the resident entertainment at Jewish summer resorts in the Northeast known as the Borscht Belt. The jokes they made at that time ranged from physical comedy to word play to a tradition of one-liners made at the expense of (Jewish) women (the most infamous being Henny Youngman's signature line, "Take my wife . . . please"). In the mid-twentieth century, dialect humor reigned supreme as the children of immigrants (most notably, Mickey Katz), mocked the accents and manners of their parents. Borscht Belt comics (e.g., Milton Berle, Sid Cesar, Mel Brooks, Woody Allen, among others) emerged as mainstream successes, reaching beyond the majority-Jewish audiences of the Catskills in the postwar period. On their heels, other Jewish comics achieved broad appeal in the 1980s and 1990s, namely Jerry Seinfeld, Paul Reiser, Richard Lewis, and Garry Shandling, among others. By the end of the twentieth century, Jews dwarfed other ethnic minorities on television sitcoms even as they made room for black, Latino, and much later, Asian comedians to achieve similar success among white mainstream (read: Christian) audiences. While Seinfeld and

Reiser's television personae made attempts to mask their Jewishness to reach the widest possible network audience, the Jewishness of *Seinfeld* and *Mad About You* remained unmistakable. In addition to a few overt references to Seinfeld's Jewishness on the series, everything about his character's milieu screamed "New York Jewish" even without addressing it (the fact that he played a version of himself, a stand-up comedian, provides only one of a myriad of codes for his Jewishness). On both Reiser's and Seinfeld's shows, the loud, over-involved Jewish mother figured predominantly in fashioning their sons' Jewishness as did their characters' relationships with WASPy women.[3] With the rise of other ethnic comedians and perhaps in response to Seinfeld's reserve about his own ethnicity, men like Jon Stewart, Seth Rogen, and Adam Sandler made a habit of regularly pointing directly to their own Jewishness as a means to confide in their audience and generate trust (Stewart), to express a charming but "funny" vulnerability (Rogen), or to point ironically to Jewish powerlessness (Sandler's "Chanukah Song," for example).

The Jewish vulnerability played up by Stewart, Rogen, and others is part of a tradition of what some have labeled "Jewish self-hatred," wherein Jews adopt the antisemitic stereotypes lobbed against them, including a general notion of Jewish men being weak or effeminate.[4] As male comics played up their passivity, they also played up an idea of Jewish women as sexually, financially, and emotionally aggressive. This image of the Jewish woman operates in stark contrast to the "weak" Jewish man who in the Old Country devoted his life to Torah study and passed his effeminate tendencies to his male progeny even as they attempted to adopt secular, bourgeois norms of masculinity.[5] This propensity to characterize Jewish men as weak and Jewish woman as aggressive led to a tradition of Jewish performance as a kind of transgendering. Whereas men comics, epitomized by nebbishy figures like Woody Allen, have constructed Jewish personae dependent on being physically slight, "indoorsy," and effeminate, women like Amy Schumer and Lena Dunham enact their Jewishness by acting like "men." That is to say, they joke openly and in great detail about sex and their bodies, make extensive use of profanity, and generally make self-confidence a central and implicit part of their comedic personae. This is the phenomenon at the heart of Schumer's "She's a lady" billboard.

At the turn of the twenty-first century, Jewish studies and gender studies intersected. Scholars generated a library of arguments about the divergent historical, social, and religious paths and possibilities for Jewish women and men. For example, Riv-Ellen Prell's *Fighting to Become Americans* makes the claim that tensions between Jewish men and women mirror the broader tensions between Jewish and gentile Americans, as men deflect the antisemitic accusations they experience onto Jewish women. In this way, greed, emotional excess, and status-seeking become traits of Jewish women, reflected in the stereotypes of the overbearing Jewish mother and the Jewish American Princess. Paula Hyman made a related claim in her book about gender and Jewish history, demonstrating how the processes and outcomes of Jewish assimilation differ radically for men and women. In secularizing Western Europe as in the United States, men distanced themselves from the responsibility for transmitting Jewish tradition to the next generation by placing the onus entirely on women and then blaming women for ever-increasing secularization (Hyman 134–70). In the realm of Jewish comedy—as might be expected of the comedic—these processes are inverted. Here, Jewish men embrace the stereotypes they once so eagerly eschewed (and adopt new stereotypes), while Jewish women comics seem keen to evade such stereotyping. In comedy, Jewish men are the ones to proclaim their Jewishness regularly in public, while Jewish women do so only selectively if at all.

Men like Jon Stewart rely heavily on Jewishness as part of their act and regularly "come out" as Jews as a mechanism to engender laughter. "I'm a Jew," Stewart confessed during an interview with NBA star Charles Barkley, "I can't dunk. So we all have our limitations" (*The Daily Show with Jon Stewart*, 3 Jan. 2012). Or, consider the scene from *Knocked Up* when Katherine Heigl's character compliments Seth Rogen's curly hair. She asks if he uses any special product to achieve the look and he responds, "It's called Jew." In both cases, the audience already knows the men are Jewish. In both cases, the fact of their Jewishness is not on its own funny. But calling it out, especially when contrasted with a 6'7" basketball star or a classically beautiful blond actress, draws a laugh from the viewer. Sig Altman sums up the power of these kinds of confessions in his book on Jewish comedy. Referring to a talk show that aired in the 1960s, he recounts an interviewee who,

> in the course of a totally serious discussion, made the quite serious remark, "I looked it up in the Jewish Encyclopedia." There immediately followed a burst of laughter from the studio audience, which obviously sensed a joke about to materialize, or perhaps saw one already born. The laughter rather suddenly subsided, however, as the collective realization apparently dawned that no joke was in fact intended at all. Nevertheless, the comic quality of the word "Jewish" in the public consciousness had been perfectly demonstrated. (Altman xvii)

As Altman's work establishes, this confessional comic device dates back at least to the 1960s. While there were a substantial number of successful, popular, Jewish women comedians during the '60s and '70s (following Tucker, Barth, and Fields, there were Joan Rivers, Madeleine Kahn, Gilda Radner, etc.), they did not employ this device. They were far more likely, not unlike their descendants in Schumer et al., to joke about the pitfalls of sex, dating, marriage, and womanhood. When these women reference their Jewishness, it lacks the self-derision and confessional quality that characterizes Jewish men's comedy.

A most striking example of this comes from one of Amy Schumer's stand-up bits where she talks about growing up as a member of the only Jewish family in her town. She tells the story of the other school children calling her "Amy Jew-mer" and throwing handfuls of pennies at her. The punchline to her sad story is, "excuse me, this is *awesome*. . . . I was like, make it rain! Such a good summer" (*CC Presents: Amy Schumer*). She goes on to talk about an evangelical woman attempting to share the "good news" of Jesus Christ. Amy recounts her response:

> "Ma'am I'm so sorry, but my people are Jewish." And she's like, "that's ok, your people just haven't found Jesus yet." And I was like, "um . . . no, like, we found him . . . maybe you haven't heard the *bad* news?"

While there is no denying the Jewishness of these jokes, they are marked by pride and hyper-confidence rather than the vulnerability and self-ridicule of the male comics of Schumer's generation (and generations past). The "limitations" of Jewishness about which Stewart joked are present in the jokes' setups—antisemitism, accusations of deicide—but not in the punchlines of Schumer's comedy. Here, Jewishness is a (potentially naïve) power play wherein Schumer understands something her anti-Jewish interlocutors do not.

The parenthetical Jewishness of Schumer's comedy, more so than the scholars Seidman discusses, allows explicit Jewishness to come to the fore from time to time. But Jewishness itself is not the butt of the joke as it has been for male comics for decades. In fact, male comedians have become so accustomed to using Jewishness as a punchline that critics have begun to question whether the joke still works. A critic from *Vulture* magazine described the passé quality of the ongoing Jewish joke in his review of the 2015 holiday movie, *The Night Before*: "There's a lot of stuff about [Rogen's character] being Jewish, because apparently that's still funny—or maybe it's just funny *because* it's not funny anymore" (Ebiri). The weak or vulnerable Jewish male joke has achieved so broad a reach that even contemporary non-Jewish comedians rely on this mode as well. Josh Lambert writes about Eddie Murphy, Steven Wright, Anthony Jeselnik, and Louis CK all "killing" with "non-Jewish Jew jokes" (Lambert). Because the Jewish jokes of Jews like Stewart have become so mainstream, or, in Altman's terms, "the comic quality of the word 'Jew'" has become so deeply engrained in American comic consciousness, these non-Jewish comedians found their own way in to laughing with (or occasionally at) Jews. Beyond that, non-Jewish comedians have adopted the "weak Jewish man" act and applied it to their own ethnic backgrounds. Louis CK is the twenty-first century's master of non-Jewish self-derision, joking at the expense of his Catholic upbringing, and regularly referring to himself as "an asshole." Newcomer Aziz Ansari created an entire series out of his act of being romantically, charmingly self-deprecating and the child of Indian immigrants (*Master of None*).

UNAPOLOGETICALLY (JEW)-ISH

While contemporary non-Jewish men comics have adopted what might be called "classic" Jewish humor, the latest Jewish women comics are taking Jewish comedy in ever-new directions. Rachel Bloom's character Rebecca Bunch on *Crazy Ex-Girlfriend* peppers her dialogue with Yiddish terms and references her New York Jewishness on occasion, especially to create contrast with the middle-class inland suburb of Los Angeles where she lives in the show. In one memorable scene, Rebecca's mother (played by Tovah Felshuh) comes to visit her and sings a glorious Broadway-inspired ballad filled with passive-aggressive insults called "The Jewish Mother Song." While Rebecca's character struggles mightily in her love life, her Jewishness is not a source of insecurity for her. She holds her ground confidently against her overbearing mother as the woman challenges every one of her life's decisions. Likewise, in one of the series' first episodes, Rebecca's boss hires her to be his personal divorce lawyer. When he describes his wife's lawyer as, "one of those real smart Jewish guys," Rebecca quickly interrupts with "I'm sorry, I'm Jewish." In spite of her rhetorical apology here, Rebecca is unapologetically Jewish. Her boss ends up being quite excited that "my Jew went to Harvard and Yale!" Rebecca concludes the exchange with, "Let's circle back about the Jew thing because that's a conversation that we need to have" ("Josh Just Happens to Live Here!"). The particularities of Jewishness offer an opportunity for generational conflict with the mother, and for comic awkwardness with her new boss. But the joke is never on Jewishness itself. For Rebecca, "Jewish identity is a non-issue" (Zaltzman). In other words, Jewishness plays here as it does in *Broad City* and Schumer's stand-up, as a basis for a joke and an unexpected opening for foregrounding these women's unabashed confidence.

One of Schumer's other notable (and viral) sketches featured some of the most successful, multiple award-winning actresses of the past thirty years. In "Last Fuckable Day," Patricia Arquette, Julia Louis-Dreyfus, and Tina Fey are having an elegant picnic to celebrate Louis-Dreyfus's reaching this moment: "in every actress's life, the media decides when you finally reach the point where you're not believably fuckable anymore." The joke here lies in the ridiculous reality that leading-lady roles diminish exponentially for women as they age, whereas male actors regularly maintain their statuses as sex symbols well into their sixties. But the joke also lies in the unmistakable beauty of Dreyfus, who, after decades of television success may just now, at fifty-five, be reaching a new career peak as the star in her HBO hit, *Veep*. Schumer's sketch calls out a system that places arbitrary demands on women's youth and beauty. But at the same time, in showing the women *celebrating* their arrival at this stage of their lives, Schumer undermines the perceived value of "fuckability" as a worthy goal to which all women should aspire.

This is Schumer's double move: a beautiful, successful woman spotlighting the unjust standards surrounding women's beauty while also undercutting ideas about women's desires to meet these standards. Or as one writer described it, Schumer "poke[s] just as hard at young single women, in their blinkered vanity, as she does at the toxic messages that surround them" (Nussbaum). This maneuver lies at the core of Schumer's feminist humor and the humor of many in her cohort. Lena Dunham, the creator of HBO's *Girls* takes a similar approach in preempting public critique of her body by displaying it shamelessly on-screen. "The nudity is a confrontation," writes Paul Schrodt of *Esquire Magazine*. "Why are some appalled by it? Why does she flaunt it? What does she think of it? The show projects our insecurities back at us, makes us deal with them."

In these examples, the women's (comically exaggerated) confidence is not explicitly Jewish. But if male comics' repeated references to their own weaknesses read as Jewish, then as these women gain visibility, their occasionally absurd displays of sexual or emotional or professional confidence begin to read as Jewish, too. Put another way, their feminism, even when not placed within a Jewish context, may be inextricable from their Jewishness, just as Seidman demonstrated of the parenthetically Jewish feminist scholars.

Part of what makes these women's performances feminist is the way they stand in contrast to the trend in stoner-slacker comedies made popular by the prolific director/producer Judd Apatow. Jewish actors Adam Sandler, Seth Rogen, Jason Segal, and Jonah Hill have played clumsy, unattractive, unambitious all-around immature Jewish "schlubs" who refuse to succumb to the demands of the adult world. In so doing, they also manage to attract unlikely goddesses played by gorgeous women like Katherine Heigl, Drew Barrymore, and Emma Stone. So commonplace in the beginning of the twenty-first century as to become its own genre of romantic comedy, these neo-schlemiel comedies received some backlash from feminists, including one famous occasion from one of the film's stars.[6] Feminists wondered why successful, attractive women would adore such clumsy, videogame playing, unkempt, porn-obsessed boys.

Interestingly, the critiques that label Apatow a misogynist have been undermined by his more recent work with woman-run comedies. Beginning with the blockbuster *Bridesmaids*, Apatow appears to have abandoned screwball boy comedies in favor of feminist television and filmmaking. He is the producer behind Schumer's film *Trainwreck* as well as Dunham's series *Girls*. Both Schumer and Dunham speak of him with great affection (as a feminist, too), belying the earlier feminist critique. If Apatow's films like *Knocked Up* and *Anchorman* depended on the (goyish) women characters being the mature, nagging foils to juvenile-acting Jewish men, then Apatow's feminist turn with *Girls* and *Trainwreck* may lie in his willingness to showcase (Jewish) women behaving childishly. "I just like immaturity," Apatow is quoted as saying, "I like to show people struggle and try to figure out who they are" (Zakarin). In using his success with these earlier projects to bring *Girls* and *Trainwreck* to wide audiences, Apatow has been heralded as "the unlikely feminist" (Rapkin).

Apatow's Jewish boys use their Jewish vulnerability to comic effect; Apatow's (Jewish) women use their hyper-confidence in the same way. In *Knocked Up*, for example, Rogen's character did not need to be expressly Jewish for the storyline to operate, but his Jewishness added a dimension of humor to the film and punctuated the unlikeliness of the romance that blossomed between his and Heigl's characters. When the women in Apatow's worlds are Jews, their Jewishness, as with Seidman's feminists, is relegated to the parenthetical. In *Trainwreck,* for example, Schumer's character is marked as coming from an Irish Catholic family (owing partly to the actor who plays Amy's father in the film, Colin Quinn).[7] In Apatow's oeuvre alone, Jewishness consistently serves as a punchline for men and a (parenthetical) premise for women.

The marginality of Jewish women's Jewishness is intrinsically related to the marginality of Jewish women generally. Historically excluded from the central locales of Jewish life in Central and Eastern Europe—*cheder, yeshiva, beys medresh*—ashkenazic women instead occupied gentile, or at least not explicitly Jewish, realms. As breadwinners, women worked in the marketplace, necessitating knowledge of non-Jewish languages. But by the nineteenth century, while Jewish girls' education continued to observe the dictum that they not engage with Torah study, the education many received followed the custom of Western Europe's aristocracy rather than the more functional business lessons of an earlier era. Jewish girls took piano lessons and learned to speak German and French.

Iris Parush writes, "unlike the strictness which characterized the education of boys, the education of girls was marked by neglect on one side and manifest permissiveness on the other" (74). Although writing about Jews in Poland and Russia in the nineteenth century, the attitudes toward Jewish women Parush describes are made manifest among Jewish women entertainers of the 2010s. With a handful of notable exceptions, female comedians have historically been one step removed from the mainstream; producers tended to see women's filmmaking as niche (directed toward women). Men's comedy is for everyone, women's comedy is for women—this unspoken contract in the entertainment world is a reflection of how men and women are seen. Men, specifically straight white men, are neutral, unmarked. Women are marked. In comedy, Jewish men are marked as Jewish. Jewish women are marked first as women and only secondarily, parenthetically as Jewish.

NEGLECT AND PERMISSIVENESS

That women's comedy has only in the past fifteen years become both mainstream and highly desirable recalls the kind of neglect Parush described. It was only after twenty-five years on air that *Saturday Night Live* employed a woman as a head writer: another feminist comic (albeit not a Jewish one) Tina Fey. She and *SNL* co-star Amy Poehler then went on to head up massively successful sitcoms, which led to the newest generation of young women-centered network comedies: *New Girl* (Fox), *The Mindy Project* (first on Fox, now on Hulu), *Jane the Virgin* (CW), *Crazy Ex-Girlfriend* (CW), among others. Then, of course, came the cable and streaming hits: Schumer's series (Comedy Central),

Dunham's *Girls* (HBO), *Broad City* (Comedy Central), *Unbreakable Kimmy Schmidt* (Netflix), and so on.

As was the case for Jewish girls and women in nineteenth-century Europe, this neglect may partly serve to explain the permissiveness that followed. These women comedians play boldly with television convention. *Jane the Virgin* bucks the half-hour sitcom format in favor of an hour-long comedy/telenovela; Schumer's show is a bizarre combination of sketch comedy and on-the-street interviews; *Crazy Ex-Girlfriend* seamlessly transforms the Broadway musical genre into an award-winning television series; *Broad City* converts a web series to a half-hour comedy without suffering from gratuitous modifications to the characters who made the web shorts so popular.

In some ways, we may imagine this permissiveness in genre and form extending to the brand of comedy these women espouse. They talk about sex and bodies in ways men do not, and not only because they are talking about women's, rather than men's, bodies. Consider, for example, one of Schumer's most frequently quoted punchlines: "I get labeled a sex comic. But if a guy got up onstage and pulled his dick out, everybody would say: 'He's a thinker'" (Fussman). Male comedians may joke about the relative merits of a woman's body, but they rarely joke about the merits of a woman's performance in bed. Lena Dunham's *Girls* brings the question of sexual pleasure to the fore by showcasing sex act after awkward sex act—not hesitating to film bodies from unflattering angles or show characters wanting to, but not succeeding in, having a great time. In the very first episode of *Broad City*, Ilana initiates a Skype session with her best friend Abbi in order to discuss plans for the day ("What a Wonderful World"). When Ilana moves the camera, Abbi (and the viewer) spots Ilana's paramour on top of her and the couple admits they are having sex during the Skype session! Schumer also jokes about which sex acts she has and has not performed, and why. In part, male comics may not have access to the same kind of material for fear of "punching down" or being too dangerously demeaning toward women to be considered funny. In other words, women's position beneath men in the social hierarchy is part of what permits them to make certain jokes that would be taboo for men. This is not unlike when comedians of color joke about race in ways inaccessible to white comics. To return to Parush's formulation, women's comedy is marked by both neglect and permissiveness.

On the flip side of the question of permissiveness in content lies Jewish female comics' access to traditional Jewish humor. If their Jewishness remains in the realm of the parenthetical, it may not be entirely by choice. Take Lena

Dunham's 2015 contribution to the "Shouts & Murmurs" comedy section of *The New Yorker*. In "Dog or Jewish Boyfriend: A Quiz," Dunham draws upon many of the classic tropes once considered antisemitic, which later became an engrained part of Jewish comedy. The Jewish boyfriend in Dunham's piece is cheap, asthmatic, and has an overbearing mother. He's a hairy hypochondriac with a weak stomach. A quick pass over Jon Stewart's joke work on *The Daily Show*, Woody Allen's film repertoire, *Seinfeld*'s (ambiguously Jewish) George Costanza, and Larry David's fictionalized version of himself on *Curb Your Enthusiasm*, even Philip Roth's early stories and novels, reveals how caricatures of Jewish men as weak, overly frugal, emasculated mama's boys permeate American Jewish jokelore. In spite of her participation in this tradition of Jewish humor, Dunham was skewered by the Jewish press for her piece. Even the Anti-Defamation League (ADL), the Jewish anti-bigotry watchdog group, condemned her for writing and *The New Yorker* for printing such an "offensive," "insensitive," and "troubling" essay (ADL Press Release). It may be that Dunham's parenthetical Jewishness is to blame for the public outrage at her piece. That is, perhaps readers were unaware of Dunham's own Jewishness, as it was not a hugely explicit part of her comedic persona, and were outraged at the thought of a non-Jew making jokes at Jews' expense. Or, perhaps it owes to the fact that Dunham is a woman—a fact that may not be extrapolated from her status as a parenthetical Jew. When a Jewish woman employs Jewish men's humor, she has gone too far. In being "too Jewish" with her humor, she has betrayed her status as a woman. Jewish men make Jewish jokes. (Jewish) women make women jokes. The sexual permissiveness in American Jewish women's comedy stems in part from the neglect among producers and the public that precedes these women. But once in the spotlight, restrictions emerge that draw out just how different men's and women's comedy can be.

In Seidman's work on parenthetical Jews, she highlights the performative quality of ethnic and gender identities, where Jewish academics and activists put their Jewishness into parentheses in favor of gay/feminist or other religious affiliations. She references one of Kosofsky-Sedgwick's autobiographical sketches, where she describes dressing up as Queen Esther for Purim. For Kosofsky-Sedgwick, Esther's bravery in "coming out" Jewish to her king conceals the related ways in which her actions—and their annual recollection in costume by Jewish girls—reinscribe conservative gender roles (Kosofsky-Sedgwick 72; Seidman 262). For Seidman, the young Eve-as-Esther is no more a performance than the biblical Esther; both "are simulacra, (Jewish) drag queens" (Seidman 263). Seidman and Kosofsky-Sedgwick draw out the performative qualities of gender, sexuality, and Jewishness, but there is an angle of Esther's story unexplored, one that helps explain why Jewish female comics' Jewishness is kept in parentheses. Esther, the queen of parenthetical Jewishness, is able to hide her Jewishness in a way a man in her position could not: perhaps because he is physically marked on his body by circumcision, perhaps because he is marked by his Jewish head covering, perhaps even in the way his masculinity contrasts with non-Jewish masculine ideals. Unmarked in these ways, women have the option to keep their Jewishness parenthetical. And while that possibility remains open to them as Jews, they cannot keep their woman-ness in parentheses. Thoughtful critics go out of their way to avoid lumping Schumer together with other women comedians—why must she be considered only in comparison to other women? Gender and sexuality keep trumping Jewishness for women, but never eliminating it. Jewishness surfaces, but it surfaces in parentheses. Or as Schumer articulated it, "[Judaism is] not something that I stay away from on purpose. If a reference pops into my head, I'll say it" (Handler).

Schumer is far likelier to make reference to sex and women's bodies than to her Jewishness. In fact, when asked to qualify her comedic persona with one word, she chose "slutty." In this way, she descends, as we have seen, from the "unkosher comediennes," whose night-club acts, stand-up shows, and albums "challenged the male-centered visions of female sexuality that dominated vaudeville, burlesque, and the Borscht Belt" (Del Negro 156). The overbearing Jewish mothers and Jewish-American Princesses featured in those men's bastions were replaced by "strong-minded, willful women, always ready to offset their opponent with a cheeky remark." Whereas the Jewish men comics joked about nagging women, in the acts of Sophie Tucker, Belle Barth, Totie Fields and others, their over-sized body parts "conspire to ridicule men and render them powerless." These Jewish women pridefully laid claim to the aggressive caricatures designed by men, while—as Schumer did in her "Last Fuckable Day" sketch—subverting expectations by deeming these features worthy of celebration.

CONCLUSION

A history that locates Schumer and her cohort among the inheritors of bawdy Jewish women's comedy runs the risk of oversimplifying the newer generation's context, denying agency, and forcing these women into a heritage they may well reject. In fact, the younger comics are constantly fighting against a sexist system that compares them only to other women and continues to assert that women cannot possibly be as funny as men (or in the same way). In a 2008 article about some of the emerging female comic stars, Alessandra Stanley writes, "after decades of insecurity . . . women finally feel they can look good and still be taken seriously as comics." Stanley contends that, "funny women in the old days didn't try to look their best; they tried to look comical." Despite this claim of radical change, nearly half a century earlier, in 1970, the *New York Times* published what amounts to the same article. In "The Funny Thing Is That They Are Still Feminine," the writer begins, "Time was when a woman comedian had to make herself ugly, cross her eyes, or fall down in order to get laughs" (Klemesrud 82). The article continues, "there is a new breed of funny girl emerging—one who believes that a woman can be both funny and feminine at the same time." Nevermind that no such article from the past fifty years discusses male comedians in terms of their collective attractiveness. What's interesting here is the repetition, that women's comedy has been branded as "new" for the past forty-five years. Whether female comedians can be taken seriously and whether this can happen without taking their appearance into account is a challenge Amy Schumer and Lena Dunham redirect back at their audiences and critics.

In lumping Schumer and company together here, I am guilty of participating in the trend that sees them as female comedians instead of simply comedians. But by interrogating them as Jewish women, I ask if that position allows for access to a certain (at times, limiting) variety of comedy or whether a misogynist system has left them little comedic recourse. It is not just their Jewishness but its parenthetical quality that leads me to analyze them together, as opposed to with Jewish men, whose Jewishness comes across as comically explicit. In line with Seidman, I do not want to claim that the Jewishness of Schumer, Dunham, Abbi and Ilana, or Bloom is "important or coherent in some way she is unwilling to acknowledge" (Seidman 264). But, as Seidman did for the feminist scholars, I only want to "register the pattern and subtlety of such a parenthetical Jewish identity." And then, I want to interrogate why parenthetical Jewishness appears, for now, to be a variety of marginalized identity reserved for women.

Notes

1. See the new introduction to Gina Barreca's *They Used to Call me Snow White*, for more analysis on Silverman's rape joke and its consequences for other comedians, especially pp. xxx–xxxiv.
2. Ruth Wisse's *No Joke* takes the long view, analyzing the history of Jewish humor in its European, American, and Israeli iterations. She offers up a handful of reasons for why humor might be Jewish, but her argument hinges on the prescriptive suggestion that Jews ought to take things more seriously and joke less often in times of trouble. She submits that they might work to teach others to mock themselves, so that Jews are less alone in this unsavory behavior.
3. For a detailed investigation into the potential Jewishness of these sitcoms, see Brook, *Something Ain't Kosher Here*.
4. Two seminal projects on Jewish self-hatred include Gilman and Reitter. Brook, *You Should See Yourself*, also points to Garry Shandling's character on *The Larry Sanders Show* having been consciously conceived as a self-hating Jew.
5. See Boyarin's groundbreaking text on Jewish masculinity.
6. Katherine Heigl infamously called *Knocked Up* "a little sexist" (Bennetts).
7. On Schumer's lack of Jewishness in *Trainwreck*, see Brook, "A Tale of Two (Jewish) Amys."

Filmography/TVography

Anchorman: The Legend of Ron Burgundy. Directed by Adam McKay. Dreamworks, 2004.
Bridesmaids. Directed by Paul Feig. Universal, 2011.
Broad City. Created by Ilana Glazer and Abbi Jacobson. Comedy Central, 2014–.
"CC Presents: Amy Schumer." *Comedy Central Presents*, 2 Apr. 2010.
Crazy Ex-Girlfriend. Created by Rachel Bloom and Aline Brosh McKenna. CW, 2015–.
Curb Your Enthusiasm. Created by Larry David. HBO, 2000–11.
The Daily Show with Jon Stewart. Created by Lizz Winstead and Madeleine Smithberg. Comedy Central, 1999–2015.
Friends. Created by David Crane and Marta Kauffman. NBC, 1994–2004.
Girls. Created by Lena Dunham. HBO, 2012–.
"Hack Into Broad City." cc.com, 2014–.
Inside Amy Schumer. Created by Daniel Powell and Amy Schumer. Comedy Central, 2013–.
Jane the Virgin. Created by Jennie Snyder Urman. CW, 2014–.
Knocked Up. Directed by Judd Apatow. Universal, 2007.
The Larry Sanders Show. Created by Dennis Klein and Garry Shandling. HBO, 1992–98.
Mad About You. Created by Danny Jacobson and Paul Reiser. NBC, 1992–99.
Master of None. Created by Aziz Ansari and Alan Yang. Netflix, 2015–.
The Mindy Project. Created by Mindy Kaling. Fox; Hulu, 2012–.
New Girl. Created by Elizabeth Meriwether. Fox, 2011–.
The Night Before. Directed by Jonathan Levine. Columbia, 2015.
Saturday Night Live. Created by Lorne Michaels. NBC, 1975–.
Seinfeld. Created by Larry David and Jerry Seinfeld. NBC, 1989–98.
Trainwreck. Directed by Judd Apatow. Universal, 2015.
Unbreakable Kimmy Schmidt. Created by Robert Carlock and Tina Fey. Netflix, 2015–.
Veep. Created by Armando Iannucci. HBO, 2012–.

Works Cited

12 Angry Men. Directed by Sidney Lumet, performances by Henry Fonda, Lee J. Cobb, and Martin Balsam. MGM, 1957.
"12 Angry Men." *Inside Amy Schumer*, created by Daniel Powell and Amy Schumer, season 3, episode 3. Comedy Central, 5 May 2015.
Altman, Sig. *The Comic Image of the Jew: Explorations of a Pop Culture Phenomenon.* Associated Univ., 1971.
"amyschumer." *Instagram*, 30 Nov. 2015, www.instagram.com/p/-tt2DAKUBz/?taken by=amyschumer&hl=en. Accessed 17 Aug. 2016.
"Amy Schumer Makes Sway in the Morning Laugh and Explains What 'Jew-ing It Up' Means." *YouTube*, uploaded by SwaysUniverse, 24 June 2013, www.youtube.com/watch?v=EiSYb4GLZN4.
Apatow, Judd, producer. *Anchorman: The Legend of Ron Burgundy.* Directed by Adam McKay. Dreamworks, 2004.
———, director. *Knocked Up.* Universal, 2007.
———, director. *Trainwreck.* Performance by Amy Schumer. Universal, 2015.
Ansari, Aziz and Alan Yang, creators. *Master of None.* Netflix, 2015–.
Anti-Defamation League. "Press Release: Lena Dunham's Jewish Boyfriend or Dog Quiz 'Tasteless' and Evokes Stereotypes." 27 Mar. 2015, www.adl.org/press-center/press-releases/anti-semitism-usa/adl-lena-dunhams-jewish-boyfriend-or-dog-quiz-tasteless.html?referrer=https://www.google.com/#.V1cGgr4rJE4. Accessed 13 Sept. 2016.
Barreca, Gina. *They Used to Call me Snow White . . . But I Drifted: Women's Strategic Use of Humor, With a New Introduction by the Author.* Univ. Press of New England, 2013.
Bennetts, Leslie. "Heigl's Anatomy." *Vanity Fair*, Jan. 2008.
Blacher Cohen, Sarah. "The Unkosher Comediennes: From Sophie Tucker to Joan Rivers." *Jewish Wry: Essays on Jewish Humor*, edited by Sarah Blacher Cohen, Wayne State Univ., 1987, pp. 105–23.
Bloom, Rachel. "The Jewish Mother Song," in "My Mom, Greg's Mom and Josh's Sweet Dance Moves!" *Crazy Ex-Girlfriend*, season 1, episode 8. CW, 30 Nov. 2015.
———. "Josh Just Happens to Live Here!" *Crazy Ex-Girlfriend*, season 1, episode 1. CW, 12 Oct. 2015.
Boyarin, Daniel. *Unheroic Conduct: The Rise of Heterosexuality and the Invention of the Jewish Man.* Univ. of California, 1997.
Bridesmaids. Directed by Paul Feig, produced by Judd Apatow. Universal, 2011.
Broad City. Created by Ilana Glazer and Abbi Jacobson. Comedy Central, 2014–.
Brook, Vincent. "A Tale of Two (Jewish) Amys: Winehouse and Schumer." *Mediascape*, 27 Aug. 2015, www.tft.ucla.edu/mediascape/blog/?p=2505. Accessed 17 August 2016.
———. *Something Ain't Kosher Here: The Rise of the "Jewish" Sitcom.* Rutgers Univ., 2003.

———. "'Y'All Killed Him, We Didn't': Jewish Self-Hatred and *The Larry Sanders Show.*" *You Should See Yourself: Jewish Identity in Postmodern American Culture*, edited by Vincent Brook, Rutgers Univ., 2006, pp. 144–59.
"CC Presents: Amy Schumer." *Comedy Central Presents*, 2 Apr. 2010.
Crazy Ex-Girlfriend. Created by Rachel Bloom and Aline Brosh McKenna. CW, 2015–.
Curb Your Enthusiasm. Created by Larry David. HBO, 2000–11.
The Daily Show with Jon Stewart. Created by Lizz Winstead and Madeleine Smithberg. Comedy Central, 3 Jan. 2012.
Del Negro, Giovanna P. "The Bad Girls of Jewish Comedy: Gender, Class, Assimilation, and Whiteness in Postwar America." *A Jewish Feminine Mystique? Jewish Women in Postwar America*, edited by Hasia Diner, Shira Kohn, and Rachel Kranson, Rutgers Univ., 2010.
Dunham, Lena. "Dog or Jewish Boyfriend? A Quiz." *New Yorker*, 30 Mar. 2015.
———, creator. *Girls*. HBO, 2012–.
Ebiri, Bilge. "Seth Rogen & Co. Indulge in Christmas Spirit, Jewish Jokes, and Too Many Drugs in *The Night Before*." *Vulture*, 21 Nov. 2015.
Freud, Sigmund. *Jokes and Their Relation to the Unconscious*. Translated by James Strachey, Norton, 1960.
Fussman, Cal. "Amy Schumer: What I've Learned." *Esquire*, 14 Jan. 2015.
Gilman, Sander. *Jewish Self-Hatred: Anti-Semitism and the Hidden Language of the Jews*. Johns Hopkins Univ., 1990.
"Hack Into Broad City—Yom Kippur." Season 3, episode 1. cc.com, 21 Sept. 2015.
Handler, Rachel. "Amy Schumer Does Not Need Your Approval." *Complex CA*, 14 July 2015.
Hitchens, Christopher. "Why Women Aren't Funny." *Vanity Fair*, 1 Jan. 2007, www.vanityfair.com/culture/2007/01/hitchens200701. Accessed 6 Sept. 2016.
Hyman, Paula. *Gender and Assimilation in Modern Jewish History: The Roles and Representations of Women*. Univ. of Washington, 1995.
Jane the Virgin. Created by Jennie Snyder Urman. CW, 2014–.
Janik, Vicki, editor. *Fools and Jesters in Literature, Art, and History: A Bio-Bibliographical Sourcebook*. Greenwood, 1998.
Klemesrud, Judy. "The Funny Thing Is That They Are Still Feminine." *New York Times*, 14 Jan. 1970, p. 82.
Kosofsky-Sedgwick, Eve. *Epistemology of the Closet*. Univ. of California, 2000.
Krasney, Ariela. "*Badchan* (Jester)." *Encyclopedia of Jewish Folklore and Traditions*, edited by Raphael Patai. Routledge, 2015, pp. 60–62.
Lambert, Josh. "Non-Jews Telling Jokes." *Tablet*, 13 June 2012.
"Last Fuckable Day." *Inside Amy Schumer*, created by Daniel Powell and Amy Schumer, season 3, episode 1. Comedy Central, 21 Apr. 2015.
Louis-Dreyfus, Julia, performer. *Veep*, created by Armando Iannucci. HBO, 2012–.
The Mindy Project. Created by Mindy Kaling. Fox; Hulu, 2012–.

New Girl. Created by Elizabeth Meriwether. Fox, 2011–.
Nussbaum, Emily. "The Little Tramp." *The New Yorker*, 11 May 2015.
Parush, Iris. *Reading Jewish Women: Marginality and Modernization in Nineteenth-century Eastern European Jewish Society*. Brandeis Univ., 2004.
Prell, Riv-Ellen. *Fighting to Become Americans: Assimilation and the Trouble Between Jewish Women and Jewish Men*. Beacon, 1999.
Rapkin, Mickey. "Comedy's Unlikely Feminist." *Elle*, 27 Oct. 2011.
Reitter, Paul. *On the Origins of Jewish Self- Hatred*. Princeton Univ., 2013.
Richardson, Emma Kat. "Ass-kickin' Amy Schumer is on the rise." *LaughSpin*, 20 Jan. 2011, www.laughspin.com/2011/01/20/ass-kickin-amy-schumer-is-on-the-rise. Accessed 17 Aug. 2016.
Sandler, Adam. "Chanukah Song." *Saturday Night Live*, created by Lorne Michaels, season 20. NBC, 3 Dec. 1994.
Shandling, Garry, performer. *The Larry Sanders Show*, created by Dennis Klein and Garry Shandling. HBO, 1992–98.
Schrodt, Paul. "Lena Dunham's Body is Funny." *Esquire*, 15 Jan. 2014.
Schumer, Amy (amyschumer). "Beautiful, gross, strong, thin, fat, pretty, ugly, sexy, disgusting, flawless, woman." *Instagram*, 30 Nov. 2015, 7:40am.
Seidman, Naomi. "Fag-Hags and Bu-Jews: Toward a (Jewish) Politics of Vicarious Identity." *Insider/Outsider: American Jews and Multiculturalism*, edited by David Biale, Michael Galchinsky, and Susan Heschel. Univ. of California, 1998, pp. 254–67.
Stanley, Alessandra. "Who Says Women Aren't Funny?" *Vanity Fair*, 3 Mar. 2008.
Tobin, Andrew. "Jason Segel Opens Up to Marc Maron About Childhood as Jewish Outsider." *Haaretz*, 31 July, 2015.
Unbreakable Kimmy Schmidt. Created by Robert Carlock and Tina Fey. Netflix, 2015–.
"What a Wonderful World." *Broad City*, created by Ilana Glazer and Abbi Jacobson, season 1, episode 1. Comedy Central, 22 Jan. 2014.
Wisse, Ruth. *No Joke: Making Jewish Humor*. Princeton Univ., 2013.
Zaltzman, Lior. "'Crazy Ex-Girlfriend' Is Jewish Comedy for the Truly Enlightened." *Forward*, 25 Jan. 2016.
Zakarin, Jordan. "Judd Apatow Discusses Lena Dunham's 'Girls', Penis Fatigue, and 'Anchorman 2.'" *Hollywood Reporter*, 6 Apr. 2012.

CHAPTER 4

"The Woman Thing and the Jew Thing": Transsexuality, Transcomedy, and the Legacy of Subversive Jewishness in *Transparent*

by Joshua Louis Moss

> It's like phallus is to crucifix as vagina is to Holocaust.
> — Ali Pfefferman (Season 2 of *Transparent*)

After winning the 2015 Golden Globe for Best Television Series, Musical or Comedy, and Best Performance by an Actor in a Television Series—Comedy or Musical, *Transparent* (2014–) creator Jill Soloway and star Jeffrey Tambor both profusely thanked the transgender community for their support (Riley 1). An emotional Tambor even made sure to credit Rhys Ernst, Zackary Drucker, and Jenny Boylan, three of the show's transgender consultants, as essential elements of the production team. The show's unapologetic exploration of fluid gender and sexual identities focused on the late-life decision by retired professor and family patriarch Mort Pfefferman (Tambor) to begin to live her life as Maura, an openly transsexual woman. Various plotlines followed Maura's transition and explored the ramifications taking place with her ex-wife and three adult children. The innovative semi-comedic tone and experimental form not only produced a landmark in transgender visibility on television but also established Amazon Studios as a viable producer of quality television. Yet rather than referring to the creative process or taking credit for their work on the show, both Soloway and Tambor spent the majority of their Golden Globe speeches transferring credit to the marginalized status and struggles of transgender and transsexual communities. Soloway even concluded by dedicating her award to the memory of Leelah Alcorn, a young transgender woman that had recently committed suicide.

As Soloway and Tambor's speeches made clear, *Transparent*'s critical success was directly tied to its role in breaking the taboo on transgender representations on television. In a profile in the *New York Times* in advance of season two, *Transparent* was praised for breaking new ground by visualizing previously marginalized gender identities without resorting to clichés or stereotypes (Rochlin 9). Similarly, in the *Los Angeles Times*, Tre'vell Anderson praised *Transparent* as part of an overdue Hollywood corrective taking place across film and television (Anderson 10, 20). Culture critic Wesley Morris went even further, championing *Transparent* as the most visible example of a "galactic conjuring of female energy," aligned with shows such as *Orange Is the New Black* (2013–), *Being Mary Jane* (2013–), *Broad City* (2014–), *Inside Amy Schumer* (2013–), and films such as Todd Hayne's *Carol* (2015) (11). Morris argued that *Transparent* was at the center of a pop culture movement that had launched a national discussion on gender and sexuality through the previously unseen female gaze (Morris 11). Soloway agreed with Morris, stating in an interview with *Ms. Magazine* that the show was attempting to subvert the male gaze in an effort to free storytelling from "the straight white cis male paradigm" (Kamen 1).[1]

Remarkably, outside of Jewish publications such as *The Forward* and *Tablet*, the importance of the Jewishness of the Pfefferman family was left nearly completely out of this debate (Cohen; Ivry). The rhetoric of gender advancement credited to the show is understood as independent of any Jewish subject matter. Todd VanDerWerff's gushing tribute in *Vox*, "*Transparent* Season 2 is the Best TV Show of the Year," analyzes the show's link between the epic sweep of historical events and the individual narrative without once mentioning the word "Jew" or "Jewish." A tribute by Sonia Saraiya in *Salon* credits *Transparent* with developing the female gaze by building on the nuanced work of shows such as *Mad Men* (2006–14). But despite an extensive examination of how season two engages Weimar-era Berlin's rising Nazi threat as the origins of the Pfefferman diaspora, the article does not mention Jewishness as an important distinction (VanDerWerff 1). When Jewishness is mentioned, such as in Emily Nussbaum's *New Yorker* article, "Inside Out: The Emotional Acrobatics of *Transparent*," it is positioned only as the means to extend the specificity of historical Jewish trauma into a queer space (Nussbaum 2).[2] In these readings, the Jewishness of the Pfeffermans is simply biographical detail. It provides a lens to explore what the reviewers regard as the show's real innovation, the introduction of complex transgender characters within mainstream television entertainment.

This rhetorical absence is striking. Not only because of the indelible historical link between Jewish activism and gender rights movements, but also because Jewish subject matter and motifs are so visible and centralized throughout the first two seasons. Numerous episodes are titled and structured around Jewish subjects such as sitting shiva ("Why Do We Cover the Mirrors?" season 1, episode 10), Talmudic metaphors ("The Wilderness," season 1, episode 6 and "Symbolic Exemplar," season 1, episode 7), Jewish weddings ("Kina Hora," season 2, episode 1) and attending synagogue services on the High Holidays ("The Book of Life," season 2, episode 7). Maura's son, Josh Pfefferman, begins an unlikely love affair and engagement to Raquel, one of the rabbis at a Conservative synagogue. Season 2's flashbacks to Weimar-era Berlin focus even more explicitly on the connection between libertine sexual exploration, European Jewish radicalism, and the reactionary backlash against both that the Nazis represented.

Soloway herself has repeatedly referenced the importance of Jewishness to the show. She has described it as "religious programming," discussed the importance of her Jewish background in formulating the show, and repeatedly emphasized the important connection of the Jewish diaspora to gender fluid visibility in the twentieth century (Clark and Zaritt 1). The Jewish-transgender link was also celebrated throughout Season 2's marketing campaign. One prominent billboard campaign featured the slogan "Seduce Your Rabbi!" as a Jewish joke on the taboo sexuality featured in the show. Another print campaign prominently featured in the *New York Times*, among many other publications, depicted the entire Pfefferman family posing in a Last Supper configuration in a deli booth with latkes, pickles, and pastrami sandwiches spread in front of them (*New York Times*, 6 Dec. 2015). The subversion of Christian iconography through the Pfeffermans' overt Jewishness operated as comedic incongruity, a metaphor for the usurpation of gender norms exemplified by Maura and her children.

The centrality of Jewishness to *Transparent* cannot simply be dismissed as biographical narrative filler. The queer-Jewish connection is the overlooked technique that allows *Transparent* to successfully problematize transgender identity through the familiar tropes of sitcom. The Jewishness of the Pfeffermans plays a critical role in the successful integration of gender and genre fluidity within the text. It produces, and then subverts, established comedic clichés. In invoking the familiar (wacky TV Jews) to examine previously unseen screen subject matter (complex gender fluidity without obvious resolution), the show produces an uncanny tension between form and representation that echoes its thematic engagement with the fluidity of problematic concepts such as diaspora and queerness. Transgender identity becomes safer when performed by screen Jews, the privileged avatars of historical televisual transgression. *Transparent's* groundbreaking experimentations with form and subject matter required a familiar, already "deviant," framing. Given the history of popular American film and television, it should be no surprise that that agent was the unruly, comedic Jew.[3]

TRANSCOMEDY AND TRANSSEXUALITY

The comedic-neurotic Jewishness of the five immediate members of the Pfefferman family follows six decades of established sitcom tradition. Creator Jill Soloway based *Transparent* on her father's real-life experiences transitioning into living openly as a woman. This art-into-life polysemy harks back to classic early sitcoms that featured real-life couples and families, such as *The George Burns and Gracie Allen Show* (1950–58) and *The Adventures of Ozzie & Harriet* (1952–66). Although *Transparent* has no laugh track, features magic realist and surrealistic forays, and intersperses broad comedy with melodrama and pathos, the show returns over and over to its sitcom origins. Set pieces such as family culture clash ("Mee-Maw," season 2, episode 5), ruined family dinners ("Why Do We Cover The Mirrors?" season 1, episode 10; "The Book of Life," season 2, episode 7), and embarrassing meltdowns in front of large crowds ("Kina Hora," season 2, episode 1; "Cherry Blossums," season 2, episode 4) are straight out of the established tropes of situation comedy form.

The impact of the transgender journey of Mort into openly living as Maura, or Moppa to her children, serves as the program's central narrative spine. But despite this gender-bending premise and the complex and deft development of Maura's character in Season 1, she also follows established, family sitcom patriarch/matriarch tropes. Season 1 establishes Mort/Maura as an ironic twist on *Father Knows Best* (1954–62), a patriarch-turned-matriarch with a better understanding of gender fluidity than her clueless, befuddled children. But Season 2 undermines this through increasingly comedic self-effacement. Maura struggles with her new identity, often falling back on her established patriarchal status when confronted or in trouble. These comedic sequences suggest the familiar sitcom parent comically out of touch both with her children's needs and the contemporary pop culture landscape she clings to. While the show takes great pains not to reduce Maura to a comedic stereotype, her journey is also not idealized or romanticized. Her residual masculine privilege eventually becomes, in season two, the central character flaw mined for comedy in classic sitcom tradition. She resembles a diverse series of sitcom protagonists including Ralph Kramden (Jackie Gleason) in *The Honeymooners* (1955–56), Lucille Ball in *I Love Lucy* (1951–57), Archie Bunker (Carroll O'Connor) in *All in the Family* (1971–81), the crotchety Costanza parents (Estelle Warner and Jerry Stiller) in *Seinfeld* (1990–98), and Jay Pritchett (Ed O'Neill) in *Modern Family* (2009–).

One of the central techniques of *Transparent's* sitcom identification locates in the incongruity between Mort's already flawed, neurotic Jewish masculinity and Maura's efforts to reject that history once she has fully transitioned. Mort/Maura's problematic inability to fully transition is an example of what Lee Edelman describes as the heterosexual gender binarism that remains at work in most queer formulations (207). In Edelman's understanding, the heterosexual male can safely masquerade as a female because the very boldness of this choice reinforces a variation of hetero-masculine confidence. To address this problematic, the show focuses on the Jewishness of Maura and, by extension, the other Pfeffermans. Maura's ex-wife, Shelly (Judith Light), a Yiddish-cracking Jewish mother, is an even more identifiable sitcom stereotype. She exemplifies the archetype of the Jewish matriarch, a mix of the folksy Yiddishe Mama wisdom of Molly Berg (Gertrude Berg) on *The Goldbergs* (1949–57) with the abrasive sarcasm of Silvia Fine (Renee Taylor) on *The Nanny* (1993–99). But Maura and Shelly are not stable sitcom stereotypes. They are presented as confounding mixes of contradictions and confusion. They are at times savvy elders. At other times they are embarrassingly inadequate parent figures. They offer updated versions of six decades of sitcom patriarchs and matriarchs. But these clichés are presented as fractured and incomplete. The sitcom archetypes that they both evoke and subvert exist as unstable genre signifiers. Just as Mort transitions uneasily into Maura, *Transparent* transitions uneasily between comedic and dramatic forms.

The archetype of comedic-neurotic Jewishness is central to this thematic link between destabilized gender and genre. The adult Pfefferman children, the eldest, Sarah (Amy Landecker), the middle child, Josh (Jay Duplass) and the youngest, Ali (Gaby Hoffman), are next-generation urban Jewish characters straight out of this heyday of urban Jewish visibility in the 1990s sitcom. But, as Vincent Brook has shown, visible Jewishness in 1990s-era situation comedies was a complex mix of ethnic otherness and assimilated whiteness that reflected an emphasis on pluralist multiculturalism (16–20). The Jewishness and sexual confusion of the Pfefferman children resurrect and reproduce this ambiguity between visible difference and polyglot inclusion. Each is triggered by Maura's transition to reevaluate their connections between love, intimacy, sexuality, and gender identity. Sarah's relationship and divorce from Len (Rob Huebel) and aborted wedding to Tammy (Melora Hardin) follow comedic Christian-Jewish weddings from *Rhoda* (1974–78) to *Will and Grace* (1998–2004). Jay's romance, engagement, failed pregnancy, and breakup with Rabbi Raquel (Kathryn Hann) come across as updated variations of the intense comedic banter between Paul (Paul Reiser) and Jamie (Helen Hunt) on *Mad About You* (1992–99). Ali's childlike refusal to commit to a career and cruel indifference to her worshipping friend-turned-lover Sydney Feldman (Carrie Brownstein) recalls the immature, narcissistic single life as depicted on *Seinfeld* (1990–98) and *Friends* (1994–2004). The transgressive sexual subject matter of *Transparent* is given breathability due to these familiar Jewish sitcom set pieces and archetypes.

Transparent relies on, but also subverts and fractures these familiar sitcom elements.[4] Following the experimentations of innovative quasi-sitcoms such as *Curb Your Enthusiasm* (HBO, 2000–11), *Louie* (FX, 2010–) and *Orange is the New Black* (Netflix, 2013) episodes break away from comedic genre traditions to blend pathos and melodrama with formal experimentation. Languid pacing and elliptical cutting repeatedly blur or disrupt coherent screen time and environment. Scenes that begin as comedic set pieces often transition into dreamlike theatricality or thematic cross cutting. These deviations from conventional sitcom expectations become an extension of both characters and subject matter. They produce a hybrid show that ultimately and uneasily situates between comedy and drama. One of the show's writers, Cate Haight, described how Soloway likes to refer to this tense form of humor with the term, "*funcomfortable*" (Thurm). Soloway's neologism is important. It appears to identify incomplete, semi-humor as an intentionally transgressive comedy technique. In keeping with experimental sitcoms in the quality television era, "funcomfortable" humor accompanies *Transparent's* break from both normative comedy and sitcom genre traditions.

Fragmented, transgressive humor in contemporary global media is a concept that I have previously defined as "transcomedy" (Moss 2–4).

Transcomedy is intentionally unresolved humor fragments that emerge as both a reaction and a response to the circulations and collisions of transnational media across both spatial and imagined borders. Transcomedy produces comedic incongruity not in the catharsis of resolution but in the tension state of the unresolved, half-formed joke. This visualizes conflicting constructions of power and marginalization at work within presumptively singular or cohesive media artifacts. It does this by removing, and therefore critiquing, the presumption that all humor has a dominant (singular) reading strategy. The audience waits for a clear comedic catharsis that never arrives. The lack of comedic catharsis becomes its own joke, a representation of what Frantz Fanon describes as the fractured duplicity of the postcolonial subject (169–171). In post-Fanonian postcolonial theory, the marginalized figure can never fully congeal within the dominant ideological framework in which they reside. Transcomedy exemplifies this paradox. It produces humor when the spectator recognizes fracture as an irreducible form. The joke is that the joke, much like the subaltern, marginalized figure, can never fully resolve.

The "funcomfortable" humor technique on *Transparent* exemplifies transcomedy. The comedic fumbling, narcissism, and myopia of the Pfeffermans at first appears to mimic the dysfunctional family paradigm of sitcom tradition. But laughing at the Pfeffermans as they explore various queer and transgender identities is also potentially an act of cruelty. This destabilization of whether it is okay to laugh at the everyday foibles of queer, taboo, and transgressive gender and sexual formulations destabilizes the good/evil binaries inherent to social problem entertainment. It also challenges established sitcom tropes. The lens of marginalization removes clear comedic context. It remains unclear whether Maura and her family are the subject of comedic catharsis. They operate as wandering comedic signifiers, fractured exemplars of both Jewish and sitcom identities that oscillate uneasily between comedic and dramatic states. Yet this oscillation is critical. It allows *Transparent* to expand its musings on fluid identity beyond the text and into the show's themes of transgression and allusionism to sitcom past.

Transparent establishes this link between genre disruption and gender fluidity in the pilot episode ("Pilot"). The episode follows two simultaneous transitions as parallel intergenerational narratives. Mort Pfefferman makes the determination that after years of secretly living as transgender, he will now begin to openly transition to a female identity. At the same time, Mort's oldest daughter, Sarah, is coming to terms with the fact that not only that she is cheating on her husband with Tammy, her college girlfriend (Gillian Vigman in the pilot, Melora Hardin in the series), but may actually be falling in love with her. As a mother of two, Sarah is transitioning from heterosexual suburban marriage into a new LGBT identity. The pilot ends at the moment both father and daughter discovers the other's hidden identity. This comedic set piece, the mutual revelation as both narrative and comedic catharsis, could easily be at home in an episode of *Friends* or *Seinfeld*. Except that *Transparent* problematizes humor in the exchange. The conclusion remains uneasy, both semi-comedic and semi-tragic.

The next four episodes of season one ("The Letting Go," "Rollin," "Moppa," and "Wedge") are primarily character and plot specific. They focus on Mort's transition into Maura, and how, to varying degrees, it is received by and subsequently affects his ex-wife and three children. In episode six, "The Wilderness," *Transparent* begins to introduce the entangled history of twentieth century Jewish visibility and sexual transgression in both Europe and the United States. Josh, a successful record producer, emotionally immature manchild, and mostly disconnected Jew, decides to seek help for his distraught state over his father's transformation by consulting a young female rabbi, Raquel. Ali begins her emotional investigation of issues dredged up by Maura by going back to college and eventually pursuing a graduate degree in gender studies. Both institutions, the synagogue and the academy, offer Jewish traces for the Pfefferman children to unearth the source of the emotional struggles experienced by their patriarch-turning-matriarch. Both intellectual/spiritual pursuits quickly transition into romantic ones. Josh begins to date Raquel. Ali begins a flirtatious relationship with one of the teaching assistants in the gender studies program, Sydney.

Episodes 7 ("Symbolic Exemplar") and 8 ("The Wilderness") bring Jewish themes to the center of this interplay between intellectual, spiritual, and erotic drives. Josh's romance and seduction of Rabbi Raquel and Ali's journey into queer academia are both acts of intergenerational Jewish diaspora disconnected from its past. Josh's erotic fixation on Raquel is tied both to her Jewishness and his panic at his father's transition from male to female. The erotic-traumatic link is made clear when Raquel visits Josh early in their courtship and he encourages her to put on her *kippah* (skull cap) because it turns him on sexually. When Josh accidentally impregnates Raquel, he learns of the news as both sit in an empty *mikvah*, the ritual Jewish purification bath reserved for orthodox women. The empty *mikvah* externalizes the incomplete Jewishness both are experiencing. As *The Forward* points out, Josh interrupts Raquel as she is preparing to read the Torah portion "Bemidbar," or "The

Wilderness," also the title of the episode (Cohen). The Torah portion refers to how God came to Moses in the wilderness and spoke to him of those that would gain entrance into the Promised Land. Josh and Raquel are framed as wandering diaspora searching for meaning through romantic and sexual desire. But this sublimation of inherited trauma is alienation redirected into the erotic/sexual realm.

The tenth episode of season one concludes this thematic link between Jewishness and the broken family unit in "Why Do We Cover the Mirrors?" After the death of Ed, Shelly's second husband, the Pfeffermans prepare to sit *Shiva*, a Jewish mourning ritual. The various broken relationships of each Pfefferman children converge as they gather around the proverbial family dinner table. Raquel refuses to continue her relationship with Josh. Ali struggles with her desires for Sydney. Sarah considers leaving Tammy and returning to her husband. Another facet of the fractured Jewishness of the Pfeffermans emerges in the form of Colton (Alex MacNicoll), a teenage evangelical Christian who is revealed to be Josh's previously unknown son from his teenage affair with his mid-twenties former babysitter, Rita (Brett Paesel), seventeen years earlier. Rita gave the child up for adoption, something the Pfeffermans purportedly did not know about. A family in Overland Park, Kansas, raised him, but Colton was determined to meet his biological parents and locates Josh.

The devoutly Christian Colton enters the Pfefferman family as a classic sitcom incongruity. He serves as an ironic physiognomic contrast, a conventionally masculine American opposite to both Maura's transgender identity and Josh's Jewish *nebbish*. In the final sequence of the episode, Colton joins the Pfeffermans when they sit down to a *Shiva* meal of bagels and lox. Colton wears a cross around his neck. He is tall, with short hair and striking blue eyes. He signifies normativity as its own form of intervention and transgression, an abstract, noble Christian purity entering the neurotic, self-contained world of the Jewish Pfeffermans. Colton is a haunting specter, the product of Josh's illicit teenage sexual experiences at the hands of his babysitter while his indifferent parents were focused on their own lives and issues. Yet Colton is also there to forgive them for their sins. As an embodiment of heterosexual Christian purity entering a Jewish *Shiva* meal, Colton contrasts with but also reveals the Jewish-queer link at work through multiple generations of Pfeffermans.

TRANSETHNICITY

The first episode of season two ("Kina Hora") solidified this link between gender fluidity and the crisis of Jewish identity in the Pfefferman clan. The title of the episode, "Kina Hora," is a Jewish expression that warns one not to brag about good fortune lest that good fortune turn bad. The episode begins as one of good fortune for the Pfefferman family attending the beautiful wedding of Sarah and her fiancée Tammy Cashman (Melora Hardin) at a lavish reception in Palm Springs. The joyous embrace of Sarah and Tammy's families serve as an idyllic introduction in which gay marriage rights, thanks to *Obergefell v. Hodges*, finally have been achieved. No social, moral, or cultural obstacles, at least in Southern California, exist to prevent the legal union of Sarah and Tammy. Yet, as the episode title suggests, the crime of hubris soon leads to disaster. The insurmountable obstacle to the marriage of Tammy and Sarah is not simply Sarah's incomplete acceptance of her lesbianism/bisexuality. It is also compounded by the incompatible WASP/Jewish interplay of the two families.

This incompatibility is established in the episode's opening shot, a nearly four minute long take in which the neurotic Pfeffermans are asked to pose for the wedding photographer. The dysfunctional nature of the family is revealed as they banter and struggle to pose with varying degrees of frustration, narcissism, and confusion. The increasingly frustrated photographer struggles to focus the Pfefferman family long enough to smile for the picture. The photographer starts by asking them to say "Sydney Loo," a confusing request that none of the Pfeffermans understand. Shelly responds with the tart, "How about a Jewish reference?" The apparently non-Jewish photographer responds by requesting they shout out, "I want a little wine." Shelly's response, "That's a little antisemitic," inspires the frustrated photographer to conclude by requesting they all just say "Happy Hanukah!" The Pfeffermans quickly give up and walk away in different directions. The Cashman family, filled with smiling people, then enters to pose for their family photograph. The contrast is striking. The joke of the sequence is clear. Even as prohibitions on gay marriage give way to new freedoms, other cultural conflicts remain.

Transparent's deployment of WASP/Jewish wedding conflict solidified the show's link between genre traditions and gender transgression. The wedding plays out as a disjointed, dream-like sequence in which the calm, blonde-haired, blue-eyed Tammy stares blissfully into the camera, while Sarah experiences panic, fear, and crisis. These feelings are amplified when she witnesses Tammy perform the "traditional father-daughter dance" with her gender normative, Anglo-Saxon father at the reception. The camera lingers on

Sarah as she watches Tammy dance with her father. Sarah then turns and looks at her "Moppa," Maura. Much of the humor of the sequence locates in Sarah seeing her father-turned-mother not through her own eyes but through that of the Christian-normative gaze. The contrast between Tammy's masculine square-jawed, silver-haired, Christian father relocates Maura into the embodiment of the Jewish deviant.

Moments later, Sarah has a panic attack on the toilet and is joined by Josh, Ali, and Raquel. She refuses to go through with the marriage, declaring "I hate her and I hate her stupid family. Those fucking WASPs!" Her meltdown, partially tied to her confusion over her own sexuality, is further triggered by her epiphany that Jewish and WASP queerness produce their own form of incompatibility. The quartet of Jewish singles subsequently begins a near Talmudic debate over when a marriage is technically legal. As the voice of authority, Rabbi Raquel informs Sarah that a Jewish wedding is only a pageant ritual and by itself is not legally binding. The notion of the wedding as theater gives Sarah comfort. She declares the wedding off. An added layer of humor in the sequence locates in the familiarity of the set piece. WASP/Jewish wedding conflict, and such conflict in general, are established comedic tropes. In *Transparent*, Jewish narcissism remains contrasted with Christian decorum even in a queer formulation.

The WASP/Jewish interplay between the Pfeffermans and Cashmans in "Kina Hora" locates *Transparent* once again firmly in American popular entertainment traditions. Israel Zangwill's highly influential play, *The Melting Pot* (1909), and films such as *The Cohens and the Kellys* (1926), *Private Izzy Murphy* (1926), and *Abie's Irish Rose* (1928), depicted the madcap banter of Catholic and Jewish families trying to come together around the Christian-Jewish wedding. A generation later, in the late 1960s, neurotic, carnal Jews became the privileged embodiment of counterculture angst and the sexual revolution. In novels, Jewish characters such as Moses Herzog in Saul Bellow's *Herzog* (1964) and Alexander Portnoy in Philip Roth's *Portnoy's Complaint* (1969) used sexuality directed at Christian partners to lash out at the constraints of bourgeois society. Wedding disruption became a frequent visualization of these changing generational mores. Benjamin Braddock (Dustin Hoffman) disrupting the wedding of Elaine Robinson (Katherine Ross) to Carl Smith (Brian Avery) in *The Graduate* (1967) and the neurotic altar panic of Jewish lawyer Harold Fine (Peter Sellers) in *I Love You Alice B. Toklas* (1968) offer two prominent feature film examples. The cruel narcissism of nice Jewish boy Lenny Cantrow (Charles Grodin) abandoning his Jewish wife (Jeannie Berlin) on their Miami honeymoon to chase his "Shiksa" fixation, Kelly Corcoran (Cybill Shepherd) in *The Heartbreak Kid* (1972) offers another.

A more recent update to this comedic conjugal tradition can be seen in the antics between the Jewish Focker family (Ben Stiller, Dustin Hoffman, Barbra Streisand) and the WASP Byrnes family (Teri Polo, Robert DeNiro, Blythe Danner) in *Meet the Parents* (2000), *Meet the Fockers* (2004), and *Little Fockers* (2010). The clash of the WASP Byrnes and Jewish Focker families in those films riffed on the notion of Jews as perverted sexual deviants in the paranoid mind of the Anglo-Saxon patriarch, Jack Byrnes (DeNiro). Similar comedic pairings can be traced throughout television history, from the counterculture ethos of the Irish-Jewish marriage of Bridget (Meredith Baxter) and Bernie (David Birney) at the center of *Bridget Loves Bernie* (1972) to the Larry/Cheryl (Larry David and Cheryl Hines) marriage on *Curb Your Enthusiasm* (1999–). In each of these examples, screen Jews functioned as unruly deviations from the default Anglo-Christians they romance, or, as with Sarah vis-à-vis Tammy in *Transparent*, occasionally disrupt, upset, and reject.

Maura, Josh, Ali, and Sarah operate as continuations of this Jewish-gender unruliness. Each of the adult Pfefferman children seeks out transgressive parent figures as externalizations of neurotic familial fracture. Josh's teenage relationship with Rita and fixation on a rabbi as his mother/savior are both efforts to locate the parent figure that Mort/Maura was/is unable to fulfill.[5] Ali's flirtations with older men and women are related events emerging out of a primary traumatic diaspora brought about by the wandering, lost father. The children's issues problematize the simplification that Mort/Maura's struggle to realize her inner desires to live as a woman is inherently noble and virtuous. Her efforts at self-fulfillment have a cascading, residual effect on her children. Underage sexuality and oedipal flirtations symbolize related traumas. Mort's alienation results in intergenerational transference. Sarah, Ali, and Josh's subsequent confusions and struggles become extensions of Mort's closeted, alienated lifestyle. This diasporic wound is both self-inflicted and passed onward to the next generation as residual pain and transferred memory.

EPIGENETICS AND THE DIASPORA PROBLEMATIC

The first academic definition of diaspora was introduced in the 1930s. It was initially defined by historians as referring only to the Jewish Babylonian exile in the sixth century BCE. Later uses, again applied only to Jews, referred to networks of Jewish refugees that had spread out across northern Africa and into Europe after the Roman destruction of the Second Temple in Jerusalem in 70 CE. By the 1960s, influenced by the work of Frantz Fanon, diaspora studies expanded to consider transnational studies of imagined communities and subcultures in a number of postcolonial and neocolonial contexts. Arjun Appadurai, building on Frederic Jameson and Benedict Anderson, summarizes this shift as a process of locating communities formed outside of spatial, geographic and historical linearity (Appadurai 26–29). Modern Israel's rise and subsequent military annexation of Gaza and the West Bank, in 1967, undercut Jewishness as a powerless community (Anteby-Yemin 60–71). These developments led scholars to argue that Jewish diaspora no longer fell under the same rubric as other marginalized cultures and communities.[6] This created a problematic in the academy. William Safran, for example, argues that Jewish diaspora remains discursively distinct and excluded, even as diaspora studies has created a multiethnic reading strategy across numerous global, transnational and displaced peoples and cultures (10–11). Donna Robinson Divine agrees, noting that theorists following Edward Said often exclude Israel from neocolonial discussions (208–9). Divine argues that this fundamentally misreads Said. According to Divine, Said's notion of a relational Orientalism between both Arab and Jew in *Orientalism* (1978) "presented an entangled discourse that resisted reading Israel's occupation of Palestinian lands through a simple colonizer/colonized binary" (Divine 185–86).[7]

By the early 1990s, scholars began to critique the term "diaspora" itself as problematic and overdetermined. It was disparaged as a simplified catch-all expression for numerous distinct cultural formulations. These included a revised focus on voluntary and involuntary labor migrations, cultural and political exiles, and numerous identity-based cultures or subcultures such as marginalized variations of gender and sexuality. In response to this problematic, Hamid Naficy argued for the need to draw distinctions between diaspora and exile (3–5). Naficy argued that conceiving of "diaspora" should not invoke a desire for spatial or geographic return, as would be found in the exile of displaced peoples (5). Instead, "diaspora" should be understood as an internal construction, a relational and fluid understanding of identity in constant negotiation between the individual and the culture in which she resides.

This notion of a fluid, problematic understanding of diaspora recurs throughout *Transparent*. This locates in the show's intersection of Jewish and queer themes. In the eighth episode of Season 1 ("Best New Girl"), the show flashes back to 1994, the same historical period when the term "diaspora" began to be critiqued in the academy.[8] On the cusp of college, eighteen-year-old Sarah (Kelsey Reinhardt) leaves for Santa Barbara to attend a protest over the exploitation of migrant workers. Fifteen-year-old Josh (Dalton Rich) is openly carrying on a sexual affair with the twenty-something Rita (Annabel Marshall-Roth). And thirteen-year-old Ali (Emily Robinson) is halfheartedly preparing for her impending bat mitzvah. Mort has the opportunity to join Mark/Marcie (Bradley Whitford), his newly acquired transgender friend, at a secret cross-dressing resort on the same date of Ali's bat mitzvah. Mort uses Ali's expressed disinterest in her bat mitzvah as the excuse to cancel it and begin pursuing his eventual gender transition. This pursuit is at once both a liberating act of a closeted transgender adult and a traumatic act of emotional abuse of his youngest daughter. The canceled bat mitzvah by a transgender woman is also ironic. The female version of the bar mitzvah was a recent development towards gender equality in Reform and Conservative Jewish culture. Mort's cancellation of the event suggests a paradox, a severing of assimilated Jewish cultural life at the moment each of the Pfeffermans begin to explore their individual sexual identities.

The episode's historically situated intersection between Maura's first public emergence as a woman and Ali's subsequent alienation from her Jewishness follows Naficy's understanding of diaspora as an internal, subjective experience. Mort leaves for his trip, leaving the young Ali alone at the house. When one of the hired bat mitzvah caterers shows up, having failed to receive notice of the cancellation, she is revealed to be an androgynous woman dressed in a tuxedo. Ali performs her *havtorah* portion (Torah reading) for the woman as a seductive, implicitly taboo erotic dance. Her improvised ritual of Jewish maturity is not produced in synagogue. Instead it locates in the approving gaze of an adult stranger.

"Best New Girl" articulates the diaspora problematic at the heart of *Transparent*. Mort's alienation and wandering are both subjective and individual to his lived experience. Yet this alienation influences his daughter's isolation from her Jewish identity. This notion of inherited trauma connects Mort's journey of gender alienation to Ali's Jewish displacement. The Los Angeles beach serves as the structuring spatial motif for generational alienation. With nothing left to do on what was her bat mitzvah day, Ali leaves her house and travels to the beach. She meets a man in his twenties and flirts with him, lying to him about her age. Mort's indifference to Ali's bat mitzvah indirectly contributes to Ali's first efforts to lie about her identity, a thematic continuation of her father's dissimulation. This is presented in tandem with Mort/Maura's seduction of one of his fellow cross-dresser wives (Michaela Watkins) at his retreat. The crossing of boundaries in this flashback episode, whether married or underage, locates sexual taboo as the expression of thematic and transcultural diaspora being experienced by both generations of Pfeffermans.

In Season 2, *Transparent* furthers the entanglement between Jewish and queer diaspora when Ali begins researching her academic thesis in feminist studies just weeks after coming out as gay ("New World Coming," season 2, episode 3). Ali excitedly discovers the concept of "epigenetics," the theory that inherited trauma is passed generationally to children through DNA. Ali's search for meaning is once again the impetus to flashback to the intergenerational origins the Pfefferman diaspora. Only this time the episode returns to 1933 where Ali's grandmother, Rose (Emily Robinson), now a teenager, enters the Institute for Sexual Research run by Dr. Magnus Hirschfeld (Bradley Whitford).[9] The teenage Rose seeks out her brother, Tante Gittel né Gershon (Hari Nef) who has begun living openly as a woman at the institute. The German-Jewish Hirschfeld and his pioneering Institute for Sexual Research, founded in Berlin in 1919, are based on historical fact. This blurring of the show's exploration of history through fiction. Rose eventually moves over the course of season two from Berlin, where she barely escapes the Nazis, to Boyle Heights, a section of Los Angeles which from the early- to the mid-twentieth century served as the primary residential enclave for Ashkenazi Jews in the city.[10]

Ali's exploration of epigenetics is counterpointed by one of Maura's central plot lines in season two, as to whether she will visit her dying mother and reveal that she is now living as a woman. In the first episode of season two, "Kina Hora," Maura is shamed by her sister, Bryna (Jenny O'Hara) for not visiting their aged mother, Rose (Shannon Welles), who is approaching death in an assisted living facility. Ali's academic investigation and personal-is-political flashbacks perform a creative version of epigenetics, reflecting the inherited trauma of Maura and Rose. This crystallizes in flashbacks in which the young Rose witnesses both the personal (her brother) and political (Dr. Hirschfeld) as Jews attempting to sustain their bold effort to liberate sexual identity in the face of the impending crush of Nazism. Rose's role as witness to the Jewish-queer connection as an inciting incident of her Diasporic wanderings locates the origin trauma of displacement at the dysfunctional center of the Pfefferman family.[11]

In the next episode, ("Bulnerable," season 2, episode 6), Ali attempts to impress a radical lesbian poet, feminist scholar, and UCLA professor, Leslie

(Cherry Jones), by wooing her with her proposed graduate school thesis.[12] Leslie also happens to be a former academic colleague of Mort's who once suffered a professional setback due to his (hypocritical) aversion to her sexual politics. Leslie becomes an object of both Ali's erotic and professional aspirations. At one point, the two are smoking pot and sitting together naked in Leslie's Jacuzzi. Ali remarks that she's increasingly thinking about the connection between "the woman thing" and "the Jew thing" and awkwardly proposes her thesis subject as "Phallus is to crucifix as vagina is to Holocaust." The much older, highly accomplished Leslie laughs off Ali's flippant reductionism. Instead she suggests that Ali refocus her scholarship on her personal narrative rather than attempting to locate a grand thesis of history. The sequence is both ironic and self-reflexive. Ali's proposal to Leslie is itself one of eroticism and taboo. She offers facile commentary on the meta-mythic link between multigenerational Jewish displacement trauma and marginalized gender identity not as academic insight but as sexual entendre. Ali's grand thesis may have validity. But, as Leslie insists, the radical path of the feminist requires a relocation of this inquiry.

Leslie's dismissal of Ali's Jewish-gender connection reflects the Jewish diaspora problematic that Naficy describes at the center of diaspora studies. "The Personal is Political" manifesto of second wave feminism also becomes writ, in this exchange, as the artistic creative expressions of counterculture radicalism. Yet Leslie dismisses Ali's Jewish-queer connection. She instead suggests that Ali pursue a personal story as her thesis concept. This is complicated by the fact that Leslie is also in the process of seducing Ali, itself a taboo act of cultural transgression. Leslie is a venerated scholar with the southern twang of an American cowboy. Her large, upper middle class house is filled with the creature comforts of privilege. This tension between Leslie as a paradoxical embodiment of both institutional Anglo-Saxon academic accomplishment and marginalized, rebellious queer/dyke academic scrambles the boundaries of power and resistance, normativity and taboo as it plays out in her erotic interest in Ali. In Leslie's erotic courtship of Ali, the personal and the political converge through the crossing of boundaries in the sexual realm. As with Sarah's rejection of Tammy and Colton's impact on Josh, Leslie's Anglo-Saxon otherness becomes the mirror by which Ali pursues the reunification of her fractured self.

TRANSGRESSING THE SITCOM

For over sixty years, American situation comedy has remained one of the most stable and consistent of entertainment genres. Despite ethnic distinctions and changing sociopolitical contexts, the comedic beats and gender interplay of *The George Burns and Gracie Allen Show* and *I Love Lucy* appear remarkably similar to contemporary prime-time comedies such as *Black-ish* (2014–) and *Fresh Off the Boat* (2015–). But, as Kathleen Rowe's influential work on gender unruliness on *Roseanne* (1989–97) has demonstrated, the sitcom contains a remarkable ability to introduce transgressive subject matter without offending mainstream audiences. Scholars such as Darrell Y. Hamamoto and Lynn Spigel have shown how fantastical family sitcoms of the 1960s such as *The Munsters* (1964–66), *The Addams Family* (1964–66), *I Dream of Jeannie* (1965–70), and *Bewitched* (1964–72) hid transgressive forms of gender in seemingly innocuous sitcom plot lines (Hamamoto 61–65; Spigel 107–10). Norman Lear's controversial 1970s-era sitcoms privileged feminist icons such as Maude Findlay on *Maude* (1972–78). In the 1980s, alt-families such as same gender parents on *Perfect Strangers* (1986–93), *My Two Dads* (1987–90), and *Full House* (1987–95) and the racially integrated families on *Diff'rent Strokes*(1978–86) and *Webster* (1983–89) subverted the gender and racial codes of the traditional postwar (white) nuclear family. In the 1990s, *Ellen* (1994–98) and *Will and Grace* (1998–2004) brought unapologetic gay representations to the mainstream while HBO's *Dream On* (1990–96) and *Sex and the City* (1998–2004) demonstrated how the familiar tropes of sitcom humor could easily adapt to explicit subject matter and nudity.

The central strategy sitcoms deploy to engage controversial political and cultural topics focuses on the familiar archetypes of the family. A brief flurry of ethnic, working-class sitcoms in the early 1950s, including the Jewish sitcom *The Goldbergs* (1949–56), gave way to homogenized whiteness throughout the 1960s (*Father Knows Best* [1954–63], *The Dick Van Dyke Show* [1961–66], etc.). Spurred by the Civil Rights movement and identity politics, the 1970s saw a revived ethnic visibility. Black, Latino, Irish, Italian, and Jewish dysfunctional, suburban, middle-class families became a staple of the sitcom approach, as they continue to be , from the aforementioned *Black-ish* and *Fresh Off the Boat* to *Jane, the Virgin* (2014–) and *The Real O'Neals* (2016–). These ethnic families recall the genre's vaudevillian origins. But they also provide an easily identifiable, safe framework for any subsequent comedic exploration of taboo subject matter. Vaudeville ethnic comedy embraced the profane as part of its burlesque origins. The prime-time ethnic sitcom hints at these transgressions as one of the central modes of its comedic address.

Transparent fits in with these genre traditions at the moment it appears to break from them. The show can only uneasily be classified as a sitcom. The deployment of uncomfortable transcomedy tropes prevents resolution and scrambles genre identification. But this resistance to narrative norms is in keeping with the long history of the sitcom as one of television's boldest and most controversial forms. The unapologetic, everyday Jewishness of the Pfefferman family grounds the show's exploration of various configurations of gender and sexual identity. Yet, as creator Jill Soloway has noted, it is the show's Jewishness, not queerness that has provoked the most profound backlash on social media.[13] One reason may be that *Transparent* looks back at the twentieth century from a perspective of sublimated trauma and displaced identities. It returns to the twentieth–century diaspora problematic explored from both Jewish and academic perspectives. But it does so by collapsing the grand sweep of history into the fictionalized, neurotic, familiar, yet non-normative Jewish sitcom family. The wandering diasporic Jewishness foregrounded by the Pfefferman family operates as the central framing device for the show's formal and thematic experimentations. By privileging screen Jews as safely neurotic sitcom archetypes, *Transparent* opens space for an expansive exploration of previously overlooked communities. The Jewishness of the Pfeffermans is critical precisely because the comedic-neurotic insider/outsider duality of screen Jewishness has been used for decades to queer dominant Anglo-Saxon power in popular screen media. *Transparent* identifies and embraces this tradition while also transporting it into new, expansive comedic, and Jewish, territory.

Notes

1. "Cis-gender" refers to one who identities with the biological and culturally coded gender one was assigned at birth.
2. Emily Nussbaum cites the moment Sarah visits her spurned (non-Jewish) fiancée Tammy (Melora Hardin) on Yom Kippur to ask for forgiveness for canceling their wedding a few weeks earlier. Tammy's refusal to forgive Sarah's narcissism, her flippant "Happy Yom Kippur," is understood by Nussbaum as a sitcom trope. Nussbaum describes Sarah as an updated version of Larry David and of Hanna Horvath, Lena Dunham's narcissistic character on *Girls* (HBO, 2012–). Despite this obvious Jewish connection, Sarah's misanthrope is a comedic experimentation of form. In this reading, Jewishness on *Transparent* presents nothing more than biographical filler, elements necessary for narrative specificity but only superficially relevant to the real cultural innovation that the program performs.
3. The timing of the show's subject matter was also fortunate. Not only did the Supreme Court legalize gay marriage months after the show premiered, but popular Olympian and tabloid centerpiece Bruce Jenner began to transition into openly living as a woman, Kaitlyn Jenner.
4. This ambiguity of form is certainly not unique to *Transparent*. The two most prominent innovators of streaming television, Amazon and Netflix, both rely on what Jason Mittell calls "Forensic Fandom," a quality television marketing strategy in which programs require dedicated viewership to unpack the complexity and nuances within the text (263–68).
5. This culminates at the end of Season 2 when Shelly's new boyfriend, Buzz (Richard Masur), a Jewish volunteer Shelly meets at synagogue, tells Josh that he has to begin the process of mourning the loss of his father, causing Josh to break down crying. The emotional sequence takes place after Buzz and Josh have rescued a duck with a broken wing from Shelly's condo pond. The metaphor of the broken wing exemplifies the trauma Josh has carried in the absence of engaged parenting and how it informs his subsequent efforts (and failures) at sustaining relationships.
6. Sander Gilman locates a solution to this diaspora problematic, arguing that Fanon's psychoanalytic reading of colonialism required him to "decorporealize the Jew, to remove the Jewish body from the category of the body at risk" (198–99). Once modern Israel was founded, Jewish bodies could no longer locate within the Fanonian double readings of the colonized other. Gilman argues that Jewish bodies play a critical and contested role in negotiating the legacy of European colonial violence in the mass media age.
7. Said points out that what the western Jew gained in the new masculinities bestowed on him as a result of Israeli military success, the Arab (male) lost, noting (his) shift

8. from exoticized and fetishized (as in *The Sheik*) to that of defeated, emasculated and militarily weak (186).
8. 1994 had already been established as an important date, the only time stamp visible in the otherwise abstract collection of home movie VHS images that made up the opening title sequence in Season 1.
9. Furthering the link between Ali's diasporic wanderings and inherited memory, the teenage Rose is played by Emily Robinson, the same actress that played the teenage Ali in "Best New Girl." Another actor from that episode, Bradley Whitford, appears as Magnus Hirschfeld. This example of casting fluidity shows how *Transparent* scrambles the signifiers of the historical, the fictive, and the imagined as poetic exemplars of the fluidity of identity.
10. For more on the how Boyle Heights developed its Jewish identity, see Sanchez.
11. Sander Gilman (244) and Daniel Boyarin (85) have shown how feminist and Jewish movements were conflated in Europe at the turn of the twentieth century through discourses of queerness. The simultaneous emerging of the Zionist and Suffragette movements increased associations between the already suspect masculinity of increasingly emancipated Jewish men and the rising visibility of female agency. However, as Boyarin has shown, the notion of Jewish men as passive and resistant to confrontation was also central to Talmudic Jewishness, a philosophy that embraced meekness as an exemplar of Jewish masculinity.
12. Further blurring the art-into-life experimentation of the show, Soloway modeled Leslie on Eileen Myles, a radical feminist poet with whom she had entered into a romantic relationship with during the writing of Season 2 (Barnes).
13. In regard to the volume of vehement antisemitic commentary directed at the show, Soloway observed, "It's more controversial to be 'Jewy' these days than to be trans" (Kamen 2).

Works Cited

Abie's Irish Rose. Directed by Victor Fleming, performances by Charles "Buddy" Rogers, Nancy Carroll, and Jean Hersholt. Paramount Famous Lasky Corp., 1928.
The Addams Family. Created by David Levy, performances by John Astin, Carolyn Jones and Ted Cassidy. Filmways Television, 1964–66.
The Adventures of Ozzie & Harriet. Performances by Ozzie Nelson, Harriet Hilliard, and David Nelson. Stage Five Productions and Volcano Productions, 1952–66.
All in the Family. Created by Norman Lear, performances by Carroll O'Connor, Jean Stapleton, and Rob Reiner. Bud Yorkin Productions, Norman Lear/Tandem Productions, 1971–79.
Anderson, Tre'Vell. "Agents of Change: Hollywood Has a Long Way To Go." *Los Angeles Times*, 20 Dec. 2015, Calendar Section.
Anteby-Yemin, Lisa. "Ethiopian Jews, New Migration Models in Israel and Diaspora Studies." *Bulletin du Centre de recherche français à Jérusalem*, vol. 15, issue 1, 2004, pp. 60–71.
Appadurai, Arjun. "Disjuncture and Difference." *Theorizing Diaspora: A Reader*, edited by Jana Evans Braziel and Anita Mannur, Blackwell, 2003, pp. 295–310.
Barnes, Brooke. "Eileen Myles, the Poet-Muse of *Transparent*." *The New York Times*, 16 Jan. 2016, mobile.nytimes.com/2016/01/17/fashion/eileen-myles-jill-soloway-girlfriend-transparent.html. Accessed 30 Aug. 2016.
Being Mary Jane. Created by Mara Brock Akil, performances by Gabrielle Union, Lisa Vidal, and Raven Goodwin. Akil Productions and Breakdown Productions, 2013–.
Bellow, Saul. *Herzog.* Viking, 1964.
"Best New Girl." *Transparent*, season 1, episode 8, 26 Sept. 2014.
Bewitched. Created by Sol Saks, performances by Elizabeth Montgomery, Dick York, and Dick Sargent. Ashmont Productions and Screen Gems Television, 1964–72.
Black-ish. Created by Kenya Barris, performances by Anthony Anderson, Tracee Ellis Ross, and Marcus Scribner. Wilmore Films, Principato-Young Entertainment, and Cinema Gypsy Productions, 2014–.
"The Book of Life." *Transparent,* season 2, episode 7, 11 Dec. 2015.
Boyarin, Daniel. *Unheroic Conduct: The Rise of Heterosexuality and the Invention of the Jewish Man.* Univ. of California, 1997.
Bridget Loves Bernie. Created by Bernard Slade, performances by David Birney, Meredith Baxter, and Harold J. Stone. Screen Gems Television and Thornhill Productions, 1972–73.
Broad City. Created by Ilana Glazer and Abbi Jacobson. Comedy Central, 2014–.
Brook, Vincent. *Something Ain't Kosher Here: The Rise of the "Jewish" Sitcom.* Rutgers Univ., 2003.
"Bulnerable." *Transparent*, season 2, episode 6, 11 Dec. 2015.

Carol. Directed by Todd Haynes, performances by Cate Blanchett, Rooney Mara, and Sarah Paulson. Number 9 Films, Dirty Films, and Film4, 2015.

Clarke, Diana, and Saul Noam Zaritt. "Yiddish on *Transparent*: A Talk with Jill Soloway and Micah Fitzerman-Blue." *Geveb*, 1 March 2016, ingeveb.org/blog/yiddish-on-transparent. Accessed 30 Aug. 2016.

Cohen, Debra Nussbaum. "How Jill Soloway Created 'Transparent', The Jewiest Show Ever." *The Forward*, 21 Oct. 2014.

The Cohens and the Kellys. Directed by Harry A. Pollard, performances by Charles Murray, George Sidney and Vera Gordon. Universal, 1926.

Curb Your Enthusiasm. Created by Larry David. HBO, 2000–11.

The Dick Van Dyke Show. Created by Carl Reiner, performances by Dick Van Dyke, Mary Tyler Moore, Rose Marie and Morey Amsterdam. Calvada Productions, 1961–66.

Diff'rent Strokes. Created by Jeff Harris and Bernie Kukoff, performances by Gary Coleman, Todd Bridges, and Conrad Bain. Embassy Pictures, Embassy Television, and Norman Lear/Tandem Productions, 1978–86.

Divine, Donna Robinson. "The Middle East Conflict and Its Postcolonial Discontents." *Postcolonial Theory and the Arab-Israel Conflict*, edited by Philip Carl Salzman and Donna Robinson Divine, Routledge, 2008, pp. 885–88.

Dream On. Created by David Crane and Marta Kauffman, performances by Brian Benben, Denny Dillon, and Wendie Malick. Kevin Bright Productions, MCA Television Entertainment (MTE), and St. Clare Entertainment, 1990–96.

Edelman, Lee. *No Future, Queer Theory and the Death Drive*. Duke Univ., 2004.

Ellen. Created by Carol Black, Neal Marlens, and David S. Rosenthal, performances by Ellen DeGeneres, David Anthony Higgins, and Joely Fisher. Black-Marlens Company and Touchstone Television, 1994–98.

Fanon, Frantz. *Black Skin, White Masks*. Grove, 2008.

Father Knows Best. Created by Ed James, performances by Robert Young, Jane Wyatt, and Billy Gray. Rodney-Young Productions and Screen Gems Television, 1954–62.

Fresh Off the Boat. Performances by Randall Park, Constance Wu, and Hudson Yang. Fierce Baby Productions, Detective Agency, and 20th Century Fox Television, 2015–.

Friends. Created by David Crane and Marta Kauffman. Warner Bros. Television, and Bright/Kauffman/Crane Productions, 1994–2004.

Full House. Created by Jeff Franklin, performances by Bob Saget, John Stamos, and Dave Coulier. Jeff Franklin Productions, Lorimar Telepictures, and Lorimar Television, 1987–95.

The George Burns and Gracie Allen Show. Performances by George Burns, Gracie Allen, and Bea Benaderet. CBS and McCadden Productions, 1950–58.

Gilman, Sander. *Jewish Self-Hatred: Anti-Semitism and the Hidden Language of the Jew*. Johns Hopkins Univ., 1990.

———. *Making the Body Beautiful: A Cultural History of Aesthetic Surgery*. Princeton Univ., 1998.

Girls. Created by Lena Dunham, performances by Lena Dunham, Allison Williams, and Jemima Kirke. Apatow Productions. HBO, 2012–.

The Goldbergs. Created by Gertrude Berg. NBC, 1949–56.

The Graduate. Directed by Mike Nichols, performances by Dustin Hoffman, Anne Bancroft, and Katharine Ross. Lawrence Turman, 1967.

The Heartbreak Kid. Directed by Elaine May, performances by Charles Grodin, Cybill Shepherd, and Jeannie Berlin. Palomar Pictures, 1972.

The Honeymooners. Created by Jackie Gleason, performances by Jackie Gleason, Art Carney, and Audrey Meadows. Jackie Gleason Enterprises and Paramount Television, 1955–56.

I Dream of Jeannie. Created by Sidney Sheldon, performances by Barbara Eden, Larry Hagman, and Bill Daily. Screen Gems Television and Sidney Sheldon Productions, 1965–70.

I Love Lucy. Performances by Lucille Ball, Desi Arnaz, and Vivian Vance. Desilu Productions, 1951–57.

I Love You Alice B. Toklas. Directed by Hy Averback, performances by Peter Sellers, Jo Van Fleet, and Leigh Taylor-Young. Warner Brothers/Seven Arts, 1968.

Inside Amy Schumer. Created by Daniel Powell and Amy Schumer. Comedy Central, 2013–.

Ivry, Sara. "'Transparent' is the Most Jewish TV Show in a While—And It's Great." *Tablet Magazine*, 1 Oct. 2014, www.tabletmag.com/scroll/185735/transparent-is-the-most-jewish-tv-show-in-a-while--and-its-great/. Accessed 31 Aug. 2016.

Jane, the Virgin. Created by Jennie Snyder Urman, performances by Gina Rodriguez, Andrea Navedo, and Yael Grobglas. Poppy Productions, RCTV, and Electus, 2014–.

Kamen, Paula. "*Transparent*'s Jill Soloway on Inventing the Female Gaze." *Ms. Magazine*, 6 Nov. 2014.

"Kina Hora." *Transparent*, season 2, episode 1, 30 Nov. 2015.

"The Letting Go." *Transparent*, season 1, episode 2, 26 Sept. 2014.

Little Fockers. Directed by Paul Weitz, performances by Ben Stiller, Teri Polo, and Robert De Niro. Universal Pictures, Paramount Pictures, and Relativity Media, 2010.

Louie. Created by Louis C. K., performances by Louis C. K., Hadley Delany, and Ursula Parker. FX, 2010–.

Mad About You. Created by Danny Jacobson and Paul Reiser, performances by Paul Reiser, Helen Hunt, and John Pankow. In Front Productions, Nuance Productions, and TriStar Television, 1992–99.

Mad Men. Created by Matthew Weiner, performances by Jon Hamm, Elisabeth Moss, and Vincent Kartheiser. Lionsgate Television, Weiner Bros., and AMC, 2007–15.

Maude. Created by Norman Lear, performances by Bea Arthur, Bill Macy, and Conrad Bain. Bud Yorkin Productions and Norman Lear/Tandem Productions, 1972–78.

"Mee-Maw." *Transparent*, season 2, episode 5, 11 Dec. 2015.

Meet the Fockers. Directed by Jay Roach, performances by Ben Stiller, Robert De Niro, and Blythe Danner. Universal Pictures, Dreamworks SKG, and Tribeca Productions, 2004.

Meet the Parents. Directed by Jay Roach, performances by Ben Stiller, Robert De Niro, and Teri Polo. Universal Pictures, DreamWorks SKG, and Nancy Tenenbaum Films, 2000.

The Melting Pot. Written by Israel Zangwill. Washington, DC, 1909.

Mittell, Jason. *Complex TV: The Poetics of Contemporary Television Storytelling*. New York Univ., 2015.

Modern Family. Created by Steven Levitan and Christopher Lloyd, performances by Ed O'Neill, Sofia Vergara, and Julie Bowen. Levitan/Lloyd, 20th Century Fox Television, and Steven Levitan Productions, 2009–.

"Moppa." *Transparent*, season 1, episode 4, 26 Sept. 2014.

Morris, Wesley. "Women in Love, Then and Now." *The New York Times*, 31 Jan. 2016.

Moss, Joshua Louis. "Defining Transcomedy: Humor, Tricksterism, and Postcolonial Affect from Gerald Vizenor to Sacha Baron Cohen." *International Journal of Cultural Studies*, 28 July 2015, http://ics.sagepub.com/content/early/2015/07/16/1367877915595476.abstract. Accessed 31 Aug. 2016.

The Munsters. Created by Ed Haas and Liebmann, performances by Fred Gwynne, Al Lewis, and Yvonne De Carlo. CBS and Kayro-Vue Productions, 1964–66.

My Two Dads. Created by Danielle Alexandra and Michael Jacobs, performances by Paul Reiser, Greg Evigan, and Staci Keanan. Columbia, Michael Jacobs Productions, and TriStar Television, 1987–90.

Naficy, Hamid. *Home, Exile, Homeland: Film, Media, and the Politics of Place*. Routledge, 1999.

The Nanny. Created by Fran Drescher et al., performances by Fran Drescher, Charles Shaughnessy and Daniel Davis. CBS, Highschool Sweethearts and Sternin & Fraser Ink, 1993–99.

"New World Coming." *Transparent*, season 2, episode 3, 11 Dec. 2015.

Nussbaum, Emily. "Inside Out: The Emotional Acrobatics of *Transparent*." *The New Yorker*, 4 Jan. 2016.

Orange Is the New Black. Created by Jenji Kohan, performances by Taylor Schilling, Danielle Brooks, and Taryn Manning. Netflix, 2013–.

Perfect Strangers. Created by Dale McRaven, performances by Bronson Pinchot, Mark Linn-Baker, and Melanie Wilson. Lorimar Productions, Lorimar Telepictures, and Lorimar Television, 1986–93.

"Pilot." *Transparent*, season 1, episode 1, 27 Aug. 2014.

Private Izzy Murphy. Directed by Lloyd Bacon, performances by George Jessel, Patsy Ruth Miller, and Vera Gordon. Warner Bros., 1926.

The Real O'Neals. Created by Joshua Sternin and Jennifer Ventimillia, performances by Martha Plimpton, Jay R. Ferguson, and Noah Galvin. Windsor & Johnson, Di Bonaventura Pictures Television, and ABC, 2016–.

Rhoda. Created by James L. Brooks, Allan Burns, and David Davis, performances by Valerie Harper, Julie Kavner, and Lorenzo Music. MTM, 1974–78.

Riley, Jenelle. "Amazon, *Transparent*, Make History at the Golden Globes." *Variety*, 11 Oct. 2015, variety.com/2015/tv/news/amazon-transparent-make-history-at-golden-globes-1201400485/. Accessed 31 Aug. 2016.

Rochlin, Margy. "A Heroine Evolves Further Still." *The New York Times*, 20 Nov. 2015.

"Rollin'." *Transparent*, season 1, episode 3, 26 Sept. 2014.

Roseanne. Created by Matt Williams, performances by Roseanne Barr, John Goodman, and Laurie Metcalf. Wind Dancer Productions, Carsey-Werner Company, and Paramount Television, 1988–97.

Roth, Philip. *Portnoy's Complaint*. Random House, 1969.

Rowe, Kathleen. "Roseanne: Unruly Woman as Domestic Goddess. *Screen*, vol. 31, issue 4, Winter 1990, pp. 408–18.

Safran, William. "Deconstructing and Comparing Diasporas." *Diaspora, Identity, and Religion: New Directions in Theory and Research*, edited by Khachig Tölölyan, Carolin Alfonso and Waltraud Kokot, Routledge, 2004, pp. 9–29.

Said, Edward. *Orientalism*. Vintage, 1978.

Sanchez, George. "'What's Good for Boyle Heights is Good for the Jews': Creating Multiculturalism on the Eastside During the 1950s." *American Quarterly*, vol. 56, issue 3, 2004, pp. 633–61.

Seinfeld. Created by Larry David and Jerry Seinfeld, performances by Jerry Seinfeld et al. West-Shapiro and Castle Rock Entertainment, 1989–98.

Sex and the City. Created by Darren Star, performances by Sarah Jessica Parker, Kim Cattrall, and Kristin Davis. Darren Star Productions, HBO, and Sex and the City Productions, 1998–2004.

The Sheik. Directed by George Melford, performances by Rudolph Valentino, Agnes Ayres, and Ruth Miller. Paramount, 1921.

Spigel, Lynn. *Welcome to the Dreamhouse: Popular Media and Postwar Suburbs*. Duke Univ., 2001.

"Symbolic Exemplar." *Transparent*, season 1, episode 7, 26 Sept. 2014.

Thurm, Eric. "*Transparent*: 'Symbolic Exemplar'/'Best New Girl' Somebody That I Used to Know." *The A. V. Club* 17 Oct. 2014, www.avclub.com/tvclub/transparent-symbolic-exemplarbest-new-girl-210619. Accessed 31 Aug. 2016.

Transparent. Created by Jill Soloway, performances by Jeffrey Tambor, Amy Landecker, and Gaby Hoffman. Picrow and Amazon Studios, 2014–.

Transparent. Advertisement. *New York Times,* 6 Dec. 2015, Arts and Leisure p. 18.

VanDerWerff, Todd. "*Transparent* Season 2 is the Best TV Show of the Year." *Vox* 13 Dec. 2015, www.vox.com/culture/2015/12/13/10021938/transparent-season-2-review-amazon. Accessed 31 Aug. 2016.

Webster. Created by Stu Silver, performances by Susan Clark, Alex Karras, and Emmanuel Lewis. Emmanuel Lewis Entertainment Enterprises, Georgian Bay Productions, and Paramount Television, 1983–89.

"Wedge." *Transparent*, season 1, episode 5, 26 Sept. 2014.

"Why Do We Cover the Mirrors?" *Transparent*, season 1, episode 10, 26 Sept. 2014.

"The Wilderness." *Transparent*, season 1, episode 6, 26 Sept. 2014.

Will and Grace. Created by David Kohan and Max Mutchnick, performances by Eric McCormack, Debra Messing, and Megan Mullally. KoMut Entertainment, Three Sisters Entertainment, and NBC Studios, 1998–2006.

CHAPTER 5

Eastern-European Fatalism in Minnesota: The Mournful Destinies of *A Serious Man*

by Howard A. Rodman

Jewish humor has long been a staple of American cinema; yet Jews themselves have been at best a sub-staple. One thinks of Felix Bressart's Greenberg in *To Be or Not To Be* (1942); Everett Sloan's Bernstein in *Citizen Kane* (1941); Rod Steiger's Sol Nazerman in *The Pawnbroker* (1965); Richard Benjamin's Neil Klugman in *Goodbye, Columbus* (1969); Barbra Streisand's Jewish commie in *The Way We Were* (1973); Richard Dreyfuss's hustling resort-hotel waiter in *The Apprenticeship of Duddy Kravitz* (1974); Ben Stiller's eponymous lead in *Greenberg* (2010); and of course Alvy Singer, Isaac, Cliff Stern et al., in the films of Woody Allen, raising urban Jewish neurosis to the level of an art form.[1] But far more often, even as Jews write and direct films, the characters they depict are not Jewish at all. For instance, I would posit that at least half the Italians in 1950s/1960s American cinema were just Jews by other means—c.f., Ernest Borgnine's Marty Piletti in Sidney Aaron "Paddy" Chayefsky's *Marty* (1955), or Tony Curtis's Sidney Falco in the Clifford Odets (né Gorodetsky)/Ernest Lehman *Sweet Smell of Success* (1957). Alternatively, Jewish characters have often been rendered as ambiguously "ethnic": see, for instance, Joe Morse, played by John Garfield (né Jacob Julius Garfinkle of Rivington Street) in Abraham Polonsky's *Force of Evil* (1948), recognizable as Jewish to those who know the code, but never explicitly specified as such.

In contemporary American cinema a Jewish man can be the humorous sidekick, a Jewish woman the symbol of rapaciousness, as if Jonah Hill and Sarah Silverman were less actors than archetypes. The depiction of Jews in contemporary cinema is, sadly, largely confined to the secular dyad of schlubby guy[2]/greedy gal.

Every once in a while, though, Jews are allowed to be Jews—which is to say, we're like everyone else, and yes some of us are funny, and some of us are also depressed, and some of us have unfortunate hair growing out of our noses and ears, and some of us are even spiritual. Richard Gere's Saul Naumann in *Bee Season* (2005), adapted by Naomi Foner from Myla Goldberg's novel, is a professor of religious studies, one of those rare movie Jews who's allowed to practice Judaism—the other exceptions being the title roles in *King of Kings* (1961), *The Last Temptation of Christ* (1988), and *The Passion of the Christ* (2004). (But as Lou Reed would say, those were different times.)

Saul Naumann believes life should be lived by the precepts of his religion. In short, he is that *rara avis* among Jews in American cinema, a serious man (although his transformation from a cantor in the novel to a professor in the film is itself a form of secularization). But it took Joel and Ethan Coen to bring to the screen a character unabashedly serious, unabashedly Jewish, unabashedly intellectual, unabashedly spiritual, and unabashedly fucked. And it is this last that is, perhaps, the most noteworthy. Because while Jews in American cinema are often allowed to play *schlemiels*—Tony Curtis in *Sweet Smell of Success*, Mark Rydell in the Robert Altman/Leigh Brackett re-reading of Raymond Chandler's *The Long Goodbye* (1973)—it takes the Coens to allow a Jewish character to go full *schlimazel*.[3] Michael Stuhlbarg's Larry Gopnik in the Coens' *A Serious Man* (2009) is smart but not funny, a man facing his ruination with all the implacability of Buster Keaton standing in front of a falling house. His life is coming apart and he doesn't know why—and that, the Coens seem to be saying, is humor enough.

Gopnik's doomstruck character is the very embodiment of a form of Eastern European fatalism—or as my grandmother would put it, "If I were a candlemaker, the sun would never set." This is not the Judaism of aspiration, or the Judaism of deep and abiding faith in liberation. This is the faith of those who know that things will only get worse. *A Serious Man* is sprinkled with more than a little Yiddish: an A to Z lexicon of Yiddishisms and Hebrewisms found in *A Serious Man* would include *agunah, bar mitzvah, bupkes, chacham, dybbuk, gett, goy, haftorah, hashem, kabballah, macher, mazel tov, mensch, mitzvah, nu, rabbi, reb, shabbas, shtetl, shiva, shul, torah,* and *Zohar*. The words are used to shackle, to burden, to remind Gopnik of the weight of the past, never to offer the promise of a more golden future. (Not on this shore, and likely not on the other, either.)

The movie comes at us in distinct parts: a prologue, in black and white, set in the Old Country in an unspecified era, perhaps the late 1800s; and the main body of the film, in a desaturated color palette shot by the extraordinary Roger Deakins, set in Saint Louis Park, a suburb of Minneapolis, in 1967 (but a far cry from *The Mary Tyler Moore Show*'s Minneapolis of 1970–77).

The prologue has no strict narrative connection to the larger film: it's a standalone, serving more to establish sensibility than causation. In the prologue—all in Yiddish, with subtitles—a man, Velvel, tells his wife Dora that on his way home in the snow he met, and was aided by, Reb Traitle Groshkover, Pesel Bunim's uncle, from Lodz, who studied under the Zohar reb in Krakow. Her first words, succinct and sufficient: "God has cursed us." Dora tells him that Reb Groshkover has been dead for three years, and that what he saw could only be a *dybbuk*. Bad enough for sure, until a knock comes at the door and there is Groshkover—whom Velvel, heavy with a sense and tradition of obligation, cannot fail to invite in. Reb Groshkover (played with sly, understated wit by the late Fyvush Finkel) maintains that he never died—what more proof be needed than that he is standing there? Dora, convinced he's already dead, plunges an icepick into his chest. And contrary to her expectations, he bleeds. Says Groshkover to Velvel, "What a wife you have!" And sensing by the pick in his chest that he's not welcome, Groshkover leaves Velvel and Dora's house to venture out into the snowstorm (and, presumably, to die, of blood loss or hypothermia, whichever comes first).

Groshkover's Parthian shot: "One does a *mitzvah* and this is all the thanks one gets?" After he departs Velvel says simply: "Dear wife. We are ruined." She demurs unconvincingly—but the curse lingers, transmigrates, perhaps to land on the shoulders of Larry Gopnik, who has no apparent relationship to Velvel and Dora other than that he's damned.[4]

Gopnik's woes are manifold. He's a physics professor up for tenure, the certainty of which ebbs with each passing incident.[5] His wife is leaving him, having taken up with the bearded, platitude-spouting Sy Ableman. The *goy* neighbor next door is building a shed on his property. Accommodating his wife's wishes, Gopnik moves out to a motel; and his brother Arthur, having failed at everything, moves in with him.[6] When Gopnik's wife's fiancé dies in an accident, it's Gopnik who's stuck with the funeral expenses. His children are annoying at best, amoral at worst. In a dream he explains to his students:

"Even if you don't understand any of this, you'll still be responsible for it on the exam"—a sentiment that could be used, with little or no alteration, as an *explication de texte* for his life. Climbing on the roof to fix his TV antenna he spots the other-side neighbor, Mrs. Samsky, sunbathing provocatively—and in giddy intoxication, falls off the roof. A subsequent visit to Mrs. Samsky—"Actually I haven't been home a lot recently. I, uh, my wife and I are, uh, well, she's got me staying at the Jolly Roger . . ."—couldn't be more awkward. The rabbis whose help Gopnik and his son seek—Rabbi Scott, Rabbi Nachtner, and ultimately Rabbi Marshak—are each of them older, wiser, and more useless than the last. In short: it's a modern Job story, with doctors and lawyers rather than prophets bearing the bad news. Gopnick is pursued by a student (and a student's father) to take a bribe, which he at first refuses, keeping his honor but losing much else, and then, finally, accepts. And immediately following: a call from his internist, who wants to discuss, in person, the results of an X-ray. Just when things couldn't get worse, a tornado approaches. The film ends.

From the moment we meet him, Larry Gopnik tries assiduously, dutifully, charmlessly to be a good man. His goodness does not seem to divert in any way the stream of catastrophe. At the end of the film, when in a moment of weakness he receives the envelope full of cash as *quid pro quo* for a passing grade, he is no more or less doomed than he'd been throughout. Is this the destiny of sun-never-sets, born in Lodz, now finding good home in Minnesota? Or is this a less specific, more pervasive curse: the curse of being human?

Jews in movies are funny. Larry Gopnik is not funny (although the film in which he resides most certainly is). Jews in movies aren't really Jewish. Larry Gopnik is Jewish in every aspect. Jews in movies—again, with the exception of biblical epics—don't typically concern themselves with questions of high moral seriousness. Larry Gopnik thinks of little else. Jews in movies are always searching for success (c.f., the character "Mark Zuckerberg" in *The Social Network* [2010]); Larry and Arthur seem to search only for the path of righteousness. Jews in movies can be side characters in the drama of someone else's social mobility (Bernstein in *Kane*; Jerry Heller in *Straight Outta Compton* [2015]), but are rarely allowed, as here, their full subjectivity, surrounded by a world of their own. Suburbia, whether old-money East (*The Swimmer* [1968]), or new-money West (*Over the Edge* [1979]; *Edward Scissorhands* [1990]), are in movies populated by WASPs—but the Coens' suburbia hardly has a one, save for the shed-building neighbor. (Even the home-wrecker Sy Ableman and the seductress Vivienne Samsky, contrary to movie stereotype, are bagel eaters.) But because this was, as Todd McCarthy uncharitably noted in *Variety*, "the kind of picture you get to make after you win an Oscar," the Coens were able to tell the story of people not unlike themselves and those they grew up with. (The film's protagonist, like the Coens' parents, is an academic.) Working within a contained, constrained budget, they could exercise their sense of existential disaster to the fullest.[7] Yet while the settings and characters are Midwestern, the sensibility is pure Eastern European: the knowledge that at any moment, for no reason at all, the pogrom might descend. As his personal world falls apart, Larry Gopnik wonders, why me? The answer he receives is straight outta *shtetl*: Why not you?

The Jews in American cinema bow more to Mammon than to God: if cinematic Jewish protagonists yearn for anything, it's assimilation, success, or the canny conflation of both. When Charley Davis (John Garfield), in the Polonsky/Rossen *Body and Soul* (1947) is told by his mother that it would be better to shoot himself than to fight for money, he replies, "You need money to buy a gun!" Moe Green (Alex Rocco, for once an Italian playing a Jew) in *The Godfather* (1972) is depicted as a savvy businessman who built a city in the desert; Hyman Roth (Lee Strasberg) in *The Godfather: Part II* (1974) is the incarnation of capitalism itself. Even in the Sholom Alaichem adaptation *Fiddler on the Roof* (1971), Topol/Tevye's most memorable song is "If I Were a Rich Man." But in *A Serious Man* the striving isn't for upward mobility, unless the "upward" in that phrase might connote heaven. And though the concerns are typical mid-century suburban concerns—adultery, poverty, dentistry—they're presented here as text to a far more intrusive subtext, one defined by Eastern European *yeshiva bocher*[8] conundrums. The ultimate rabbi, Marshak (played by the noted Beckett scholar/interpreter Alan Mandell), seems at first to dispense neither wisdom nor advice to Gopnik's son. Instead he quotes (or Talmudically misquotes) popular song: "When the truth is found. To be lies. And all the hope. Within you dies. Then what?" And, after several long moments of silence, "Grace Slick. Marty Balin. Paul Kanta. Jorma . . . Somethin." Summing it up: "These are the membas of the Airplane." He nods a couple of times. Then: "Interesting." Then: "Here." Finally: "Be a good boy."

His ultimate admonition goes all the way back to early cinematic history, to what is arguably the first feature-length talkie, *The Jazz Singer* (1927), in which Warner Oland's Cantor Rabinowitz's son Jackie, instead of going into the family business, wants to sing jazz. Jackie Rabinowitz—later Jack Robin (Al Jolson)—has to decide between a Broadway opening night performance, and returning to join his dying father, singing Kol Nidre at the Yom Kippur service. Of course Jack becomes Jackie once more, forsaking for the moment the lights of Broadway for the candles of his people. He has been, as Rabbi Marshak would put it, "a good boy."

But what the Coens are doing with their faith here is far more subversive—and I would argue, far more truthful. Good boys grow up to be good men, and good men suffer and die as all men do, and all good women, too. The redemptions of the new world can't hold a candle to the curse of the old. Bad things happen, worse things happen, and then there's a tornado. The setting may be Minneapolis, the music may be played by electric guitars, but in the Coens' shtetl-cursed Saint Louis Park, righteousness is no guarantee of anything, and even the best among us will find ourselves visited by every misery—and worse, will never know why. It's a Judaism older, less kind, than usually purveyed by American cinema, and for that reason alone, far more compelling.

Notes

1. On the smaller screen there's Jerry Seinfeld in *Seinfeld* (1989–98), a show famously about Nothing; and *Seinfeld* co-creator Larry David in the crypto-autobiographical *Curb Your Enthusiasm* (2001–11).
2. Members of the so-called "Jew Tang Clan" of Apatovian schlubbs would include Jonah Hill, Seth Rogen, Jason Segel, Jason Schwartzman, Michael Cera, and Paul Rudd.
3. The distinction between *schlemiehl* and *schlimazel* has been defined this way: the former is the clumsy waiter who spills soup, the latter the hapless customer upon whom the soup is spilled. See Thomas Pynchon's Benny Profane in *V.* (1963): " 'Ah, *schlemihl*,' he whispered into the phosphorescence. Accident prone, *schlimazzel*. The gun would blow up in his hands."
4. Joel Coen, in a remark of no probative value whatsoever, says "It doesn't have any relationship to what follows, but it helped us get started thinking about the movie" ("*A Serious Man* Production Notes," www.focusfeatures.com/article/a_serious_man_production_notes?film=a_serious_man).
5. This is perhaps the only other American feature film to use tenure as a plot point, with the possible exception of the 1988 remake of *D.O.A.*
6. Arthur loses money gambling, scribbles gnomically in a notebook—could he perhaps, for all of his pain, be one of the *Lamed Vav Tzadikim*? One of the thirty-six righteous men who cause the Lord to utter, "I will spare all the place for their sakes"?
7. As Ethan Coen noted, "When you're making a movie about a Jewish Midwestern community in 1967 and Fred Melamed is the sex guy, they don't give you a lot of money" ("*A Serious Man* Production Notes").
8. Boy Torah scholar.

Works Cited

A Serious Man. Directed by Joel and Ethan Coen, written by Joel Coen & Ethan Coen, performances by Michael Stuhlbarg, Richard Kind, and Sari Lennick, cinematography by Roger Deakins. Focus Features, StudioCanal, and Relativity Media, 2009.

"A Serious Man Production Notes." *Focus Features* 2 Oct. 2009, www.focusfeatures.com/article/a_serious_man_production_notes?film=a_serious_man. Accessed 25 Aug. 2016.

The Apprenticeship of Duddy Kravitz. Directed by Ted Kotcheff, screenplay by Mordecai Richler, performances by Richard Dreyfuss, Micheline Lanctôt, and Jack Warden. Astral Bellevue Pathé, CFDC and Duddy Kravitz Syndicate, 1974.

Bee Season. Directed by David Siegel & Scott McGehee, screenplay by Naomi Foner from the novel by Myla Goldberg, performances by Richard Gere, Juliette Binoche, and Flora Cross. Bee Season Productions, Fox Searchlight Pictures, and Bona Fide Productions, 2005.

Body and Soul. Directed by Robert Rossen, original screenplay by Abraham Polonsky, performances by John Garfield, Lilli Palmer and Hazel Brooks. Enterprise Productions, 1947.

Citizen Kane. Directed by Orson Welles, written by Herman J. Mankiewicz & Orson Welles, performances by Orson Welles, Joseph Cotton, and Dorothy Comingore. RKO Radio Pictures and Mercury Productions, 1941.

Curb Your Enthusiasm. Created by Larry David. HBO, 2000–11.

D.O.A. Directed by Annabel Jankel and Rocky Morton, screenplay by Charles Edward Pogue, story by Charles Edward Pogue and Russell Rouse & Clarence Greene, performances by Dennis Quaid, Meg Ryan, and Charlotte Rampling. Bigelow Productions, Silver Screen Partners III, and Touchstone Pictures, 1988.

Edward Scissorhands. Directed by Tim Burton, screenplay by Caroline Thompson, story by Tim Burton & Caroline Thompson, performances by Johnny Depp, Winona Ryder, and Dianne Wiest. 20th Century Fox Film, 1990.

Fiddler on the Roof. Directed by Norman Jewison, screenplay by Joseph Stein, from the play by Joseph Stein, adapted from stories by Sholem Aleichem by special arrangement with Arnold Perl, performances by Topol, Norma Crane, and Leonard Frey. Mirisch Production Company and Cartier Productions, 1971.

Force of Evil. Directed by Abraham Polonsky, screenplay by Abraham Polonsky, from the novel by Ira Wolfert, performances by John Garfield, Thomas Gomez, and Marie Windsor. Enterprise Productions and Roberts Pictures, 1948.

The Godfather. Directed by Francis Ford Coppola, screenplay by Mario Puzo and Francis Ford Coppola, based on the novel by Mario Puzo, performances by Marlon Brando, Al Pacino, and James Caan. Paramount Pictures and Alfran Productions, 1972.

The Godfather: Part II. Directed by Francis Ford Coppola, screenplay by Francis Ford Coppola & Mario Puzo, based on the novel by Mario Puzo, performances by Al Pacino, Robert De Niro, and Robert Duvall. Paramount Pictures and the Coppola Company, 1974.

Goldberg, Myla. *Bee Season.* Bantam Doubleday Dell, 2000.
Goodbye, Columbus. Directed by Larry Peerce, screenplay by Arnold Schulman, from the novel by Philip Roth, performances by Richard Benjamin, Ali MacGraw, and Jack Klugman. Willow Tree, 1969.
Greenberg. Directed by Noah Baumbach, screenplay by Noah Baumbach, story by Jennifer Jason Leigh & Noah Baumbach, performances by Ben Stiller, Greta Gerwig, and Jennifer Jason Leigh. Scott Rudin Productions and Twins Financing, 2010.
The Jazz Singer. Directed by Alan Crosland, play by Samson Raphaelson, adaptation by Alfred A. Cohn, titles by Jack Jarmuth, performance by Al Jolson. Warner Bros., 1927.
King of Kings. Directed by Nicholas Ray, screenplay by Philip Yordan, performances by Jeffrey Hunter, Siobhan McKenna, and Hurd Hatfield. MGM and Samuel Bronston Productions, 1961.
The Last Temptation of Christ. Directed by Martin Scorsese, screenplay by Paul Schrader, from the novel by Nikos Kazantzakis, performances by Willem Dafoe, Harvey Keitel, and Barbara Hershey. Universal Pictures, and Cineplex Odeon Films, 1988.
The Long Goodbye. Directed by Robert Altman, screenplay by Leigh Brackett from the novel by Raymond Chandler, performances by Elliott Gould, Nina van Pallandt, and Sterling Hayden. E-K-Corporation and Lion's Gate Films, 1973.
Marty. Directed by Delbert Mann, story and screenplay by Paddy Cheyefsky, performances by Ernest Borgnine, Betsy Blair, and Esther Minciotti. Hecht-Lancaster Productions, 1955.
The Mary Tyler Moore Show. Created by James L. Brooks and Allan Burns, performances by Mary Tyler Moore, Edward Asner, and Gavin MacLeod. MTM Enterprises, 1970–77.
Over the Edge. Directed by Jonathan Kaplan, written by Charlie Haas & Tim Hunter, performances by Matt Dillon, Michael Eric Kramer, and Pamela Ludwig. Orion Pictures, 1979.
The Passion of the Christ. Directed by Mel Gibson, screenplay by Benedict Fitzgerald and Mel Gibson, performances by Jim Caviezel, Monica Bellucci, and Maia Morgenstern. Icon, 2004.
The Pawnbroker. Directed by Sidney Lumet, screenplay by Morton Fine & David Friedkin, from the novel by Edward Lewis Wallant, performances by Rod Steiger, Geraldine Fitzgerald, and Brock Peters. Landau Company and the Pawnbroker Company, 1965.
Pynchon, Thomas. *V.* Lippincott, 1963.
Seinfeld. Created by Larry David and Jerry Seinfeld, performances by Jerry Seinfeld et al. West-Shapiro and Castle Rock Entertainment, 1989–98.
The Social Network. Directed by David Fincher, screenplay by Aaron Sorkin, based on the book by Ben Mezrich, performances by Jesse Eisenberg, Andrew Garfield, and Justin Timberlake. Columbia Pictures, Relativity Media, and Scott Rudin Productions, 2010.
Straight Outta Compton. Directed by F. Gary Gray, screenplay by Jonathan Herman and Andrea Berloff, story by S. Leigh Savidge & Alan Wenkus and Andrea Berloff,

performances by O'Shea Jackson Jr., Corey Hawkins, and Jason Mitchell. Universal Pictures, Legendary Pictures, and New Line Cinema, 2015.

Sweet Smell of Success. Directed by Alexander Mackendrick, screenplay by Clifford Odets and Ernest Lehman, from the novel by Ernest Lehman, performances by Burt Lancaster, Tony Curtis, and Susan Harrison. Norman Productions, Curtleigh Productions, and Hill-Hecht-Lancaster Productions, 1957.

The Swimmer. Directed by Frank Perry, screenplay by Eleanor Perry, from the story by John Cheever, performances by Burt Lancaster, Janet Landgard, and Janice Rule. Columbia Pictures, Horizon Pictures, and Dover Productions, 1968.

To Be or Not to Be. Directed by Ernst Lubitsch, screenplay by Edwin Justus Mayer, original story by Ernst Lubitsch and Melchior Lengyel, performances by Carole Lombard, Jack Benny, and Robert Stack. Romaine Film, 1942.

The Way We Were. Directed by Sydney Pollack, written by Arthur Laurents, performances by Barbra Streisand, Robert Redford, and Bradford Dillman. Columbia Pictures, Rastar Productions, and Tom Ward Enterprises, 1973.

CHAPTER 6

"If Jewish People Wrote All the Songs": The Anti-Folklore of Allan Sherman

by Jeffrey Shandler

A number of years ago I was in a store with a friend of mine. There was music playing, and my friend, hearing a familiar melody, began singing along: "My Zelda, My Zelda, she took the money and ran with the tailor." I smiled, recognizing the words to a song on an Allan Sherman record I'd often heard as a kid in the early 1960s, as, apparently, had my friend as well. But then he stopped and listened more closely to the recording. "Those aren't the right words," he said, looking puzzled. I listened too and quickly realized the cause of his confusion.

"That's the original," I explained. "It's Harry Belafonte singing 'Matilda.'"
"What do you mean 'original'?" he asked.
"It's a parody," I replied. "'My Zelda'—it's a send-up of 'Matilda.'"
"Oh! I never heard of it," my friend answered, looking rather disappointed. "But Allan Sherman's still original," he insisted. "Anyway, he's *my* original."

It is not only noteworthy that my friend and I both remember the words to Allan Sherman's "My Zelda" decades after the album on which it appears had been released and long since we'd last listened to it. It is also remarkable that, for my friend, this song exists for him not as a parody of another song, but as the "original." His understanding of the song has provocative implications; while Sherman's parody loses one register of meaning, as much of its humor relies on familiarity with "Matilda" as performed by Belafonte, "My Zelda" acquires added value when thought of as an "original" work. Doing so situates Sherman's artistry not merely, or even primarily, as a spoof of something else but as having an inherent worth in its own right as an example of American Jewish popular culture. Indeed, Sherman's parodies of familiar folksongs are revealing artifacts of Jewish life in mid-twentieth-century America. In addition to their comic portrayal of middle-class American Jews at the time, Sherman's recordings raise questions about what might constitute "original" American Jewish folkways.

*****

In October 1962, Warner Brothers issued a long-playing record album entitled *Allan Sherman's Mother Presents My Son, the Folk Singer: Allan Sherman Singing Very Funny Folk Songs*. This LP consists of ten numbers, all parodies of songs widely familiar to the American public, culled from a range of folk repertoires: African American, English, French, Irish, and Jamaican. Allan Sherman, an American Jew who worked in New York and Los Angeles as a television writer and producer, composed the mock lyrics and performed them, accompanied by a group of instrumentalists and, on some numbers, by other singers. The album was recorded live at a party in Hollywood before an audience of Sherman's family, friends, and entertainment industry colleagues.

My Son, the Folk Singer quickly became a bestseller. Warner Brothers' fastest selling album at the time, it sold 65,000 copies in its first week, 500,000 in its first month, and eventually sold well over one million copies. This success established Sherman's national prominence as a musical parodist. All three of his "My Son" recordings—*My Son, the Folk Singer* was followed in 1963 by *My Son, the Celebrity* and *My Son, the Nut* —reached number one in sales on the US album charts (Cohen, *My Son, the Book* 5). In addition to recording another half-dozen LPs, Sherman performed his parodies in live concerts and on television variety shows during the 1960s.

Though his fame proved to be short-lived—Sherman died in relative obscurity and penury in 1973—his parodies have found a niche in American popular culture. Rhino Records issued two "best of Allan Sherman" compilations in 1979 and 1990, followed by a boxed set of six CDs of Sherman's work in 2005. *There Is Nothing Like a Lox*, a CD of thirteen Sherman parodies never before released, was produced by Rock Beat Records in 2014. A search of YouTube in 2016 yielded thousands of videos featuring one or more of Sherman's recordings or clips of his appearances on television.[1] Though his oeuvre does not seem to have entered the repertoires of other professional singers or comedians, it has inspired similar comic songs, such as Christine Nelson's 1966 album *Did'ja Come to Play Cards or to Talk*,[2] and has even become the subject of parody itself.

Allan Sherman was born Allan Copelon (following his parents' divorce, he took his mother's maiden name as his surname) in Chicago in 1924. During college he performed some of his earliest musical parodies, such as war-themed spoofs of songs from the Rodgers and Hammerstein musical *Oklahoma!*; these include a number titled "Everything's Up to Date in Berchtesgaden" (Cohen, *Overweight Sensation* 52). After college and military service, Sherman came to New York in 1945. Hoping to make a career as a songwriter, he found work writing jokes for comedians such as Jackie Gleason and Joe E. Lewis. This led to Sherman's involvement in television during its early years, working as a writer or producer for several variety shows, such as *Cavalcade of Stars* and *Broadway Open House*. During this period, Sherman continued to write song parodies. Prominent among these were Jewish-inflected spoofs of Broadway tunes, including a full-length parody of Lerner and Loewe's musical *My Fair Lady*, which Sherman tried to produce but was unable to do so, due to legal problems of copyright infringement.

Sherman's work in television continued throughout the 1950s. He helped produce *I've Got a Secret* and other game shows, as well as another popular variety program, *The Steve Allen Show*. In 1961, Sherman moved from New York to Hollywood to work for CBS. In California, he became a popular guest at entertainment industry parties, where he performed his parody songs with great success. This eventually led to an agreement with Warner Brothers to produce an album of his parodies. For this recording, Sherman elected to spoof folksongs rather than Broadway numbers, in part to avoid legal challenges to their publication; the result was *My Son, the Folk Singer*. Though his use of folksongs as the basis for his parodies may have been expeditious, it proved to be a defining feature of his first well-known works.

Sherman is best remembered for songs from this and the subsequent "My Son" albums. In addition to demonstrating a mastery of pun and dialect rhyme, some of his lyrics are noteworthy for their deft satire of American Jewish life in the early 1960s. Sherman's humorous observations about work, popular culture, family life, and relations between the sexes or between parents and children were then the stock-in-trade of many American joke writers and stand-up comedians. What distinguished Sherman's comedy is his Judaized spoofing of well-known folksongs to address these topics. Through this device, Sherman lampooned not only American Jewish life but also the songs he parodied as well as their singers. Indeed, Sherman mocked the very idea of the folksong and of folk culture itself.

Sherman's performance of his parodies and the way that audiences responded to them were also key to his mockery of folk singing. His debut album pokes fun at a spate of folksingers, including Burl Ives, Theodore Bikel, and especially Harry Belafonte, who had become celebrities in the United States during the 1950s in large measure due to the recording and broadcast media. For example, in "My Zelda," Sherman invites different groups in the audience (such as "members of Hadassah") to sing along with him, in a comic imitation of Belafonte's similar practice during live concerts, thereby extending this parody of "Matilda" to a sendup of the folksinger's interactive style of performing.

Belafonte's performances were well known to Americans through occasional appearances on television and especially a series of popular long-playing albums, the first appearing in 1954. Other songs he recorded that Sherman subsequently parodied include "Water Boy" and "Jump Down, Spin Around" (like "Matilda," issued on the 1955 LP *Belafonte*). Though best known at first for music from his native Jamaica, Belafonte also performed African American, French, and Irish folksongs, as well as blues numbers, Christmas carols, show tunes, and even the occasional Jewish song.[3]

The medium of the long-playing album was as important to the success of the "My Son" recordings as it was to the careers of Belafonte, Bikel, and Ives. Sherman's parody extended to this new means of disseminating their performances, including the cover art and liner notes of his albums. The "My Son" recordings appeared at a strategic moment in the history of the long-playing record. Though the technology of $33^{1}/3$ RPM records had been pioneered before World War II and commercial production of LPs had begun in the late 1940s, the format entered its prime in the late 1950s and early 1960s. At this time a growing number of recording artists made innovative use of this longer format, and the "age of the album" came to dominate the commercial recording industry, surpassing recordings of individual songs on small 45 RPM discs.

In addition to the possibility of recording longer works, which had its greatest impact on classical music and jazz, LPs enabled performers of all kinds to compile sequences of shorter pieces—especially popular songs, which, by dint of the limitations of early sound recording technology, were still typically about three minutes long—within a strategic structure. Individual songs on an LP might follow the order of numbers in a Broadway musical or a live concert, and popular singers such as Bing Crosby and Frank Sinatra created original sequences by recording thematic albums, such as collections of love ballads or

Christmas songs. Performers of traditional folksongs recorded LPs that demonstrated the international range of their repertoire. At the same time, a new generation of folk musicians—Joan Baez, Bob Dylan, Peter, Paul and Mary, among others—used long-playing records to integrate into a traditional folk repertoire their own compositions, many of which addressed contemporary social issues, thereby articulating a link between established folk music and their new songs.

Though short, humorous monologues and sketches had been issued on 78 RPM discs since the early twentieth century, the LP provided expanded possibilities for recording comic routines as well. Among American comedians who issued popular LPs in the late 1950s and early 1960s were Shelly Berman, Lenny Bruce, Dick Gregory, Bob Newhart, Mort Sahl, and Jonathan Winters, as well as the comedy duos Mel Brooks and Carl Reiner, Bob Eliot and Ray Goulding, Mike Nichols and Elaine May, and the Smothers Brothers. Some of these recordings document live performances, providing listeners with a sense of how these comedians interacted with audiences in nightclubs.

Sherman's first albums straddle the new use of long-playing records made by both folksingers and comedians. He was not the only performer to do so. Most famously in this period, the Smothers Brothers also recorded mock folksongs, beginning with the 1961 album *The Smothers Brothers at the Purple Onion*. But whereas the Smothers' parodies are salacious or frivolous (e.g., "Tom Crudely," a sendup of "Tom Dooley"), Sherman's rely on a comic Judaization. In this respect as well, Sherman was not alone. Other postwar American Jewish comic performers, most notably Mickey Katz, issued recordings of Jewish spoofs of familiar songs. However, their humor relied on bilingual wordplay for their comedy, which assumed knowledge of Yiddish language and culture, as borne out by such titles as "Borscht Riders in the Sky" (Katz's spoof of Stan Jones's "Ghost Riders in the Sky") and "Geshray of De Vilde Kotchke" (Katz's sendup of Terry Gilkyson's "Cry of the Wild Goose").[4]

The distinctive conceit of Sherman's mock lyrics are, as he is quoted saying in the liner notes to *My Son, the Folk Singer*, "What would happen if Jewish people wrote all the songs—which, in fact, they do." In another note on the back of the album cover, Sherman's former employer Steve Allen explains that, "unlike those forms of Jewish humor which, because they involve such a high percentage of Yiddish words and private allusions, are difficult for us gentiles to appreciate, this package has an almost universal appeal."

What marks the parodies on the "My Son" albums as Jewish is not, as Steve Allen notes, a matter of having access to insider vocabulary or traditional lore. Sherman's lyrics for these recordings contain altogether no more than a half-dozen Yiddish words or a few passing allusions to traditional culturally specific phenomena such as Jewish holidays or foods. Rather, Jewishness is signaled more frequently by such linguistic elements as the first or last names of characters—e.g., Yetta, Mr. Meltzer, Mrs. Goldfarb—as well as by rhetorical devices typical of the English spoken by urban American Jews who were the children or grandchildren of Yiddish-speaking immigrants. These elements include idiomatic renderings of Yiddish expressions, such as "How's by you the family?" in Sherman's song "Sarah Jackman," a parody of the French folksong "Frère Jacques," as well as dialect rhyming and punning, as in a verse from his parody of the Mexican Hat Dance (recorded on *My Son, the Celebrity*), which rhymes "Calcutta" (pronounced "Calcuddah") with "butter" ("buddah") and "another"—or "an udder" ("anuddah"). Dialect is an essential element of the title of Sherman's single most popular song, "Hello Muddah, Hello Faddah" (which appeared in 1963 on the album *My Son, the Nut* as well as on a 45 RPM single), a number that does not spoof a folksong but sets lyrics to a melody from the "Dance of the Hours" ballet in Amilcare Ponchielli's 1875 opera *La Gioconda*.

The audible presence of an enthusiastic audience of Sherman's acquaintances is also understood as an important marker of the Jewishness of the "My Son" albums. On these recordings one hears Sherman's family and friends howl with knowing laughter and applaud wildly at key moments—all of which signal to listeners what is to be savored as well as how. Thus, Judy Harris, a fan of Allan Sherman recordings, writes on her website:

> One of the great delights of listening to these recordings is the fun that both Sherman and the audience seem to be having. I am not Jewish and know next to no Yiddish, but just to hear the screams of the audience when he exhorts "members of Hadassah" to sing along to My Zelda adds to my pleasure. I don't think these recordings would be as enjoyable if they did not have this audience feedback.

Sherman's mock folksongs situate Jewishness in the milieu of his contemporaries: middle-class American Jews who live in or near major urban centers. Thus, the songs mention such locales as the Catskills, Levittown, Miami, Shaker Heights, and Brooklyn's Ocean Parkway, and they include characters who work in the garment industry, sales, accounting, and advertising. There is, moreover, a sensibility in Sherman's parodies that the recordings identify as Jewish. For example, the liner notes to *My Son, the Folk Singer* urge the reader to listen to these songs, in which Sherman "expresses his own Jewish acceptance of another's plight but, as well, his Jewish disapproval of a person taking on airs just because he's oppressed" (album back cover). As this issue is not addressed explicitly in the parody lyrics, it implies that the act of parody is itself a distinctively Jewish idiom. Jewishness is thus defined by a self-conscious difference in relation to the sensibilities of others, a distinction with which Jews are familiar and against which they take measure of themselves. The skewing of folksongs through this parodic sensibility constitutes a performance of Jewishness. Sherman is, in effect, the inverse of another Midwestern Jewish musician who changed his last name, Bob Dylan (né Robert Zimmerman), whose eponymous first album appeared the same year as *My Son, the Folk Singer*. Whereas Dylan's performance of American folksongs facilitated a refashioning of himself that obscured his Jewish identity, Sherman remakes the international repertoire of folksingers as if "Jews wrote all the songs." To be an American Jew, Sherman intimates, is to be parodic—that is, to engage in polemically motivated acts of imitation that, according to literature scholar Simon Dentith, define parody (9).

Typical of comical parodies in general, the humor in Sherman's "My Son" recordings is generated by a risible disparity between the songs' original lyrics and his mock versions. As is true for all parodies, comical or not, familiarity with the original is key to their appreciation. In this case, the disparity is a cultural one—a gap between the various ethnic worlds evoked by the original songs and a Jewish parody-world. Sherman's parodies compound this cultural disparity by identifying Jews both as familiar types and as cultural outsiders. In his mock folksongs Jewishness is not merely substituted for conventionalized images of Englishness, Irishness or Frenchness, but is juxtaposed against them. Similarly, Sherman characterized his mediocre singing voice, in contrast to the "beautiful and legitimate and lush" sound of the instrumental and choral accompaniment to his vocals, as key to articulating this disparity: "You're looking into Tiffany's most elegant show window, and in the middle of the window is a black velvet pillow, and right in the middle of the pillow is an onion. That's me" (Allen n.p.).

"Sir Greenbaum's Madrigal," recorded on *My Son, the Folk Singer*, exemplifies Sherman's use of parody to articulate the cultural disparity between Jews and others. The hero of this spoof of "Greensleeves" is a reluctant knight who considers his life of chivalry "not right for a boy who is Jewish" and eventually abandons it for "a position in dry goods." This number is not only a Judaized sendup of an English folksong that mocks a mythical vision of "Merrie Olde

England"; it also uses this parodic device to satirize folksong performers and enthusiasts who endorse this romanticized image of the past. As the agent of Sherman's satire is a Jew—conceptualized as a cultural outsider both in England of yore and in the American present—the satire has a double edge. On one hand, Sherman's lyrics imply, Jews were (and are) not cut out for robust virility, exemplified by knighthood; on the other hand, Sir Greenbaum is portrayed as more sensible, if less intrepid, than his gentile comrades. He prefers the comforts of suburban middle-class life to that of chivalry, deflating its heroic image by, for example, characterizing medieval armor as "a pair of aluminum pants." The ridiculed Sir Greenbaum gets the last laugh.

The double-edged nature of his satire resonates with Sherman's glib, yet telling, assertion that his recording reveals "what would happen if all the songs were written by Jews—which, in fact, they are." Very likely he had in mind the many Jews of Tin Pan Alley, Broadway, and Hollywood who wrote everything from Christmas carols to cowboy ballads to New England sea shanties. These composers and lyricists not only created new repertoire for the American public but also disseminated it in radically different ways from the traditions of the folk singer—namely, through the modern, urban marketplace, in the form of sheet music sales, theatrical performances, films, radio and television broadcasts, and recordings. At the same time, other performers—ranging from Belafonte and Ives to Baez and Dylan—were themselves transforming the art of the folksong through the release of highly successful commercial recordings, even as these performers strove to invoke the cachet of a genuinely pre-modern aesthetic on these albums by cultivating an informal performance style, employing traditional instrumentation, offering anecdotes on the source and context of songs, and recording before live audiences—all to simulate the intimate, unpolished, "homespun" authenticity of folk music.

By using the folksong as the conceit for his satire, Sherman assailed the conventional integrity of folk culture and, therefore, of folk identity. Whereas the romantic notion of folk culture, rooted in the defining work of the eighteenth-century German critic Johann Gottfried Herder, conceptualizes it as the distinctive expression of the inherent spirit of a particular people, Sherman demonstrates, through parody, that this music is something that can be imitated, commodified, and thereby transvalued. He, too, can sing to the accompaniment of "authentic" instruments—and so harps, flutes, drums, castanets, marimbas, mandolins, and tambourines punctuate his performances, according to various ethnic conventions. He, too, can pose on the album cover of *My Son, the Folk Singer* in bare feet and with shirt unbuttoned, head thrust back and strumming a guitar, or break down the formal performer/audience barrier on the concert stage. In the parodic world of Allan Sherman, folk music is not a received tradition, the unique expression of a pre-modern people, but is something manipulated, manufactured, and marketed. What Sherman offers is a kind of "anti-folklore"—that is, a work that both reproduces and subverts conventional folkways.[5] This anti-folklore, Sherman further implies, is an appropriate folk expression of the modern Jew, who is portrayed in these recordings as a rootless cosmopolitan, an inveterate dealer in commodities, and as inherently risible.

In this regard, Sherman's images of the Jew and of Jewish culture both resonate with scholarly perspectives, such as the notion of the Jew as archetypal middleman minority,[6] and play provocatively with antisemitic accusations that Jews, as a people who have no legitimate folklore of their own, merely appropriate the traditions of others. Moreover, in the aftermath of the Holocaust, Sherman's anti-folklore implicitly asks what Jews in America might now consider their folk heritage to be, following the recent destruction of the centuries-old center of Jewish culture in Europe.

Sherman's most elaborate use of anti-folklore to address contemporary American Jewish culture can be heard in his one parody of a Jewish song, which appears on his second album, *My Son, the Celebrity*. In "Harvey and Sheila," a spoof of the modern Hebrew song "Hava Nagila," Sherman replaces the original lyrics exhorting Zionist pioneers to sing and rejoice with the story of the eponymous American Jewish couple. Harvey and Sheila meet in New York City, fall in love, marry, move to California, have children, achieve prosperity, and become Republicans. The couple's rapid rise is voiced through the mock-lyrics' extensive use of abbreviations (CPA, IBM, MIT, PHD, PBX, RCA, JFK, PTA, TWA, XKE, GOP, VIP), culminating in the observation that this success could only take place "in the USA."

Sherman exploits a key element of how "Hava Nagila" is usually performed to enhance his comic portrait of contemporary American Jewish life. Over the course of the song's three stanzas, the tempo increases from slow to fast (a performance convention of an East European Jewish *hora*, on which the hasidic-inspired melody of "Hava Nagila" is based). This acceleration, combined with the linguistic device of abbreviations, underscores the message of the lyrics, which both celebrate and mock the fast-paced upward mobility of middle-class American Jews in the Eisenhower and Kennedy years. The result is Sherman's most deft and complex satire of American Jewish life. By replacing hasidic and Zionist celebrations of the joy of singing and dancing with an account of the pursuit of professional and material success in the American mainstream, Sherman leaves listeners to ponder the tacit implication of the cultural price Jews might be paying for this success.

"Harvey and Sheila" also marks the culmination of Sherman's parodic Jewish anti-folklore. Beginning with some of the numbers on his second albums, he moved beyond the mock-folksong format, writing parodies of Broadway tunes, Gilbert and Sullivan songs, theme songs from movies, and rock-and-roll numbers. These parodies were also often satirical, but they no longer relied regularly on Jewishness to create the comic disparity. Rather, they tended to be built increasingly on a generational, rather than cultural distance, as the middle-aged Sherman complained about teenagers, the Beatles, avant-garde theater, dieting, computer technology, advertising, and the urban jungle. By turning from subversive satirist to conservative curmudgeon and relying less on Jewish idioms, Sherman may have been looking to expand his repertoire and his audience, but his later albums never rivaled the commercial success of the "My Son" series.

Though Sherman initially mocked folk music's commodification by the recording industry, it was the source of his own success. The popularity of Sherman's first albums in the early 1960s transformed his parodies, which he had been performing for years at private gatherings, into popular culture on a national scale. In a tribute to Sherman, published in the booklet accompanying one of the CD reissues of Sherman's parodies, Steve Allen recalls an oft-repeated anecdote that "President John F. Kennedy was overheard singing 'Sarah Jackman, how's by you?' as he hurried though the lobby of the Carlisle Hotel in New York." Allen also recalls, "At one point it seemed as if every twelve-year-old child in the country was singing 'Hello Muddah, Hello Faddah'" (Allen n.p.). The facility with which sound recordings allow listeners to hear, on demand, the same performance as often as desired enabled Sherman's songs to enter a national repertoire in a matter of months. Unlike most "traditional" folksongs, his parodies are too closely associated with Sherman's performance of them to have entered any other professional performers' repertoire or to have encouraged the creation of variants or additional verses. Instead, the fixed nature of the recorded performance, heard over and over again, promotes memorization by the listener and enables vicarious participation in the performance by singing or lip-synching along. These activities constitute a new folk music practice, centered on recurrent playing of recorded performances. Listening to these recordings was primarily a domestic activity, providing auditors with vicarious access to a posh Hollywood party or nightclub and the fantasy of being part of a larger, "insider" audience.[7] For the many middle-class American Jews who purchased and listened repeatedly to Sherman's first albums, the comedy was also self-reflexive, simultaneously mocking and celebrating their lives in ethnic urban enclaves or suburban communities, including their professions, social practices, foodways, and aspirations.

Sherman's "My Son" albums appeared during a threshold moment of American Jewish self-representation in the public sphere. In 1961 Levy's rye bread launched a longstanding ad campaign that informed the American public, "You don't have to be Jewish" to love Levy's "real Jewish" rye bread. These print ads featured photos of an Irish policeman, an Italian cook, as well as an American Indian, African American, and Asian American, all savoring Levy's rye bread. As I have noted elsewhere, this ad campaign "offers an especially complicated message for Jews. Jewishness is not only a tempting possibility for Gentiles, it is an option for American Jews as well—*they* don't 'have to' be Jewish, either." Here, Jewishness is configured as "something both indelible and consumable. People may or may not be Jewish; it is a matter of election through purchase—but the product (and the act of ingesting it) *is* Jewish reliably and authentically" (Shandler 190).

Sherman's mock folksongs entered the American Jewish repertoire at this moment and, paradoxically, became part of its culture. Like the ads for Levy's rye bread, his songs transgress ethnic boundaries as they problematize the notion of Jewish authenticity while also tacitly staking a new claim for its possibility. This possibility was soon realized in other recordings that enacted a similar comic expression of an American Jewish culture founded in ambivalence, including the aptly titled 1965 LP *You Don't Have to Be Jewish*. Both this album and its successor the following year, *When You're in Love, the Whole World Is Jewish*, feature an ensemble of performers in sketches and comic songs. Allan Sherman's notion that his songs reflect "what would happen if Jewish people wrote all the songs—which, in fact, they do," also presaged later interest in the Jews of Tin Pan Alley, including by author Philip Roth. In his 1993 novel *Operation Shylock*, the protagonist offers a provocative, subversive disquisition on the Jewishness of some of Irving Berlin's best-known contributions to American popular song a half-century earlier:

> The radio was playing "Easter Parade" and I thought, But this is Jewish genius on a par with the Ten Commandments. God gave Moses the Ten Commandments and then He gave Irving Berlin "Easter Parade" and "White Christmas." The two holidays that celebrate the divinity of Christ—the divinity that's at the very heart of the Jewish rejection

of Christianity—and what does Irving Berlin brilliantly do? He de-Christs them both! Easter he turns into a fashion show and Christmas into a holiday about snow. (157)

Allan Sherman's most famous song, "Hello Muddah, Hello Faddah," has itself become the subject of parody in a Yiddish song, titled "Hello Mameh" (Toiv). This number was recorded in 1987 by Country Yossi and the Shteeblehoppers, one of several groups of musicians who create Judaized mock lyrics—in both English and Yiddish and mixes thereof—to a variety of popular American songs, which are targeted to a young Brooklyn-based Orthodox Jewish audience.

Country Yossi's "Hello Mameh" is set to Ponchielli's ballet music and retains the conceit of Sherman's original lyrics, written in the form of a letter, about a boy's suffering while attending summer camp. But there are telling differences: not only does this version make extensive use of Yiddish, but when the boy promises his parents that he will behave if they bring him home, he assures them that he will be not only a good boy, per Sherman's song, but also a pious Jew. Country Yossi's parody reverses the anxious, ambivalent acculturation of Jews into an American mainstream as portrayed in Sherman's lyrics and asserts instead a proudly different American Jewishness, expressed in language and religiosity. At the same time, "Hello Mameh" evinces its creator's familiarity with Sherman's recording, and an indebtedness to his parodic anti-folklore, as would a full appreciation of Country Yossi's song by his Orthodox listeners—though, like my friend mentioned at the start of this essay, they, too, might think of "Hello Mameh" as an "original."

Thanks to the presence of Sherman's songs on CD reissues, YouTube videos, and this Orthodox takeoff, his parody has come full circle. It is now a fixture of the folklore of the American Jewish community that he satirized. This continued engagement both reinforces and complicates the significance of Sherman's anti-folkloric parodies as examples of American Jews' culture and thereby demonstrates new possibilities for considering what might constitute their folkways.

Notes

1. A search on March 3, 2016 yielded "about 17,700 results" ("Allan Sherman," youtube.com).
2. Nelson sings the duet "Sarah Jackman" with Sherman on *My Son, The Folk Singer*.
3. Belafonte recorded "Hava Nagila," on the 1957 album *An Evening with Belafonte* and "Layla, Layla" on the 1962 album *The Many Moods of Belafonte*.
4. On Mickey Katz, see Kun. Sherman recorded a Yiddishized parody song, "A Satchel and A Seck," on a 78 RPM disc in 1951. It was later issued in a compilation of comic Jewish songs sung other performers, including Fyvush Finkel, Sylvia Froos, and Lee Tully, on an LP entitled *More Folk Songs by Allan Sherman and His Friends* in 1962, "to capitalize on Sherman's new popularity" ("Allan Sherman Discography").
5. On anti-folklore, see Miron.
6. On Jews as a middleman minority, see Bonacich.
7. I thank Peter Pullman for this observation.

Works Cited

"Allan Sherman," www.youtube.com/results?q=%22allan+sherman%22. Accessed 3 Mar. 2016.

"Allan Sherman Discography," dmdb.org/discographies/sherman.disco.html. Accessed 3 Mar. 2016.

Allen, Steve. "Allan Sherman." *My Son, The Greatest: The Best of Allan Sherman*. Rhino Records, 1988. Compact disc booklet.

Belafonte, Harry, perf. *An Evening with Belafonte*. RCA Victor, 1957.

———. *Belafonte*. RCA Victor, 1955.

———. "Hava Nagila." *An Evening with Belafonte*. RCA Victor, 1957.

———. "Jump Down, Spin Around." *Belafonte*. RCA Victor, 1955.

———. "Layla, Layla." *The Many Moods of Belafonte*. RCA Victor, 1962.

———. *The Many Moods of Belafonte*. RCA Victor, 1962.

———. "Matilda." *Belafonte*. RCA Victor, 1955.

———. "Water Boy." *Belafonte*. RCA Victor, 1955.

Bonacich, Edna. "A Theory of Middleman Minorities." *American Sociological Review*, vol. 38, issue 5, Oct. 1973, pp. 583–94.

Booker, Bob, and George Foster. *You Don't Have to Be Jewish*. Kapp Records, 1965.

———. *When You're in Love, the Whole World Is Jewish*. Kapp Records, 1966.

Broadway Open House. Created by Sylvester L. Weaver Jr., performances by Milton Delugg, Jerry Lester, and Dagmar. NBC, 1950–52.

Cavalcade of Stars. Performaces by Jackie Gleason, Jack Carter, and the June Taylor Dancers. Drugstore Television, and DuMont Television Network, 1949–52.

Cohen, Mark. *My Son, the Book*. Rhino Entertainment, 2005. Booklet included in CD boxed set *My Son, The Box*.

———. *Overweight Sensation: The Life and Comedy of Allan Sherman*. Brandeis Univ., 2013.

"Dance of the Hours." *La Gioconda*. Composed by Amilcare Ponchielli, 1875.

Dentith, Simon. *Parody*. Routledge, 2000.

Gilkyson, Terry, composer. "Cry of the Wild Goose." Performance by Frankie Laine. Mercury, 1950.

Harris, Judy. "Allen Sherman," users.bestweb.net/~foosie/sherman.htm. Accessed 27 July 2015.

I've Got a Secret. Created by Allan Sherman and Howard Merrill. CBS, Mark Goodson-Bill Todman Productions, and Telecast Enterprises, 1952–67.

Jones, Stan, composer. "Ghost Riders in the Sky." Edwin H. Morris & Co., 1948.

Katz, Mickey, perf. "Borscht Riders in the Sky."

———. "Geshray of De Vilde Kotchke."

Kun, Josh. "The Yiddish Are Coming: Mickey Katz, Anti-Semitism, and the Sound of Jewish Difference." *American Jewish History*, vol. 87, issue 4, Dec. 1999, pp. 343–74.

Miron, Dan. "Folklore and Antifolklore in the Yiddish Fiction of the Haskala." *The Image of the Shtetl and Other Studies of Modern Jewish Literary Imagination*. Syracuse Univ., 2000, pp. 49–80.

More Folk Songs by Allan Sherman and His Friends. Jubilee, 1963.

My Fair Lady. Music by Frederick Loewe, and lyrics by Alan Jay Lerner. Mark Hellinger Theatre, 1956.

Nelson, Christine. *Did'ja Come to Play Cards or to Talk?* Reprise Records, 1966.

Oklahoma! Music by Richard Rogers, lyrics by Oscar Hammerstein. St. James Theatre, 1943.

Roth, Philip. *Operation Shylock: A Confession*. Simon and Schuster, 1993.

Shandler, Jeffrey. "*Di toyre fun skhoyre*, or, I Shop, Therefore I Am: The Consumer Cultures of American Jews." *Longing, Belonging, and the Making of Jewish Consumer Culture*, edited by Nils Roemer and Gideon Reuveni. Brill, 2010.

Sherman, Allan, perf. *A Gift of Laughter: The Best of Allan Sherman, Volume II*. Rhino Records, 1990.

———. "A Satchel and A Seck." *More Folk Songs by Allan Sherman and His Friends*. Jubilee, 1963.

———. *The Best of Allan Sherman*. Rhino Records, 1979.

———. "Harvey and Sheila." *My Son, the Celebrity*.

———. "Hello Muddah, Hello Faddah." *My Son, the Nut*.

———. *My Son, the Box*. Rhino Entertainment Company, 2005.

———. *My Son, the Celebrity*. Warner Bros., 1963.

———. *My Son, the Folk Singer: Allan Sherman Singing Very Funny Folk Songs*. Warner Bros., 1962.

———. *My Son, the Nut: Allan Sherman Sings Nutty Things, This Time with Strings*. Warner Bros., 1963.

———. "My Zelda." *My Son, the Folk Singer*.

———. "Sarah Jackman." *My Son, the Folk Singer*.

———. "Sir Greenbaum's Madrigal." *My Son, the Folk Singer*.

———. *There Is Nothing Like a Lox: The Lost Song Parodies of Allan Sherman*. Rock Beat Records, 2014.

Smothers, Thomas, and Richard Smothers. *The Smothers Brothers at the Purple Onion*. Mercury Records, 1961.

The Steve Allen Show. Performances by Peggy Lee, Steve Allen, and Al Flosso. CBS, 1951–57.

Toiv, Yossi. "Hello Mameh." *Country Yossi and the Shteeble-hoppers: Captured*. Country Yossi Productions, 1987.

PART 3: UP-CLOSE AND PERSONAL

CHAPTER 7

Comedy and Corned Beef:
The Genesis of the Sitcom Writing Room

by David Isaacs

There are three things all Jews worship, God, Chinese food and wall to wall carpeting.
—Woody Allen (born Allen Stewart Konigsberg)

For over forty years I maintained my mundane, by Hollywood standards, lifestyle as a writer of Network Half-hour Comedies. Half-hour being a bit of a misnomer because the scripted content of a broadcast network sitcom these days is only about twenty-one minutes, down from about twenty-four minutes when I started working professionally back in the mid-'70s. That three-minute gap makes the challenge of telling a satisfying comic tale all the more complex. I'm sure the Networks would be more than happy to shave a few more minutes off if we could find an acceptable way to serve their audience a story without a resolution. None of this is meant as a budding senior citizen's cynical complaint. I'd gladly take on the hard work again, if for no other reason than the chance to sit around a long table spread with an all-day feast of deli and/or Chinese food, trading jokes, sports gossip, socio-political commentary and random sex talk with some of the funniest men and women you could ever meet. It's a blessing to love your work as much as I did. The money was good too, but that's not my subject this time out.

No doubt the entertainment industry has changed drastically in my lifetime. From the business plan that dictates how content is created, produced and distributed to the many platforms we now use to access our entertainment, there is little of practical consequence that remains from "the golden days." (My age obligates me to use that phrase to describe the time before Reality TV.) The one function that still flourishes is the Sitcom Writing Room. Just as practiced as far back as Radio comedies, every weekday morning a group of writers gather round a big table in a large room about ten in the morning to spend, on the average, ten hours in a constant ongoing tumult of conversation, preparing story and script for the stage and camera. Actually, very little of that all day gabfest makes it into the finished script. The large ratio of trivial chatter to final useful product will be explained later in the chapter, but suffice it to say the process itself has changed very little. Well, save for the variety of the cuisine, which for health concerns alone, has moved away from the heavy nitrate and sodium blockbuster bombs of pastrami and corned beef that killed plenty of writers in mid-joke.

A glimpse into the obvious—

Comedy is by its very nature a communal experience. The desired result of the creative effort is a response of laughter from another individual. More than one person laughing is even better. To again demonstrate my age, I'm one of the very few that still believes in the sitcom laugh track. Not so much the canned laughter that some series still indiscriminately dub in, but the real laughter of a live audience enjoying a filming of *Cheers, Everybody Loves Raymond, Seinfeld* or *Friends*. I've always felt the audience response allows the person watching the show at home to feel like part of the live experience. It's also why I believe the four series just mentioned, along with others of earlier years like *The Mary Tyler Moore Show, All in the Family, Taxi* and *I Love Lucy,* all truly, reliably funny, are much more popular in syndication than other past fare, both comedic and dramatic. Call me old fashioned but I enjoy hearing laughter more than sensing it. Or maybe I'm just lonely.

The creating of comedy in volume, in other words, cranking out twenty-one minutes each week for a full season, even a short-lived season, requires a similar kind of community. To paraphrase an overused comparison, if I craft a joke in the forest and no one laughs, is it funny? Or if a bear only seems amused does it count? There is no way to know with absolute certainty if you play in a vacuum. That is probably why you see so many teams writing comedy. Confirmation of your ability to be funny is proof positive sitting right in front of you. God knows I needed another person around all the time. There are a

Comedy and Corned Beef: The Genesis of the Sitcom Writing Room   129

few comedic Mozarts, blessed with once in a lifetime comedic chops, who are exceptions to the need to team up. My long time writing partner, Ken Levine, and I had the honor of working on a short-lived sitcom with the late, great Larry Gelbart, who in his venerable career completed the Comedy Writing Hat Trick. That is, great success in TV, Films and Theatre. (*Show of Shows, MASH, Tootsie, A Funny Thing Happened on the Way to the Forum.*) On his own Larry Gelbart could turn out literally reams of the funniest, almost lyrical dialogue that read like a gift from the Comedy Gods, and pushing the comedic Mozart comparison a bit farther, there were no corrections on the page. That is not hyperbole. Larry wrote in long hand on a legal pad and there were no corrections, i.e., cross outs, new lines on the margins . . . corrections. For a young writer like myself it was inspiring and diminishing all at once. Knowing work could be that good and just flow, but also facing the awareness that I could never reach that comedic level, let alone by myself. It's tough and maddening being just a Salieri. Then again, and this is not to brag, I made much better money than a jealous court composer and they fed me.

To switch the music referencing to a different groove, I like to think that the Sitcom Room, and I may be doing a bit of romanticizing here, is akin to an all-night jam session of fine jazz musicians. Comedy is a bit like jazz in the sense that there is a line of melody or theme that allows improvisation. For instance, Miles Davis and ensemble take a standard like "My Funny Valentine" and use their particular instruments to dig into the melody, adding texture, shading and irony, ultimately interpreting it a whole different way. Creating comedy, to stretch yet again, is similar in form. We take an old evergreen, for example, "Donald Trump," and lay out the all too familiar "melody," that is, monumental egotist, serial husband, bad orange comb over, et cetera, and just riff on the elements. Now The Donald is a subject that is almost too easy, but in the hands of some experienced comic minds the Trump song could go on endlessly . . . as it seems to do in real life.

The collaborative nature of the contemporary Sitcom Room had its origins in Radio to be sure, but in irreverence and combative spirit I believe it derives from the late night post-gig gatherings of primarily Jewish comics in the '40s and '50s. Meeting at legendary Manhattan delis like the Carnegie or Stage or, at the time popular but now extinct "cafeterias" like Kelloggs on 49th Street and "drugstores" like Hansen's on 51st Street, struggling comics, Rodney Dangerfield (born Jacob Cohen), Alan King (born Irwin Alan Kniberg) and Lenny Bruce (born Leonard Schnieder), to name a few who achieved notoriety, nursed coffee and deli till the wee hours, trading stories, riffing on "melodies" and fine tuning their comic voice. Oh, to be a fly on the food in those gatherings, which were natural extensions of the intense verbal combat of the shtetls that these young tummlers came from in Lower Manhattan, the Bronx and Brooklyn. In today's culture that honing of comic chops on street corners, in run-down nightclubs and around a deli table would be called putting in "The Ten Thousand Hours." The craft of comedy requires that amount of dedication and more. The all night joke session is also the closest thing that we have to an ongoing tradition.

> *I am as Jewish as a matzo ball or kosher salami.*
> —Jackie Mason (born Yakov Moshe Maza)

In his 1984 film, *Broadway Danny Rose,* Woody Allen brought the late night comic's table to life. The movie opens on six comedians, all of them real life veterans of mid-century standup (Sandy Baron, Morty Gunty, Will Jordan, Jackie Gayle, Howard Storm and Corbett Monica) in session at the Carnegie Deli, cracking wise and talking over each other as they introduce the saga of Danny Rose, a small-time Broadway booking agent. The scene is a wonderful re-creation of the mad, rapid-fire competition and uncensored commentary that was part of those gatherings, and is definitely still alive in any contemporary Sitcom Room. The atmosphere, not to mention the culture, is also decidedly Jewish.

That is not to say that comedy is or was exclusively the realm of Jews. No doubt we have been disproportionately represented professionally, and I imagine if there were some kind of equivalent Comedy Hall of Fame there would probably be a Mezuzah up on the main entrance and deli sandwiches named after celebrities in the basement restaurant. However, a great deal of the psychology of funny has to do with the notion of being the outsider, or in modern parlance, the outlier. Not to the manor (or manner) born and more than a bit angry about it. Certainly there has never been a cultural monopoly on that feeling. Now more than ever it's the common ground that breeds the comic point of view for all those who perceive themselves out of the mainstream.

Not to go all Freud here, but anger is at the heart of comedy, which incidentally is a hell of a healthy device to work out personal frustrations, like not being invited to the main party. (Personally I'd like to start a national dialogue on the alternative therapy of comedy for gun "enthusiasts" . . . but in the end, and being me, I'd just rather say something biting at their expense and not get involved.) So it's clearly not just Jewish territory. Still it's pretty safe to say that there is no ethnicity, religion, race, or interest group that has a history of being labeled, or identifies more as the outsider then the Jewish people. Depending on what part of the globe we are talking about it's a tight race for top outcast group, but the Jews have History of the Western World cred that goes back before Moses. Granted we are finally back in Israel, but having an ethnic and religious homeland for nearly seventy years cannot just undo thousands of years of packing quickly.

As a secular Jew there are three places I acutely feel my Jewishness: (1) Shul. When I am there for a bar mitzvah or memorial or a quick drive up during the High Holidays; (2) In any of the coastal Newports—Rhode Island, Southern California, Virginia, take your choice; (3) When I am eating lunch in a Sitcom Room. The first two for obvious and contrasting reasons, but the third for its atmosphere of camaraderie, irreverence and non-stop criticism of nearly everything including the food, which I again mention, is usually free of charge. A kvetch-fest if ever there was one to the point that even WASP, Afro-American, Latino and Asian writers leave the room still complaining in a whining East Coast accent. The influence is unmistakably there.

There are a group of us who even combine Shul with the Sitcom Room. Every Passover my writing partner and his family hold a "Comedy Seder." Around a long table, as has been the custom for several millennia, we re-tell the story of the Exodus. However, we do change the details a bit to fit TV writers. The ten plagues become the ten dumb Network notes, e.g., "I love the title, but do they all have to be Friends?" or "The script has lots of oatmeal, but no raisins." I'll take boils and locusts any day over trying to interpret that unique brand of obtuse criticism.

To write comedy, to view from the outside looking in and express your dismay and anger at the absurdity of life, no matter your race, ethnicity or heritage is to have a little Jewishness in you. Not to go all Jung here, but I like to think that is our contribution to the collective unconscious.

> *As a child my family's menu consisted of two choices:*
> *Take it or leave it.*
> —Buddy Hackett (born Leonard Hacker)

The unwritten code of the original Comics Table and subsequently the Sitcom Room is the freedom, not to mention the sanctity, of the creative space. Civility and political correctness are checked at the door. As someone once said about a novice or non-pro sitting in at the table for the first time, only the brave and reckless need enter. Thick skin is a requirement because sacred beliefs will be stepped on and cracks in personal armor are always fair game. Let me provide a personal example.

    I live with male pattern baldness. For some men, like say Jason Straham or a Patrick Stewart, who both have skulls that are not too round or too oval but just right, it can be an image enhancer. For me it is something I've gradually grown to accept as less important than my impending death, which looms ever larger, encouraging me to finish this chapter. A few years ago when I was still working regularly in the Room, my mother-in law, a dear woman who has always been one of my biggest boosters, off-handedly suggested that I should get a hairpiece to create a suddenly younger and less self-conscious me. In her words, "they make them look a lot more natural now." Now, I'm no less vain than the next cue ball, but my answer to her idea was less resentful than incredulous. "Do you know where I go to work everyday? Do you know the kind of less than gentle, encouraging folks I work with? Do you know what would happen if I left work bald one day and showed up the next with a full head of hair? It would be like sticking a steak in front of a pack of hungry, bi-polar jackals." Her sobering answer was "Why do you care about them?" It was at that moment it dawned on me that even though I possessed zero bravado I had developed an uncanny sense of self-preservation working and trading zingers with those relentless "jackals." Realizing I must walk through life hairless, vulnerable and ready to be the butt of a joke went a long way to making me comfortable in my own skin. Dying is still on the table.

> *Mass Production is craftsmanship with the drudgery taken out of it.*
> —Henry Ford (born Henry Ford)

Irony duly noted that the above quote is from one of America's most noted and virulent anti-Semites (but he made a hell of a car . . . once). Then again, I couldn't help but notice that it neatly sums up the process of the typical Sitcom Room. Artistry aside, it is the production line of comedy. To manufacture a full sitcom season or an abbreviated one is an enormous undertaking that, as I mentioned before, has a high ratio of energy and raw material to finished episode.

    In reading about the late night gatherings of the young and hungry comics of the '40s and '50s, I often wonder how much wonderful material was generated just in conversation, but never used on stage. Those jam sessions must have been wildly loud and uncensored, but unfortunately material that wasn't appropriate in mid-century nightclubs had no function. At the same time, the chance to just let go provides a creative energy to feed the entertainment machine. So enough Detroit, but the analogy is an apt one.

So a Sitcom Room runs like a figurative production line (I can't help myself, it just makes it all sound more enterprising) with upwards of a dozen people turning out episodes that generate from a simple story idea to an outline to several drafts of a script. Many of the finest comedy writers we have typically learn their craft in this atmosphere. Case in point—the staff of the early 1950s *Show of Shows*. Arguably the greatest collection of young comedy writers in one place, the room included Mel Brooks, Carl Reiner, Larry Gelbart, Neil Simon and Woody Allen, among others who went on to transcendent success. I think anyone who knows comedy would agree that it was a Room for the Ages.

Typically, and the broadcast year has become more fluid, a writing staff gathers in early summer to begin plotting a season's worth of stories and churning out drafts. The work pace picks up from there into production, going faster and faster as each week goes by and deadline inevitably catches up to preparation. The hours become longer and longer, and weekends can become workdays as well. All of that creative labor is usually relative to the series itself. A successful show will usually work more normal hours, while a show that is struggling to find it's theme, not to mention its audience, will put in whatever time is needed to break through to a series narrative that's succeeding. An eighty-hour workweek multiplied across several months is not unheard of or unexpected. But then all TV writers are obsessed with how many hours we work. It will come up in any writer–to-writer conversation. Putting in the hours is a badge of honor and something to at least be proud of after you've ruined your marriage and health just to end up with a canceled series. As an old Hollywood saying goes, "The money is great, but you spend it at Cedars Sinai."

The focus of each Sitcom Room workday is on the story and script. The story has to make narrative sense, the jokes have to come from the attitudes of the characters and they have to be funny. To concentrate on any or all of those factors and to stay on subject for ten hours straight would slowly wear down any momentum. The big lunch only adds to the general mid-day malaise. The working antidote for lost energy is constant conversation, digression in any direction, along with the unwritten rule of having the freedom to say anything, no matter how politically incorrect, and make a damn fool of yourself. For most young writers it's an acquired skill, but creatively speaking, a necessary, even vital risk. To revisit the music analogy, it's how you learn to keep your instrument in tune. The sense of openness and feeling of trust among the players is what keeps the work moving forward. Add one outsider to the mix, especially one of the series actors who many times are the butt of the humor, or any person who takes personal offence to the conversation, and the chemistry changes immediately. It's a very delicate balance.

Back in the late 1990s a female assistant working in the *Friends* writing room brought a lawsuit against Warner Brothers for sexual harassment (*Lyle vs. Warner Brothers Television Productions*). In short, she claimed that the general atmosphere and conversation of the writing staff, a few men in particular, was offensive and created a workplace that was untenable for her. I wasn't there, but my guess is that a lot of folks, male or female, young or old would agree with her charge and the suit itself. The general talk often turns to sex, which can get pretty raunchy, and truth be told that's an understatement. Yet it is part of the process that leads to the finished product. Go back to those late night tables of the '40s and '50s. Little of the social and sexual candor that was tossed around each night ever made its way in front of the microphone or to early TV (and if it was it was sanitized for the times), but working off and releasing what was churning in your gut was the real playtime. If suddenly there were an arbitrary set of rules of table decorum then it follows those rules would result in a bunch of cautious comics second-guessing their every word. The idea of a special dispensation for allowing inappropriate, even lewd speech in a particular line of work is against conventional norms and the need to bring civility and accountability to the workplace, but it is as true now as it was in the '50s. The steam of consciousness has to flow to ultimately deliver the goods.

The face of the TV industry has changed along with the business, content, technology, and delivery, and all for the better. The big table that sits in the middle of the room includes "outsiders" of all races and ethnicities and thankfully they are beginning to turn out series comedies that better reflect our still emerging mixed culture. The comedy itself may be more ironic and specific than the broader, not always so "good old days." However the best of it has that irreverence and touch of anarchy that we all relate to and cherish because it pokes at the infuriating dysfunction and absurdity of our mutual existence. I believe that inspiration to just let go and push the envelope started decades ago around a table in the back corner of the Carnegie Deli with a bunch of Shtlel Jews. That's my legend and I'm sticking to it.

Works Cited

A Funny Thing Happened on the Way to the Forum. Directed by Richard Lester, performances by Zero Mostel, Phil Silvers, and Buster Keaton. United Artists and Melvin Frank Production, 1966.

All in the Family. Created by Norman Lear, performances by Carroll O'Connor, Jean Stapleton, and Rob Reiner. Bud Yorkin Productions and Norman Lear/Tandem Productions, 1971–79.

Broadway Danny Rose. Directed by Woody Allen, performances by Woody Allen, Mia Farrow, and Nick Apollo Forte. Orion Pictures, 1984.

Cheers. Created by James Burrows, Glen Charles, and Les Charles, performances by Ted Danson, Rhea Perlman and John Ratzenberger. Charles/Burrows/Charles Productions and Paramount Television, 1982–93.

Everybody Loves Raymond. Created by Philip Rosenthal, performances by Ray Romano, Patricia Heaton, and Brad Garrett. Talk Productions, Where's Lunch, and HBO Independent Productions, 1996–2005.

Friends. Created by David Crane and Marta Kauffman. Warner Bros. Television and Bright/Kauffman/Crane Productions, 1994–2004.

I Love Lucy. Performances by Lucille Ball, Desi Arnaz, and Vivian Vance. Desilu Productions, 1951–57.

Lyle v. Warner Brothers Television Productions. No. B160528, Court of Appeal, Second District, Division 7, California, 21 April 2004.

The Mary Tyler Moore Show. Created by James L. Brooks and Allan Burns, performances by Mary Tyler Moore, Edward Asner, and Gavin MacLeod. MTM Enterprises, 1970–77.

MASH. Created by Larry Gelbart and Gene Reynolds, performances by Alan Alda, Wayne Rogers, and Loretta Swit. 20th Century Fox Television, 1972–83.

Rogers, Richard, and Lorenz Hart. "My Funny Valentine," *Babes in Arms*, 1937.

Seinfeld. Created by Larry David and Jerry Seinfeld, performances by Jerry Seinfeld et al. West-Shapiro and Castle Rock Entertainment, 1989–98.

Taxi. Created by James L. Brooks et al., performances by Judd Hirsch, Jeff Conaway and Danny DeVito. John-Charles-Walters Productions and Paramount Television, 1978–83.

Tootsie. Directed by Sydney Pollack, performances by Dustin Hoffman, Jessica Lange, and Teri Garr. Columbia Pictures, Mirage Enterprises, and Punch Productions, 1982.

Your Show of Shows. Created by Sylvester L. Weaver, Jr., performances by Sid Caesar, Imogene Coca and Carl Reiner. Max Liebman Productions, 1951–54.

CHAPTER 8

The Faemmle Business: Laemmle Theatres, Los Angeles, and the Moviegoing Experience— an Interview with Bob and Greg Laemmle

by Ross Melnick

In a December 2015 *Hollywood Reporter* article, film historian Thomas Doherty wrote that Carl Laemmle's place in American film history was assured but "Less well known is Laemmle's role as a savior of Jewish refugees from the charnel house of Nazi Germany." Laemmle, he adds, put "his money where his heart was, not just for family and friends but for any desperate supplicant." Indeed, during the 1930s, Laemmle spoke out against the rise of Adolf Hitler, pulled Universal out of Germany, and signed hundreds of affidavits to ferry "Hitler's chosen victims" out of the country and into the United States, despite its restrictive immigration policies. Those family ties saved many of Laemmle's relatives from the Nazis (Doherty). Among them were Kurt and Max Laemmle, who would build one of Los Angeles' most important theater chains from the 1930s to the 1960s and, for the last half century, create a brand name for the exhibition of foreign, independent, and art house films in the very heart of Hollywood.

In May 1928, at the age of twenty-two, Max Laemmle sailed to the United States to begin working for "Uncle Carl" ("List or Manifest," May 21, 1928). He was provided with "film selling schooling" and sent to Canada to hock Universal films to local exhibitors ("Daily Review" 2). By March 1929, he had been named a supervisor of Universal Pictures and, in 1930, was sent to Paris to manage Universal's French offices (Universal Film Société Anonyme) ("Max Laemmle, Wyler Appointed" 8). Max's brother Kurt had originally hoped to travel a different path in the petroleum business, but "his efforts were thwarted by barriers Jews faced in the oil industry at the time" (Levine 12). Instead, Kurt left their home in Stuttgart, Germany for the United States to work for Universal's San Francisco branch office in August 1932 ("Behind Keys" 19). Max, meanwhile, stayed in Paris managing the company's French sales and "inducing big French stage names" to dub Universal's sound films for the global Francophone market ("Times Square: Chatter—Paris" 39, 44). Max resigned from Universal in December 1933 ("Nephew Max Laemmle" 15). He initially hoped to become an exhibitor in Paris but instead became an independent film distributor ("Foreign Film News" 13; Max Laemmle-Film Export 20). Kurt, meanwhile, moved to Universal's sales office in Chicago. Like his brother, he also chafed under the company's low wages and resigned in 1935, taking what he considered a golden opportunity to buy the Ritz Theatre in Lowell, Indiana, during the Depression (Levine 12; "Out Hollywood Way" 14). Days later, Kurt was in Los Angeles, already "looking over local theatre properties" (". . . Los Angeles" 2).

By now, Kurt's daily concerns were as much personal as they were professional. Max and his parents, Sigmund and Alice Laemmle, were still in Europe and the growth of fascism began to alarm him. (Max and his wife Bertha had just had their first child, Robert, on September 5, 1935, in Paris ["Births" 76].) Three months later, Kurt wrote to Max, urging him to come to the United States as the clouds over Europe rolled in. "After what the Nazis do now re the Jews, just imagine what they will do after the Olympics are over," he wrote Max. "That's all they are waiting for. So you being right there, carry some of the responsibility to get our parents to a decision and action. I am glad to do my share when I am over there, but all must be prepared" (Levine 13). The letter advised Max to transfer his assets out of Europe and to enter the exhibition business in the United States (Levine 13).

It would take another three years for Max to finally leave Paris. In 1937, he planned to establish a film company in the United States with his brother Kurt that would both distribute French films and remake them ("Foreign" 5; "To Handle French Pix in U. S." 12). In April 1938, Max sailed to the United States to meet with business associates Arthur Mayer and Joseph Burstyn. He later traveled to Chicago to see Kurt and the two brothers traveled by car to California ("List or Manifest," April 27, 1938; McCarthy 7, 27). Max subsequently bought Pacific Coast distribution rights to Jean Renoir's *La Bête*

Humaine (1938) in May 1938 and, four months later, Kurt and Max purchased the Franklin Theatre in the Los Angeles neighborhood of Highland Park ("To Distribute 'Human Beast'" 10; "Theatres-Exchanges," September 28, 1938, 23). The duo bought the Glassell Theatre (later renamed the Dale) in nearby Glassell Park that December and soon added the Park Theatre in Highland Park as well ("Theatres-Exchanges," December 28, 1938, 20; Levine 19). With his business secure, Max returned to France in 1939 and retrieved Bertha and Robert and sailed to the United States in March 1939 ("List or Manifest," March 26, 1939). He also persuaded his parents to finally leave Stuttgart and move to Los Angeles. "We got out just in time," he later recalled (McCarthy 7, 27).

In Los Angeles, Max had still not given up on the distribution business, but he was grateful to be in the United States and in the picture business ("Max Laemmle on Coast" 22). "These [cinemas] afforded us a livelihood for several years" (McCarthy 7, 27). In the early 1940s, Kurt swapped one Ritz for another, selling his faraway Ritz Theatre in Lowell, Indiana in 1942 and buying another Ritz Theatre in Inglewood, California ("About People of the Theatre" 32; Levine 13). During the war, the Laemmles' theaters—not yet called Laemmle Theatres—were key centers for a home front audience. Frank Whitaker recalled the Park Theatre years later as a place "where housewives escaped a few hours from dull chores, where young girls waited for the war to end and loved ones to come home, where teenagers worshipped their movie idols and children were dropped off Saturday while Mom went shopping" (Whitaker 74).

When the war came to an end and Hitler's destruction became well known, the Laemmles, like many Jews in the motion picture industry, worked hard to repatriate refugees in displaced persons camps and other victims of the Holocaust. In 1948, Max Laemmle became a vice president of the Southern Regional chapter of ORT—the Organization for Rehabilitation Through Training—while Kurt's wife, Alyse Laemmle, became the Regional Extension chair of a women's chapter of the Jewish benevolent organization ("ORT Plans Luncheon, Program" C2; "ORT Screen Unit Forming" A5). Kurt and Max were key members of the Theatres and Exchanges Division of the Motion Picture division of the United Jewish Welfare fund alongside local exhibitors such as Sid Grauman and Sherrill Corwin ("UJW Theatres Division Pledges Up" 38). Alyse later became vice-president of the Women's Organization for Rehabilitation Through Training, touring Europe and working to help refugees repatriate to the United States, Canada, and Israel. Back in the States, she also started selling insurance in 1951 and quickly became one of the top selling insurance saleswomen in Southern California (Vierhus C3).

Kurt and Max, meanwhile, began to move the circuit west in the 1940s, responding to demographic shifts within the city. They bought the Los Feliz Theatre in 1947 and it became the flagship of the circuit for decades. But by the mid-to-late 1950s the Laemmles' theater business was struggling as audiences dwindled due to television and other postwar changes. Kurt stayed on as a financial partner in the theater business but joined his wife in selling insurance. By then, the only theater left for Max to manage was the Los Feliz Theatre on Vermont Avenue. Drawing on his European background and sensibilities, Max re-crafted the Los Feliz from neighborhood house to art house. Increasingly, he recalled later, "I'd take a fling at something foreign. I was knowledgeable about foreign films, and they did better than a poor American film, so I drifted into showing them more often, then permanently" (Diamond G1). It was the birth of what is today Laemmle Theatres, a distinctive brand of theaters and programming that has catered to a more eclectic palate and moviegoer ever since. Max brought in the waves of the moment: Italian neorealism, French New Wave, Japanese art cinema, American avant-garde, and independent film, and buttressed these selections with documentaries, retrospectives and film series, and the more sophisticated films from the Hollywood studios.

In 1961, while Max and Bertha were away, their son Robert (Bob) took a break from his job at a bank to manage the Los Feliz Theatre—the last stand of the family business. When Max returned, Bob was brought on board to spearhead a new expansion effort in Pasadena and other locations. During the 1960s, Max and Bob Laemmle opened the Esquire in Pasadena (1964) and the Regent (1966) and Plaza (1967) theaters in Westwood (Levine 20, 29). The move to art house programming in the 1960s cemented Max's reputation as a local tastemaker and cultural figure and he was honored by the Los Angeles County Board of Supervisors in 1963 with a commendation for his "continuing contribution to the culture of Los Angeles through the screening of outstanding art cinema, for his interest in student and professional artistic endeavors and his furtherance of intercultural appreciation" ("Max Laemmle Honored by Supervisors" D9). By 1965, *Los Angeles Times* critic Kevin Thomas wrote, "Today, there are more places to see art films in Los Angeles than ever before, but only the Cinema, the Europa, and Laemmle's Los Feliz would be considered 'first-rate'" ("L.A. Lags" M17). Thomas added, a half-century later, "There was a tremendous amount of detail work put into each film and as far as I know, no other theater ever in fifty years did this kind of personalized, focused marketing. And all of this intense, imaginative and creative effort is the foundation of the whole Laemmle chain" (Levine 69). In the era before home video and saturation booking, all of this attention to detail could pay off handsomely as a hit film could play for months or even years at a single theater. Claude Lelouch's *A Man and a Woman* (1966), for instance, played at the Regent Theatre for more than two years ("Three-Year Run at Regent" NC1). (The Regent Theatre made another long-term run when, in an ironic twist, the theater was subleased by Uncle Carl's old studio, Universal, for two years after the Lelouch film played out ["Universal to Sign Lease" W1].)

By the 1970s, the chain was once again expanding west. Having marched from Northeast Los Angeles to Los Feliz to Westwood, the Laemmles' next cinema was a new twin theater—then a novel concept—the Monica Twin, in Santa Monica. The art house's opening ads promoted the chain's legacy as a family business exclaiming that the Monica Twin was "Max & Robert Laemmle's New Concept in Deluxe Twin-Theatres—Where Comfort, Beauty & Service Match the Quality of Their Film Presentations" (Monica Twin Advertisement D14). Despite a challenging industrial climate, Bob Laemmle told *Boxoffice*, "There's nothing wrong with this business that showmanship can't correct" ("Los Angeles" W6). The following year, the Laemmles took over the Royal Theatre in West Los Angeles, where the company's offices still remain. They also grabbed the Westland Twin in West Los Angeles and the Music Hall in Beverly Hills in 1974, and, branching out to the suburbs five years later, the Town Center 5 in Encino in 1979 (Levine 20, 21).

Throughout the 1970s, Laemmle Theatres' eclectic programming brought global cinema to Los Angeles audiences increasingly starved of art house films as Hollywood began ramping up its production of blockbusters and family films in the late 1970s and early 1980s. "The Hollywood film wants to know how the bank was robbed," Bob explained in 1977. "The foreign [film] wants to know who robbed the bank." He added, "We screen an average of five films a week, and we're not just seeing them but developing ideas for promotion. We see our part in a film as creative, not just a business proposition. We want people to see it and we want to have everybody involved come out making money, or there won't be more films" (Diamond, G1). Max Laemmle was honored again in 1973 with the Chevalier of the Order of Arts and Letters from France's Minister of Cultural Affairs for the circuit's dedication to French cinema and French film series and festivals ("Max Laemmle" 30). By then Laemmle Theatres had become well known for their international programming and as the home of the Israeli Film Festival ("Israeli Film Festival Is Set" W1).

Laemmle Theatres added the Continental in West Hollywood in 1980, the Grande 4-plex in downtown (1984), the Fine Arts in Beverly Hills (1985), and the Colorado in Pasadena in 1986 ("Max Laemmle" 30). From a death spiral in the late 1950s to a golden moment for art cinema in the 1980s, *Boxoffice* declared "The Neighborhood Art House" as "a very hot property" by 1982: "Once a questionable investment in the minds of many exhibitors and tainted by tales of unpredictable grosses and low concession sales, the art house has survived quite nicely due to increasingly strong product, growing audiences and intelligent booking practices" (Lincoln 18). Laemmle Theatres aided and benefited from this resurgence in art house filmmaking and distribution and Max was honored in 1983, this time by the Los Angeles Film Critics Association. At the award luncheon, held at a restaurant in Universal City, Laemmle told the crowd, "I had occasion to call Universal Pictures the other day, and they asked me how to spell Laemmle." Uncle Carl may have been long forgotten by many, but Laemmle Theatres had remained a vital if still intimate part of Los Angeles's film culture (Thomas, "Laemmle Honored" 7). For Bob, their small number of cinemas was always intentional. "[A]s a family run business we go very slowly," he commented in 1983. "We believe in personal handling of our product. You have to remain small and intimate to have the time to do that" ("Laemmle: Art Exhibs" 6, 18).

After more than half a century in Los Angeles, Max Laemmle passed away in 1989. "I would have left daily film-reviewing sooner than I did," *Los Angeles Times* film critic Charles Champlin wrote at the time, "except that the dwindling, often-derivative flow of Hollywood product was interrupted by the films Max imported for his longtime base, the Los Feliz on Vermont, and later for his flagship, the Royal, and a lengthening chain of other Laemmle theaters. He was a shrewd businessman with a knack for reaching and holding the art-film audience" (Champlin E1). *Boxoffice*'s obituary may have been the most sublime, merging Max Laemmle's love for the family, the business, and the family business: "Max," the trade journal wrote, "leaves behind his brother, his wife, two children, four grandchildren, and the sixteen Laemmle screens" ("Obituaries," April 1, 1989, 18–20). His wife, Bertha, who had traveled from Paris all those years earlier, died a few months later. She, like many of the Laemmle clan, had played her own role in the company's development, overseeing the interior decorations of many of the cinemas in the chain ("Obituaries," August 16, 1989, 96, 98; "Obituaries," October 1, 1989, 95). As a final tribute, AFI Fest created an award in Max's name that "honor[s] the contribution made by exhibitors and cinemas who have established an outstanding record in the previous year of recognizing, encouraging and promoting film as an art form" (Meisel 40).

Despite the family's (and the business') loss, the Laemmle chain kept on through the 1990s. "Just as Bob once joined forces with his father Max," Peter Henne wrote in *Boxoffice* in 1997, "now Greg Laemmle is becoming a full half of the Laemmle team" (Henne 22, 153). Bob and Greg picked up their own award in 1999 from the Los Angeles Independent Film Festival—the Indie Supporter Award—"presented to individuals who have been instrumental in helping independent filmmakers realize their vision" ("Laemmles to Receive" 122). Since then, Laemmle Theatres has lost some of their key venues and added new ones. The company had to relinquish the old Los Feliz Theatre in 1987 and, more recently, the Sunset 5 and Fallbrook 7, but it has added many new screens as well, refurbished venerable locations like the Royal, and refashioned the old Monica Twin into the Monica Film Center in 2016. Bob and Greg Laemmle are now looking north to new markets and refusing to be just a lessee in favor of being a stakeholder, developer, and investor in all of their new cinemas. "The closure of the Sunset and Fallbrook locations has reinforced our feeling that as a family business we really need to be our own landlords," Greg Laemmle told *Boxoffice* in 2013. "Mall owners are looking for national-credit tenants and they do not necessarily appreciate, although they should, what we bring to the table" ("Building Community").

Today, at the Royal, the Music Hall, and other Laemmle theaters, time feels still. It's still the same business, the same family, and in many ways, the same family business. Sitting down with Bob and Greg Laemmle is to be in conversation with caretakers of a very unique family name and a very unique exhibition company and history. And one can't help wondering if, without Kurt Laemmle's urging all those years ago, Max, Bertha, and Bob might not have made it out of Paris in time. It is hard to imagine what Los Angeles's art house scene might have been without the Laemmles and their theaters. With those thoughts, and the current state of film exhibition and the world in mind, I sat down with Bob and Greg Laemmle to ask them about how their family and industry history and how their cultural identity interacts with their business, their philanthropy, and their programmatic decisions.

Ross: The founding of Laemmle Theatres in 1938 was directly affected by the difficult contours of European Jewish history.

Greg: My grandfather was in Paris where my father was born and likely would have stayed in Europe—almost certainly would have stayed in Europe—if not for the rise of Nazism.

Ross: I'm curious, of course, about your own reflections on this period. How much does your family's background play into your dedication to showing Jewish-themed films and films like *Son of Saul* that reflect upon the Holocaust and those who were unable to leave in time?

Greg: In addition to being Jewish my grandfather was European and the best parts of European culture informed his personality and so I think he was always interested in the idea of bringing world culture to the United States. And we've been an art house in some way, shape, or form almost since the beginning, and now that we're known as being an art house it's what we do. Do we make a special effort to include films that reflect the Jewish experience? Sure.

Ross: Did Max talk often about Germany and the world he and Kurt left behind? Did it have an impact on the kinds of films he booked?

Bob: There's a very interesting letter downstairs on the wall [of the Royal Theatre] from my uncle Kurt to my dad in 1935 . . . all about the awareness of what politically is going on. They were encouraging my parents to consider [leaving].

Greg: The reality is that most of the family made it out of Europe. Carl, famously, [was] known for providing affidavits for family members and even non-family members from the community. Both brothers were able to get to the United States [and] their parents came to the United States. They were able to bring many members of their spouses' families. My maternal grandmother's family lost a few family members—

Bob: Almost all. . . . My grandfather had I don't know how many brothers that were lost. My mother's parents were Russian and that's the side of the family where I have my height from. If you know Carl, he was probably 5'5" or something. I'm the total freak in the family who got to 6'5". So I understand that my grandfather, that his brothers, were all above six foot. But I don't know how many [he had]—I never really had that conversation with my mother as to how many there were. But they were all lost.

Greg: So I guess there was an impact. . . . I don't remember necessarily growing up with a sense of survivor guilt per se but I know that my grandparents, the Laemmle grandparents, worked very hard in the late '40s and throughout the rest of their life on issues related to Palestine. . . . Rather than focusing on business, it felt like they were working more for ORT and other organizations.... Whether that was a reflection of some sort of sense of guilt or just... an opportunity to do something since they had to survive for a purpose.

Bob: [Regarding Laemmle Theatres and changes in the exhibition industry] When you say Laemmle Theatres, it was not really branded.... It was obviously operated by the Laemmle brothers but there was no branding identifying them as Laemmle theaters. That didn't happen until the '60s. Basically, I did that. What prompted it really was that Walter Reade came to Los Angeles, built a theater called the Granada and also acquired the Music Hall and Beverly Canon. So here's Walter Reade, a newcomer in LA with three theaters, and they take out ads describing it as Walter Reade Theatres and I'm looking at that and we had five theaters at the time and we hadn't yet branded. We discussed it with my dad and we decided that instead of being in the Independent Theater Guide [in the newspapers] where there's no identification of ownership at all—just the theater name—that we would take out a very special guide for Laemmle Theatres. And that was really the first time that we started branding.

Greg: For quite a few years it was one theater. Neighborhood chain with six theaters and TV comes along [and the chain dwindled to just] the Los Feliz Theatre.

Bob: My uncle Kurt went into the insurance business because the one theater really wasn't enough to support two families so the decision was that my dad as the older brother would stay with the theater and my uncle went into the insurance business where he was phenomenally successful by the way. And his wife [Alyse] also went into the insurance business where she is still functioning at the age of ninety-nine. She still works and services her customers.... Whenever a question comes up and I ask my son he calls [her]. At ninety-nine, she's pretty remarkable.

Greg: My grandfather was very good at building relationships with the film critics and he was very good at building relationships with his patrons from that one single screen. I think possibly into the '60s when it was just the Los Feliz, or just starting to expand, that people knew—the cognoscenti—if you wanted to know what was going on in world cinema you talked to Max Laemmle. Max Laemmle was the local guy that had that so maybe it was reasonable to say, "There is enough awareness around this name that this is the appropriate thing to brand it to"... It wasn't so crazy to name the business after yourself [like] Bergdorf's.

Ross: The exhibition business has certainly changed since then.

Greg: I would argue that the business has basically stayed the same. Little aspects of it have changed: multiplexing, digital projection, how you communicate, [and] distribution, I mean. In the '60s you would send a letter to New York because it was too expensive to call long distance and you'd wait for the reply so the pace has picked up but, at the end of the day, we're still showing movies to an audience that comes to buy tickets.

Bob: There is one thing that precipitated the change. There was a film called *The Immoral Mr. Teas* [1959]. It was the first of what you call the pornographic films. It became a big, big success. It played at a theater called the Monica. It was on Santa Monica Blvd. near Fairfax—just west of Fairfax. With the success of that film many—in fact almost all of the theaters that were showing foreign films—converted and started showing porn. The Los Feliz was the only one that remained true to the calling because to us it wasn't just providing money, it was an interest. . . . The Los Feliz showed the real esoteric foreign films, the foreign films that nobody else wanted to play because they weren't by Truffaut, Bergman, Fellini, Kurosawa, those films we didn't get. Those played these other theaters that ended up converting to porn theaters. Now, after that conversion happened, and here we were with the Los Feliz Theatre and I got into the business, we started the expansion. . . .

Greg: Our business changed. *The* business didn't change.

Bob: There was a vacuum for us to step into, to show the bigger foreign films.

Greg: We recognized, or my Dad recognized, that the city was moving west and made a conscious effort to move with it. And the audience was expanding for these films. That was also an opportunity there.

Ross: American Jews have long been involved in motion picture exhibition, often as an outgrowth of their desire to provide entertainment and culture. How much do you see Laemmle Theatres as a community center for culture and does that draw upon a familial and ethnic desire?

Greg: Well, I absolutely see ourselves as a cultural center, as a meeting place. One of the distributors we work with, Jeff Lipsky, I want to credit him with using the concept, that the movie theater is now the modern agora. It's the place where you gather and you get information and you hear about what's going on in the world. So I do sense that. We're uncomfortable specifically branding it as a Jewish environment because it's not. We do the annual *Fiddler on the Roof* on Christmas Eve and at some venues more than half the audience isn't Jewish. It's still just fun to come out and experience that so, personally, I definitely identify as a Jew but I don't want the business to reflect that because we want the business to reflect being part of Los Angeles and Los Angeles is an incredibly multicultural city. Always has been. Even if the motion picture business has always had a particular association with the Jewish community it was also always a multiethnic environment.

Ross: There are very few other places where strangers gather together in a room, who don't know each other, for a group experience. People don't go to the same church, the same mosque, the same synagogue. Because you actually care about curating a community experience, I'm curious what your own thoughts are about what you're trying to constitute, your own sense of your audience. Because people who don't book one thousand screens, who book twenty, have a sense of who their audience is.

Greg: It varies by theater. Are we consciously trying to create something? No, there's no specific political or religious agenda at play there. We are probably trying to provide an opportunity for our patrons to become informed and aware—attuned—to what is going on in the world. So that's an opportunity to create that cultural space. If you're just playing Hollywood films ultimately you're kind of numbing your audience a little bit so by combining some of the more interesting films from Hollywood and the American independent films and documentaries, foreign language films—even the cultural events, the opera and the ballet—there's an opportunity for someone to say I'm really able to acquire a lot of information about what's going on in the world, elevated through the arts, entertained, and be mentally alert because of that. And share that experience with others, both people I don't know, which is one of the great things about cinema, but also people you know. How often do you see neighbors seeing each other at the movie theater... It's those kinds of structured and unstructured interactions that really define the space.

Ross: You've hosted the Jewish Film Festival, the Sephardic Jewish Film Festival, and the Israel Film Festival. Are those festivals you've actively reached out to or do they just know Laemmle Theatres and contact you directly?

Greg: We also host the Hungarian Film Festival, the Polish Film Festival. I think we've hosted everything but the American Nazi Party film festival. That might be a stretch. [Thinking] Well, if they paid enough. [Group laughter] We don't reach out specifically to them but we do host a number of film festivals and there's a natural affinity obviously especially when it comes to the Jewish and Israeli film festival because we're also just year round showing a number of films with Jewish themes and Israeli films. . . . It's a natural fit.

Ross: Laemmle Theatres, like the Royal, actively books *Omar* (Hany Abu-Assad, 2013) and other Palestinian films, Jordanian films, and you're showing all kinds of films from around the world—particularly the Middle East. So I'm curious about how important it is to you to have Middle Eastern films and a global menu of films that aren't going to play AMC or other theaters.

Greg: It's almost exclusively about our relationship with distributors or a producer's desire to have a film play in Laemmle Theatres. . . . I can't tell you how many times people call and say "I can't believe you're showing that movie. You're an anti-Semite and I'm never coming to see another movie at your theater." And it's like, okay, you're now not going to see all of the Israeli and Jewish-themed films if you really follow through [on that]. Look, there's a world of ideas out there and there is a level where it is our responsibility to present this. You don't want to buy a ticket, don't buy a ticket, but if you want to say that something shouldn't exist . . . But we don't bring our personal, philosophical beliefs to our programming and say "I don't agree with this film so I'm not going to play it." We did not play *The Last Temptation of Christ* [1988] partially because I didn't need to. There were plenty of other people who were playing the film. You didn't need Laemmle Theatres to play that film. Now if we didn't play [Abu-Assad's] *Paradise Now* [2005] that film might not have been seen in Los Angeles. . . . Is it an insightful film? You can't have that conversation until you've seen the film. It is our responsibility to provide an opportunity for that film to be seen. In our programming, yes, I do feel it is important to provide space for uncomfortable ideas and experiences to be available because that's the only way we're really going to learn.

Bob: We are open to talking to people. So if there is a festival, they may try to call, in the past, AMC or Mann Theatres or whatever, and they get no response. They know that if they talk to us—they know they will reach somebody who is sympathetic who will try to work with them to make something happen. . . . We probably qualify [for the Oscars], I'm guessing, eighty percent of the shorts, documentaries, independent features, because we are willing to talk to people and try to work with them to make things happen. Now that started from the very beginning, back in the '60s, where there were people who would come to us and ask the Los Feliz Theatre, "Would you please qualify this short?"

Ross: With so much attention on television these days does cinema still have the primacy and importance to reach audiences and bring them together?

Greg: It is harder now. I think it is harder now. Even the independent scene is dominated by a very marketing-driven culture. There are very few critics that can really champion a smaller film and break it through to a larger audience because at some point they're not being given the space. They don't have the power. If you can't cut together a thirty second TV spot, and not only cut it together but afford to sell it, you're not going to hit critical mass to have a film enter the cultural conversation. And yet there are still opportunities.... A film like *Ida* [2013] just hits a groove and starts finding an audience ... but these are films that are hitting a million people in the US and that's throughout all platforms.

Ross: Films don't have the same chance to play for months at a time anymore with so much foreign and art house product available.

Greg: It puts pressure on the audience. There's enough capacity that if an audience wants to make a film run long—that long tail—it's possible but it's about getting enough momentum going with the audience to make that happen and that's a little more difficult. Because the audience is consumed with what's new—"I heard that's great but this new one is coming and I saw the ads on TV."

Ross: So those kinds of windows put pressure on the ability to have a film play for a long time and find an audience.

Greg: Before the film has opened they've already set the date for the DVD so you only have a little window. The theatrical run has been curtailed in an unnatural fashion based on some of these preset issues. *Spotlight* [2015] should be going out really super wide right now through May but, at the end of the day, it's also out on this and it's out on that. What could have been a long theatrical tail for something is not going to appear for a variety of reasons. But it's ultimately about the fact that the DVD date got set.

Ross: What was the impetus for the Laemmle Charitable Foundation which donates much needed funds to charities including Bet Tzedek, the Westside Food Bank, etc.? Is this the family's interest in the notion of *Tikkun Olam*

("Healing the World")? How much does this charitable initiative reinforce the local presence of Laemmle Theatres in the community versus the national focus of your larger competitors?

Greg: The foundation was set up to provide a lasting vehicle for the family's interest in investing in the community. If you are going to make the statement that it's a multigenerational business then you have to find ways to encourage and support the younger generation as it moves into a position of leadership. Generally speaking, people make less in terms of salary in a family business than they do out in the real world . . . how do you augment that earlier generation's ability to integrate into the larger culture? So having that vehicle that provides entrée for people was something I was thinking about when I encouraged my father to start the foundation in 2000. . . . It's very focused on Los Angeles as you can see from the organizations we support. Even if they're national organizations we're very focused on what they're doing here in Los Angeles. . . . We have almost exclusively stayed away from funding Jewish organizations with the exception that we do support Jewish organizations that are providing a Jewish response to a general community issue. [The Food Bank] is a Jewish response to a general problem that's something we can get behind. . . . Personally, I've really started to see or try to see my own family's history as immigrants coming to Los Angeles and finding Los Angeles to be a welcoming community for that immigrant experience and so I like to . . . remember that you were a stranger in a strange land. We can take it from the tribal experience or take it from our own personal experience and say we came here fleeing persecution. Yes, maybe we arrived with a little more on our backs than some of the immigrants coming today but the experience is ultimately the same so how do we create here in Los Angeles a more welcoming environment, an environment that provides for the same developing opportunities to integrate into the city that we had? Because I do believe that that will actually be for the benefit of Los Angeles, and not to the detriment of Los Angeles, both economically, culturally—in all kinds of ways. I think Los Angeles has benefited incredibly from, just speaking personally about the Jewish immigration to the city, and when you look at the history of the city culturally and from a business standpoint in so many ways, all of these Jewish families who were able to settle here and make homes here, enrich the city. So I'd like to see that happen for the next generation of immigrants.

Ross: You've stated in the past that Laemmle Theatres no longer wants to be simply a lessee but a builder and operator of all of its future cinemas. With your upcoming Newhall project, how are you taking control of this process from beginning to end? Would it surprise some that you're going to Newhall?

Greg: I already talked to the Rabbi! That really does go back to the idea that Los Angeles is changing . . . and areas where you would previously say no one is interested in art film or [has] enough population and you turn around and there's three to four hundred thousand people living in the Santa Clarita Valley and they're educated. You talk about some of these neighborhoods where these art houses were and now people are coming back to them but in the '60s people were fleeing these neighborhoods. Maybe part of it was because the local neighborhood theater started showing porn films because the operator wasn't really invested in what was going on around them, they just [said], "How can I make the most money today?" There are so many parts of town where Laemmle Theatres had theaters and left and now it's time to come back. The corporate mentality is how do I make money quickly and the family business mentality is how do I plant the tree for the next generation?

Greg: How do you recruit talented individuals who are located in that area? Will they think twice about moving, taking a job in that area if living in that community means they're going to have to give up on the cafes and the restaurants and, yes, the art house movie theater that they really find important to the richness of their life. So to be able to say, "You don't have to give up on it. Look, we have it here as well." I don't think Old Town Newhall is going to be Silver Lake but if it can have some of the elements of Silver Lake that makes it a more interesting community and a richer community.

Ross: For the art house business to expand, distributors rely on circuits like yours to open new theaters and find new audiences.

Greg: Distributors do need us to expand otherwise they're going to be focused on the ancillary release . . . But if exhibition can increase then exhibition continues to become a viable and important business for distributors, for producers. But it does speak to the role of art in place making. When people say they're going to create an arts and entertainment district, what are you really trying to create? You better stop and think because just dropping a twenty-plex downtown isn't necessarily going to change anything. . . . It's the conversation we have with every community, with every developer.

Ross: Do you think movies can still bring disparate people and cultures together through cinema and the cinemagoing experience? How valuable is that in a world as unpredictable and fractious as the one we're faced with today? How does seeing movies from foreign cultures provide your audience with an opportunity for empathy and understanding?

Greg: I hope they can see that the conversations going on in some of these countries that we read about in the headlines, that the people who live in some of those countries, the individuals, are people and that the actions of the government don't necessarily reflect the concerns and desires of the people who live there. I can say that in regard to a film like *Gett* [2014]—which could be argued shows people living under a theocratic regime within Israel or apply it to the young girls in *Mustang* [2015] who just want to be young and free and yet their environment crushes their dreams but maybe can't ever destroy them completely—that's where the artists in these communities can provide voice to something that shows that what their rulers are saying in the headlines isn't always appropriate. And if we can have that conversation on an artistic level maybe we can have it on a personal level and then maybe we can begin to develop a little more trust. I would like to think that the films coming out of Iran show that beyond just the results of the recent election that the films that we see show that there's a lot more thoughtfulness than whatever Ahmadinejad wants to scream in the headlines.

Bob: You see what's going on with the film in Pakistan about honor killings [Sharmeen Obaid-Chinoy's documentary *A Girl in the River: The Price of Forgiveness* (2015)]. All of a sudden the country is reevaluating. The judicial process is changing as a result of this film. When I read that I thought, wow, this is really amazing.

Greg: So I think film can have that conversation on a current level, the way *Ida* is being interpreted both within Europe and within Poland. . . . I'm not happy at all about some of the attacks on the film but even in the attacks there's an interesting conversation to be had. Maybe we do need to acknowledge that, yes, while the Polish people were guilty of certain things there was also a lot of harm done to Poland and the Poles. We should acknowledge that. That's not necessarily the role of this one film or another film but film as a conversation can begin to provide some context for events in our recent past. . . . [Regarding the film *Les Innocentes* (2016) about Soviet soldiers' sexual assaults of Polish nuns during World War II] If you only see one or the other you're not getting a full picture of what the world is. If you have the opportunity to see both, understand both, sort of try to put them together, you may get a picture of why things are currently the way they are. And acknowledge people's pain and help everyone get past it.

Ross: What is the future of Laemmle Theatres and art house exhibition?

Greg: Ever since TV came in people have been predicting the death of exhibition. Those cries are only getting louder and louder. Certainly trying to be a small business, a family owned business, in an environment where all we see is increasing corporatization, flies in the face of any sort of reasonable business practice. But there you have it. We do believe in the future for exhibition and we believe that, I guess, that as a family business we're going to be able to survive as well—as much as the world is telling you, "Sell, sell, sell." . . . It probably becomes harder and harder for each generation to consider selling because now you bear the weight of generations. That's going to be a decision for the next group.

Works Cited

A Girl in the River: The Price of Forgiveness. Directed by Sharmeen Obaid-Chinoy, performances by Asad Jamal, Saba. HBO Documentary Films and SOC Films, 2015.

A Man and a Woman. Directed by Claude Lelouch, performances by Anouk Aimée, Jean-Louis Trintignant, and Pierre Barouh. Les Films 13, 1966.

"About People of the Theatre." *Better Theatres*, 7 Feb. 1942, p. 32.

"Behind Keys." *Variety*, 9 Aug. 1932, p. 19.

"Births." *Variety*, 18 Sept. 1935, p. 76.

"Building Community: In 75th Anniversary Year, Laemmle Theatres Looks Forward." *Film Journal International*, 16 Sept. 2013, www.filmjournal.com/content/building-community-75th-anniversary-year-laemmle-theatres-looks-forward. Accessed 20 Aug. 2016.

"Carl's Nephew Gets Try." *Variety*, 17 Sept. 1930, p. 7.

Champlin, Charles. "Max Laemmle Introduced L. A. to the Best in Foreign Movies." *Los Angeles Times* (hereafter *LAT*), 24 June 1989, p. El.

"Daily Review." *Exhibitors Trade Review*, 9 Oct. 1928, p. 2.

Diamond, S J. "At Art Movie Theaters, Real Art Is in the Selling." *LAT*, 24 Apr. 1977, p. G1.

Doherty, Thomas. "Remembering the Hollywood Mogul Who Rescued Hundreds of Germany's Jews (Guest Column)." *The Hollywood Reporter*, 29 Dec. 2015, www.hollywoodreporter.com/race/remembering-hollywood-mogul-who-rescued-851399. Accessed 20 Aug. 2016.

Fiddler on the Roof. Directed by Norman Jewison, performances by Topol, Norma Crane, and Leonard Frey. Mirisch Production Company and Cartier Productions, 1971.

"Foreign." *The Film Daily* (hereafter *TFD*), 8 Mar. 1937, p. 5.

"Foreign Film News: Laemmle's Plan." *Variety*, 13 Feb. 1934, p. 13.

Gett: The Trial of Viviane Amsalem. Directed by Ronit Elkabetz and Shlomi Elkabetz, performances by Ronit Elkabetz, Simon Abkarian, and Gabi Amrani. Arte France Cinéma, Canal+ France, and DBG, 2014.

Henne, Peter. "The Laemmle Difference." *Film Journal International*, 1 Aug. 1997, p. 22, 153.

Ida. Directed by Pawel Pawlikowski, performances by Agata Kulesza, Agata Trzebuchowska, and Dawid Ogrodnik. Opus Film, Phoenix Film Investments, and Canal+ Polska, 2013.

The Immoral Mr. Teas. Directed by Russ Meyer, performances by Bill Teas, Ann Peters, and Marilyn Wesley. Pad-Ram Enterprises, 1959.

"Israeli Film Festival Is Set for Royal in Oct." *Boxoffice*, 25 June 1973, p. W1.

La Bête Humaine. Directed by Jean Renoir, performances by Jean Gabin, Julien Carette, and Simone Simon. Paris Film, 1938.

"Laemmle: Art Exhibs Want Majors to Let Classics Units Run Freely." *Variety*, 3 Aug. 1983, pp. 6, 18.

"Laemmles to Receive Indie Supporter Award." *Film Journal International*, 1 Apr. 1999, p. 122.
The Last Temptation of Christ. Directed by Martin Scorsese, performances by Willem Dafoe, Harvey Keitel, and Barbara Hershey. Universal Pictures and Cineplex Odeon Films, 1988.
Les Innocentes. Directed by Anne Fontaine, performances by Lou de Laâge, Agata Buzek, and Agata Kulesza. Mandarin Films, Aeropian Film, and Mars Films, 2016.
Levine, Alison. *Laemmle Not Afraid . . . 75 Years of Film Exhibition in Los Angeles*. Three Thirty/Laemmle Theatres, 2013.
Lincoln, David. "Art Film Exhibition Steady Profits in a Special Market." *Boxoffice*, 1 June 1982, p. 18.
"List or Manifest of Alien Passengers for the United States." S.S. Normandie, 21 May 1928. Liberty Ellis Island Foundation.
"List or Manifest of Alien Passengers for the United States." S.S. Normandie, 27 Apr. 1938. Liberty Ellis Island Foundation.
"List or Manifest of Alien Passengers for the United States." S.S. Aquitania, 26 Mar. 1939. Liberty Ellis Island Foundation.
"Los Angeles." *Boxoffice*, 31 May 1971, p. W6.
". . . Los Angeles." *MPD*, 22 Aug. 1935, p. 2.
"Max Laemmle." *Variety*, 10 Jan. 1973, p. 30.
"Max Laemmle, Wyler Appointed." *TFD*, 28 Mar. 1929, p. 8.
"Max Laemmle Honored by Supervisors." *LAT*, 17 July 1963, p. D9.
"Max Laemmle on Coast." *TFD*, 17 Apr. 1939, p. 22.
Max Laemmle-Film Export Advertisement. *La Cinématographie Française*, 9 Jan. 1937, p. 20.
McCarthy, Todd. "Honor Vet Exhib Laemmie for Role in L.A.'s Culture." *Variety*, 23 Oct. 1985, pp. 7, 27.
Meisel, Myron. "AFI Festival Branches Out with Laemmle Theatrical Runs." *The Film Journal*, 1 June 1991, pp. 16, 17, 40.
Monica Twin Advertisement. *LAT*, 18 Feb. 1970, p. D14.
Mustang. Directed by Deniz Gamze Ergüven, performances by Günes Sensoy, Doga Zeynep Doguslu, and Tugba Sunguroglu. CG Cinéma, Vistamar Filmproduktion, and Uhlandfilm, 2015.
"Nephew Max Laemmle Loses Paris U. Post." *Variety*, 26 Dec. 1933, p. 15.
"Obituaries." *Boxoffice*, 1 Apr. 1989, pp. 18–20.
"Obituaries." *Variety*, 16 Aug. 1989, pp. 96, 98.
"Obituaries." *Boxoffice*, 1 Oct. 1989, p. 95.
Omar. Directed by Hany Abu-Assad, performances by Adam Bakri, Leem Lubany, and Eyad Hourani. ZBROS, 2013.
"ORT Plans Luncheon, Program." *LAT*, 17 Oct. 1948, p. C2.
"ORT Screen Unit Forming." *LAT*, 19 July 1948, p. A5.

"Out Hollywood Way." *MPD*, 16 Aug. 1935, p. 14.

Paradise Now. Directed by Hany Abu-Assad, performances by Kais Nashif, Ali Suliman, and Lubna Azabal. Augustus Film, Lama Productions, and Razor Film Produktion, 2005.

Spotlight. Directed by Tom McCarthy, performances by Mark Ruffalo, Michael Keaton, and Rachel McAdams. Participant Media, First Look Media, and Anonymous Content, 2015.

"Theatres-Exchanges." *Variety*, 28 Sept. 1938, p. 23.

"Theatres-Exchanges." *Variety*, 28 Dec. 1938, p. 20.

"Times Square: Chatter—Paris." *Variety*, 20 Sept. 1932, pp. 39, 44.

Thomas, Kevin. "L. A. Lags in Art Film Appreciation." *LAT*, 19 Dec. 1965, p. M17.

———. "Laemmle Honored by L. A. Film Critics Assn." *LAT*, 11 July 1983, p. 7.

"Three-Year Run at Regent for 'A Man And A Woman.'" *Boxoffice*, 14 Oct. 1968, p. NC1.

"To Distribute 'Human Beast.'" *TFD*, 24 May 1938, p. 10.

"To Handle French Pix in U. S." *TFD*, 3 Mar. 1937, p. 12.

"UJW Theatres Division Pledges Up." *Boxoffice*, 28 May 1949, p. 38.

"Universal to Sign Lease for Laemmle's Regent." *Boxoffice*, 20 Jan. 1969, p. W1.

Vierhus, Ann. "Woman Honored on Insurance Sales." *LAT*, 13 Mar. 1955, p. C3.

Whitaker, Frank. "Park Theatre Exits H. P. Scene." *Highland Park News-Herald & Journal* [Los Angeles, CA], 17 Oct. 1963, p. 74.

CHAPTER 9

An Outsider's View of Sixties America: Matthew Weiner Talks with Michael Renov about the Jews of *Mad Men*

by Michael Renov

Matthew Weiner is the creator of the hugely acclaimed series *Mad Men* which ran for seven seasons on AMC. Weiner has been the recipient of nine prime time Emmys over the course of his career as *Mad Men* creator and, before that, as a staff writer on David Chase's *The Sopranos*. Something of a cultural phenomenon, *Mad Men* was awarded a record four straight Emmys for Outstanding Drama Series and featured ninety-two episodes, seventy-three of them written or co-written by Weiner. *Mad Men* displayed a consistency of intelligence and sophistication—as well as a highly influential '60s fashion sense—that helped to set the standard for a new "Golden Age" of television. The following conversation took place over several hours in Weiner's West Hollywood offices.

Weiner: When I wrote *Mad Men* I had been working in TV for about six years already. I discovered, getting into half hour comedy, I realized something that everybody already knew, which was that this was the Jewish version of jazz.

Renov: [Laughter]

Weiner: Half-hour TV comedy was a popular mainstream entertainment that was based on a very specific ethnic rhythm and the old "think Yiddish write

British," that was still there. But even all the people I worked with who were Irish Catholic and Italians and African Americans, they were all working in this vibe that was from *The Goldbergs* and other things on radio and probably from the [Yiddish] theater and vaudeville.

So you're in this tradition and, at the same time, there are no Jewish characters in any of these shows. At the time, *Seinfeld* was the biggest thing on TV. I guess there were a couple of Jewish characters on *Friends*, Ross and Monica, but the idea that George Costanza was Italian was one of these things that no one worried about. There was a story told in the writer's room, and I don't know if this is true either, that the first season of *Roseanne* they were coming to the holidays and she goes, "So anyway, when it's Hanukkah for the Connors, . . ." and they were like, "What? The Connors aren't Jewish." And Roseanne was like, "Yes they are." And the whole idea that this tattooed working class family would be Jewish, which is what Roseanne was from, Utah I believe. . . .

So, the idea of putting Rachel Menken front and center in the pilot episode as a love interest, which meant imbuing her with physical attributes of attractiveness, this went very much against the grain.[1] Against the Woody Allen stereotype of the shrewish, ugly, cloying, frigid Jewish woman, which was a big, popular trope in the writer's rooms that I worked in.

I was going to make Rachel Menken a sex symbol, I was going to make her powerful, and I was going to use her to represent, very consciously, the straddling that was being done by that generation in their effort to assimilate. I call them the nose job generation. My parents are part of this. My mother doesn't have a nose job but they are part of this. My dad is one of the preppiest people in the world, but he is one of if not the first person in his family to go to college. And they faced a lot of antisemitism and limitations on where they could go to college. Now public school in New York City was completely blind to all of this, which is what it was intended to be.

Education was so important to this immigrant generation and maybe to Jewish culture in general. Apparently, there's this twelve block area of the lower east side, I've heard there were something between fifteen and twenty Nobel Prize winners from this neighborhood. There aren't a lot of cultures where the mother is proud to say that her son is a physicist.

Renov: [Laughter]

Weiner: I was very conscious, as a parallel to Don, because it wasn't the main story, but I wanted to show that Rachel Menken's father had an accent, and was probably embarrassed about it. I wanted to show that Rachel was supremely American but she was in two worlds. And it comes out in their relationship with Israel, and their relationship with the United States, and their relationship with their family, and their relationship to intermarriage, all of these are the big issues of assimilation. And I felt that worked great with Don and Peggy and everybody in that show because it was about the gold standard, which is how do I take whatever I have and file it down so that it fits into the WASP male standard.

But Don Draper, like a lot of guys in advertising, was from rural poverty. New York City is filled with people from West Virginia, etc., and they get suits and money and they either try to hide that or, like Conrad Hilton, eventually wear it on their sleeve. I'm talking about all different kinds of people that we would not anymore define as ethnic minorities. Being Catholic is a huge liability in a lot of these worlds. You get an ad agency like BBDO, where there's a lot of Catholics, or McCann. At the time the United States is sort of segregated into white shoe and everybody else. And something about the economic environment in the mid-fifties and the postwar, it's a free-for-all and a lot of people are slowly, by the end of the sixties, traversing all of these barriers either through money—which is a great equalizer in American culture—or through true assimilation, sometimes denial even. Actual transformation into the thing that you desire to be, a lie like Don's—you can become successful.

Renov: You were born in the middle of the decade that your show was about.

Weiner: Yes.

Renov: Was that a liability or a virtue?

Weiner: Well, now that I look at other period shows, I think the biggest liability was that I was making a period piece about a time when a huge chunk of the audience was alive. And so, you're basically dealing with people's memories which are flawed. It's not just a matter of looking things up in the *New York Times*. Someone will say, "Yeah, we had that toaster," or "We didn't have that toaster," or "No one said 'super'. Why do they say 'super'?" And I'm like, "Well it's all over [J. D. Salinger's] *Franny and Zooey*," so somebody was saying it, and it's from the forties. And I can document "bitchin" as a 1950s car word not just a 1970s surfer word. And so your research is essential, but at the same time . . . [sighs].

Here's the thing: I wanted, I put it front and center, that this world would be reliable in some way. That it would be airtight in some way because I wanted to remove the audience's ability to abstract itself from it. Even though the show's been criticized for this in various places as being this winking superiority trip on "look how smart we are now," the exact opposite was what I was trying to do. There are very few jokes like that in it. Maybe there's one in the pilot, but for the most part, it's saying "You think that you're so smart and so different, but you're not. You are a human—a human problem is a human problem."

Did I learn as time went on? There was so much time from when I wrote it to the end of the show's run. The world was transformed during the time when the show was on the air, which will be acknowledged at some point. Our conversations about gender were greeted with scorn by feminists when *Mad Men* went on the air. It took a long time for people to even understand that the show was progressive in some way.

Renov: Oh yes, I remember that very well.

Weiner: And now, it's not even up for debate.

Renov: You have the awards to prove it.

Weiner: Well, you can get awards and be regressive, believe me. But I do think that people started seeing how many women were working on the show and they acted like that's why it's about gender. None of this matters to me. I am completely oriented towards the person and personhood. That's not white or black or male or female. There are differences. I grew up in the intellectual era in college in which the word "difference" was used a lot, with scorn actually.

Because the melting pot thing had already dissolved. And the idea of quote unquote "humanism" was rejected as not specific and a lie. So all that intellectual shit aside, I am basically telling a story about human beings that I want to recognize. Do I know every kind of person who's out there? No. Do I need a writing staff to tell me that? Do I need more life experience to tell me that? Yes to all of that. Could I feel differences, having grown up in Baltimore till I was eleven, a place that was very much like 1965 in 1975. I moved to Los Angeles, which is probably like 1985 in 1975.

And, like a lot of artists, I'm an outsider. So I'm observing these things. In the beginning of the show, I referred to it a few times as science fiction until someone who wrote science fiction said, "It's not science fiction, it's historical fiction. Don't use that." And I said but I am trying to take you into a world that did exist but didn't exactly. I'm thinking of the *Star Trek* episode where they go back into the quote unquote "past."

I wanted there to be no barrier from it being over art-directed, not related to reality, looking like a Hollywood movie, being in black and white, having too much score, having titles over the film. All of these things I felt would remove the audience from the experience. And commercials, too, by the way, which I really tried to not have.

Renov: I remember.

Weiner: Yeah, I tried to not have that. And, in the end, I don't think the commercials mattered. Because the other thing that happened during the show's run was the technological revolution of the DVR. So they were thwarted because people saved these things up. They did watch the show that week, but people avoided the commercials for the most part. Or watched them because they wanted to.

Renov: Didn't you manage to keep an extra minute of the show minus commercials?

Weiner: Yeah, they wanted to add more commercials about midway through the show. A lot of the show is about the stupidity and shortsightedness of capitalism. And I was experiencing it with both the companies that made the show.[2] Something amazing was happening to them financially and they could not stop trying to eat the horse that they were riding. I don't have the pressures that they have. You know, they had to make quarterly reports, one of them was in the midst of a takeover attempt for almost six of the eight years we were on the air. And suddenly one of the companies goes public, the other one goes through the roof. But they had no understanding because neither of them understood TV and that we were in this alternate entertainment universe. They had no understanding of what was financially happening to them and were constantly short sighted. Constantly. And there's a lot of reference to it in the show. And, believe it or not, that echoed into other people's shows. In what I consider to be one of the greatest compliments as an artist, there's a *30 Rock* episode where Kabletown, because it was right during the takeover of NBC by, who was it . . .

Renov: Comcast.

Weiner: Yeah. We had had a quote when they were getting bought by McCann, the first time, where Don says, "I don't want to turn a dollar into a dollar ten, I want to build something." And I saw it echoed in the voice of Alec Baldwin's character as he was watching his business flourish financially but completely disappear. And it's a great irony, one which Oliver Stone and before him Abraham Polonsky and Rod Serling observed in their work. The dismantling of something to its parts is the wise financial move but it means people's jobs and it means money going to one person and it's the opposite of the productivity work model that the rest of us are living by.

So, all of that was in the show and looking back on it, not being from that period, I wanted it to be about the things that I was interested in. So I got to take the milieu and play against people's perception of that period. Some of the first reviews were like, "It's 1950s Manhattan," and I'm like, "No, it's 1960." Unfortunately the show was not able to undo this idea that history goes directly from *Happy Days* to Woodstock. And maybe people know about the ring-a-ding-ding years of the Rat Pack in the early sixties, but the idea of what went on before the Kennedy assassination, and how modern it is, how there is a kind of fearlessness in the height of the cold war about America.

It's Maslow's Hierarchy of Needs.[3] I do believe that. I believe that, after World War II, as this generation comes home, and it's not my theory, this "lonely crowd" has everything.[4] I don't know if it's a sociological phenomenon or an economic phenomenon, whatever it is. But you will see, if you look at the popular literature, at pop culture, and I'm including even teenage music, and look at the density and complexity and newness of that period, it's remarkable. We're not in that period right now. There's nothing new right now. People are terrified of things that are new. And you see the level of erudition that's expected from the masses at that time. You see what's on the bestseller list. You are embarrassed to be uneducated. You can't just pull out your phone and tell people who won the election in 1972. You saw an aspirational sort of pop culture—take a look at *Time* magazine and try to read it without a dictionary. And that's *Time* magazine, *Life* magazine. Widely circulated, still very pulpy you know, very populist in many ways, there's nothing more populist than *Life* magazine and you will see poets. You want to see an interview with Jean Paul Sartre? You know where it is? You know where the only interview is, I think, in English in the 1960s of Jean Paul Sartre? It's in *Playboy*. Like who are they aiming at? They might be creating insecurity in their audience but that mindset and what's coming are very interesting to me, to see how new ideas actually affected individual people.

And, as dramatists, you can't help but make that the center of people's lives. There are things like the Kennedy assassination and the Cuban Missile Crisis, Marilyn Monroe's death, later 9/11, some big, big socially galvanizing events. And America's in two wars right now. We may talk about ISIS today but, for the most part, we're gonna talk about, you know, the kids and the traffic and things like that. I've always said, "If you're in the middle of a divorce, at 9/11, it's the divorce you're gonna remember." The two will be associated with one another but you still have your own problems. And yet, when people do a historical project like this, they just go off the *New York Times*. I'm like, "Well go ahead, go off the *New York Times*. You might notice the assassination of Malcolm X is on page 4." Nobody knows it's important and then you go back and look at a timeline of the sixties in any book and it's right there. It's like the major event, and you're like, really? Nobody knew that at the time.

Renov: Georg Lukacs, a European Jewish Marxist critic, wrote this essay "Narrate or Describe." He was really writing in favor of a certain novelistic approach, pitting one approach to writing against another. On one side was someone like Zola whom he thought was very much oriented to the surface of things and therefore couldn't really penetrate very deeply into social history.

Weiner: Right.

Renov: Lukacs favored someone like Tolstoy with those big thick novels of his who could actually get inside history with his characters and narrate big events, embed his characters in those events.

Weiner: That's fascinating. I'm working in a different medium. So it's a little bit harder because there's not a lot of voiceover in *Mad Men* and the great challenge that I started off with as a goal was to dramatize internal states. I wanted to narrate internal states the way Tolstoy does, but I knew that in film you can't just say, you can't even explain that someone is somebody's sister. Believe it or not, in a scene, it's very hard to explain, it's all behavior. You can't tell someone, "She reminded him of someone he knew in high school," if you're trying to emulate reality in any way, reproduce reality. People calling each other "sis" or saying, "I haven't seen you since high school," it's really shitty drama. But I had a class in Tolstoy in college, just in Tolstoy, where in a four-month period we were supposed to read *Anna Karenina*. I did read quite a bit of it actually, but it was a ridiculous request. Because it was *Anna Karenina, War and Peace, Sevastopol Stories, Death of Ivan Ilyich*. And then at the same time, just for background, *Fathers and Sons*, which is the one that you read right away because it's really short and (Dostoevsky's) *Crime and Punishment*, just so you know what's going on in the environment. So, basically—a lifetime of work in four months. And what I found was—and this will sound incredibly naïve—and more than in reading *Madame Bovary*, I found that I recognized the behavior of these people.

I don't know if he's giving Zola short shrift in a way, because Zola is sort of like, "I'm gonna show it to you," sort of like a filmmaker. Like you're saying, "I'm gonna show it to you and you'll get it," right? It will penetrate you. Maybe Zola would have been better as a filmmaker, to let people walk through the room and see the heads turn. I always use the example of *The Story of O*, when she's walking against the soldiers. There's this incredible shot in this movie where she's walking towards her lover defiantly and the soldiers are coming in her direction and she walks through the column of soldiers as they're coming at her. You want to explain somebody's personal defiance has political ramifications? This is before that guy was standing in front of the tank in Tiananmen Square. That's what it looked like. And some writer thought it up, right? To dramatize it. So, I'm definitely in favor of narration but I'm hesitant to stick people's faces in things. I hear some French critic tell me, referring to Betty Draper, "She's so Douglas Sirk. You know, you have this reflection of the TV set." And I would say to him, "She watches those movies. She's not in those movies." When the news of her death comes to her, she's living in the tragedy of Camille. She is not Camille. People process. We talk of a post-cinematic world, post-literature world. We see ourselves as those characters, they inform our expectations.

Renov: As long as I've known you, I didn't know until I started reading other interviews with you that you wrote poetry.

Weiner: Yes.

Renov: That was your way in.

Weiner: It was my way into show business.

Renov: That's rare.

Weiner: It was my way, it was my chosen form of expression outside of comedy, which I didn't realize was running parallel the entire time. And there was a lot of comedy in the poetry. It was what I wanted to do and what I thought I would be doing. It's not like I wasn't interested in show business. I grew up in Los Angeles, like I said, from age eleven or twelve but show business was deeply discouraged on some level, the way you would discourage your children from pursuing something that was going to be fruitless and filled with heartache.

Renov: I also read that you loved reading T. S. Eliot's *The Waste Land*.

Weiner: Yes.

Renov: So the poetry you were drawn to, instead of being about these short bursts of emotion, was really about these vast expanses.

Weiner: Yes, absolutely, *The Waste Land* scene is an expansive poem. It is not *The Odyssey*. It is *The Odyssey* for a modern person. It is boiled down, it has scenes, it has footnotes, which are basically giving you the education that you need. You have your iPhone at the bottom of the page that Eliot has given you. But what I really loved about it was this timeless, historic, epic context which was kind of being demeaned and colloquialized. As if to say: this was the grandeur of our culture, this is the culture now. Are we still attached to these things? This sounds like a complicated idea but I intuitively understood this from the beginning that he was discussing heroism on, like, a Greek level in the modern world. And so when you get down to two women talking about an abortion in a bar at closing time, that snippet of incredible dialogue, it's great dialogue that he overheard. This is my world. This is how I make a living, right? And it's being put in the context of this mythology, and all the stuff that excites you when you're young. The archetype, the story that we all tell. You read *King Arthur*, and you're like, "I feel like that," you know? All of those stories and I say "us."

I still have to qualify it: this is western culture. This is the Judeo-Christian tradition. I was raised in this. It was not the only culture but it was the one that I felt attached to, so here I am, the grandchild of serfs and non-land-owning Jews, deserters from the Austrian army, tailors and fleshers, fur dressers, all these things. And yet I'm attached to this story. And I'm also looking at the world I live in and saying, "Look at the drama that he is predicting here." He is channeling a cultural dissolution and he's also offering hope. He's also saying, "The rain's gonna come." And the language, there was something about it. It's not arch. It's very common and it's surprising. It's like what I like about Cheever.

Sylvia Plath's on the far end of it because she's a little bit arch, just so crispy and surprising but very dense. It's no one's natural vocabulary. But there's something about *The Waste Land* where I was thinking, "What is this man doing?" Taking every one of these traditions and putting them in a blender and saying that we are a reference to a great tradition. And how do we live that in the modern life? He did it in a lot of his work and then you get *Ulysses* a few years later where Joyce turns a Jewish man in Ireland, in Dublin, into a Greek hero.

So my attachment is to using your education to experience the world. This is why I always hate when I hear people talk about education in terms of making a living. It's supposed to enrich your life. It's supposed to make you experience life. That is it's major goal. And that's a luxury. It means you don't have to go and mine coal right after your father dies in the mine. That's a luxury of civilization and a consequence of financial success. I'm not gonna be classist about it or ignorant that everyone has that possibility. But it is a way to traverse class and it is a way to experience life differently. And I felt the very old emotion which is that the world was disintegrating and that there was entropy.

I grew up in what will eventually be recognized as a very tense time, a time of nuclear threat, the end of the Cold War, in the '80s. There was a constant discussion that the end of the world was imminent in some way or another and that we might lose. It's how Ronald Reagan got to be the President. We were powerless; culture was slipping away. And so, if you're given the end of the world and you read a poem that's, at the time, sixty years old, seventy years old, and you think about World War I when everything theoretically changed, you can't help but think, "Well this is where we are, history repeats itself." And yet something is different. Modernism in particular was very big in my education: these are the traditions and they don't exist anymore. This is existentialism. There are no primary causes. This is reality, we're in the world of reality that none of the people of the past, none of these dreamers and poets had to deal with. Even though the literature is all about murder and kidnapping and babies being thrown off of cliffs, they were the first perhaps to live in this civilization that we're in right now where humanity itself is threatened. I spoke about these things that way then too. How do you tell an epic when there are no heroes? Right? That's a good story.

Renov: What I wanted to say about poetry and then bigger poetry, *The Waste Land*. They're still relatively small scale. You end up with a ninety-two-part television drama.

Weiner: Yeah. Which you didn't know was gonna be that way. I mean I love that it's that now and that we can talk about it like that, but you gotta remember that I built a village, and then they were like, "Hey do you want to go all the way to the ocean?" And I'm like, "Yeah!" And then the next year they were like,

"Forget it, we're done." And you can see the ocean but really every single season of the show was predicated on the idea that that was the last season of the show. And that's terrifying but also invigorating. You know, to commit to using every piece of story that you have.

Renov: Can we talk a bit about world building, about your awareness that you are building a whole world for your audience?

Weiner: You know what's weird? David Chase, when I got to *The Sopranos*, was talking about how much he admired *The Simpsons* because it was such a complete universe. And I thought, "Oh yeah, that's really true." But, it wasn't on my mind. It's one of the things that I worry about with a limited series or an anthology. Half the fun is going back to that place over time and seeing them open that door and seeing the people that you know. But, when they talk about world building? You know what, it's so reverse engineered. And there's so much conversation about what they're doing in the public. I mean, you can look back at *Cleopatra* and see them bragging about how much they spent on it and it's all a sales pitch. Whenever I hear the word "world building," I reach for my remote.

But, you know, just to get back to something we touched on earlier about Jewish identity, which is that we are outsiders. That can be ideal for the artistic temperament. I know it's also an advantage of being white, being a white minority. I see it with the Irish Catholics and with Italians who are minorities and are raised as minorities for sure and do face prejudice but can be interlopers and can catch people behaving the way they behave. It's a little harder to explain to someone who grew up in Manhattan, who's Jewish, or in Encino. I grew up in Hancock Park[5] and that line in the pilot that "having money and education doesn't take the rough edge off of people," that I overheard someone saying. And I knew that was antisemitism. That idea of "being seen as an Other," the Manhattanite might have no idea.

Renov: So even though Nat King Cole helped to integrate Hancock Park for African Americans in the 1950s, he didn't do it for the Jews?

Weiner: It's so funny because it's a Jewish neighborhood now. It's known as that and there are so many show business people living there. Los Feliz was created because show business people could not get into Hancock Park and it created some very strange bedfellows. There were gays, Jews, Walt Disney. They're all next to each other in Los Feliz because they weren't allowed into Hancock

Park. They were united by their status as show business. Old LA money didn't approve, which is, you know, only thirty years old or whatever. It's hardly the Mayflower. You gotta remind them in Pasadena that they've only been there ten years longer than everybody else. But when I was growing up, there was a sort of class culture and there was a cotillion, a restricted country club, many restricted clubs. I went to a public school with three Jews in it. I was the kid who stood up and explained Hanukkah. You don't want to be that person. And you really don't imagine being that person in Los Angeles. Now Beverly Hills? Encino? The Valley? I don't know if anybody was explaining anything there but I was in a world that was a true throwback. I overheard a lot of things and knew what it was to be Other.

There was an African American family that lived in the old Ahmanson mansion and the kid and I were friends. We both never talked about who we were or anything like that but we both knew that nobody wanted us in that neighborhood, especially not the Japanese consulate across the street. You know, it was, "There goes the neighborhood." We had bought our house from one of the prominent African American families in the neighborhood, a single guy actually. And then, the Mayor's mansion was created and Tom Bradley moved in. I was in the barbershop, where there was also a Jewish barber, by the way, but not the head barber. The head barber said something so racist. My parents are, especially when it comes to racism, very, very liberal and angry. My mother worked for the Civil Rights Commission. They're very righteous about poverty, about race. But I thought, "Oh, I'm in with the white people." And I get to overhear this shit. I did not know that people used the n-word about the mayor! And I'm talking about like 1982. I'm not a little kid. I'm in tenth grade, in high school.

But that's the outsider thing, being able to be an interloper and also having some jealousy for those who grew up in a more balanced environment or a more heavily Jewish environment. We had a secret group in my high school called "The Sons of Hitler." It was a scandal in the paper eventually, a bunch of kids writing graffiti with swastikas. They were the scions of the most powerful people in Los Angeles. I can name then. We knew it was coming from their house. So, basically, your feelings are hurt. You know? I invited everyone to my bar mitzvah, and they all said they were coming, and then nobody came. I found out later, their parents wouldn't let them.

Renov: Have you seen *Stella Dallas*?

Weiner: Yeah! [Laughter] Yeah, it's exactly like that. Years later, I found out that I would never be anything but the loud Jew.

Renov: We've already established that you're not very enamored of this notion of world building but you are quite interested in narrative.

Weiner: World building is just a slogan to me, a show business thing. I'm trying to replicate reality. So, if you are okay with working with a green screen, which I am, you're never gonna be working in reality. It's all in your imagination. If you think that, if you're relying on the actor to pretend like they're holding a suitcase, that's fine. But I wanted a much more complete version for the audience. I had read this about people like Billy Wilder, and Stanley Kubrick, and Hitchcock. I wanted to create the world for the actors so that they could live in this reality. And pick actors who had realistic behavior. You know, they were not famous people, they were not bringing in any kind of baggage for the audience. Almost nobody knew who any of these people were which is tremendous. You're making a foreign movie, you know? So they *are* those people, there's already an extra level of reality. Then you write in things like coughing and sweating and you take away the OCD nature of filmmaking, which is hard because we are all control freaks and have OCD, and say, "Okay, I want to see wrinkles on these clothes. I don't want topstick on the guy's collars because sometimes they flop a little bit. Let's let Betty Draper not have a new outfit every scene like you usually see on TV. Let's make sure that everybody doesn't have to match the drapes. Let's not pick the haircuts from right now and give them to these people because they look better. Or give a twist on the old fashioned haircut. Let's give them that old fashioned haircut like Peggy's bangs, and let's face the fact that that's what it actually looked like and it looks horrible to us." It goes with the formality. I want all the drawers full of stuff. I had a big argument with the director of the pilot, Alan Taylor. It's sort of a director's bragging rights to see how much they can do in one shot without an edit, especially an insert shot.[6] For the most part, unless they come from editing, they don't like this way of working. They think it removes the audience from the story, which is the stupidest thing in the entire world. Alan agreed with me in the end. But I wanted to show Don opening that drawer—we took an extra shot—and taking a clean shirt out of the drawer. I wanted an *insert*. Takes just as much time to light as the big dramatic scene sometimes.

Renov: I still remember that insert shot.

Weiner: Yeah, and, you know what, it was mentioned to me a lot, especially by women who found it very sexy. That Don had a drawer full of shirts. The implication was that this man wasn't going home. It's Jon Hamm, so a lot of the things he does, if the rest of us did them, would seem disgusting. I knew that these guys had a drawer full of shirts. And there's something kind of gentlemanly and formal about it. But it is a manly, period version of the walk of shame.

Renov: Okay, so, into this world, which is detailed but imperfect and tending toward verisimilitude at some level, into that world, occasionally, and over time increasingly, there is the Jewish presence.

Weiner: Yeah. Yeah. Well, from the pilot.

Renov: From the pilot absolutely, but you nuanced it so much more over time. I've got a list of Jewish characters beyond Rachel.

Weiner: Well, I would have made more of the characters Jewish in the show. I got sort of brush back pitches from my writers saying, "What are you doing?" And I was like, "What am I doing? It's Manhattan. Like, who do you think is there?" You know, when Don Draper finally goes to the *shiva*[7] and I get to very easily explain to the audience what a *shiva* is in an expositional flourish, Don gets to say, "I've lived in New York a long time. I know what it is. I brought cake." Like how could he not? Roger Sterling is high WASP, Mayflower, maybe. Pete Campbell the same. You don't think those people eat bagels? That's New York! And they're eating them all the time. It's not a surprise. The Vanderbilts knew what a bagel was. [Laughter]

Renov: Right. The fact that you've got Roger, high WASP from Season One, a couple of seasons later marrying Jane Siegel, a young Jewish woman.

Weiner: Yeah. Well, the marriage thing is an interesting thing and you see this with African Americans, with every minority. Sexuality trumps everything. Yes, it's a scandal for someone on the social registry to marry outside of his race. And that's what Jews were considered. But, a really beautiful woman . . .

Renov: Queen Esther, for example.

Weiner: Yes! Exactly. A really beautiful woman, of any form can ascend. Ava Gardner, right? Don Draper. That's what that was about. Don Draper crosses all class boundaries because he is handsome. The first African American people, other than the pejorative mammies and uncles like Uncle Ben's Rice, the first African Americans in popular advertising are beautiful women. And you open up the most segregated magazines in the world now, the high class rich people's travel magazines and the black faces you see will be these incredibly beautiful African Americans or actually Africans. That's not an achievement. It is complete objectification and sexualization. But I felt that Roger got this woman who was the next generation. And he's entitled on his third try or whatever it is, second try. But she's so beautiful it doesn't matter. But I would have made more people Jewish.

And my wife, too, everyone's saying, "What are you doing?" I said I'm trying to reflect the culture of New York and of advertising at that point. And even though there are no Jews in these agencies yet, there are Jews in every other industry. The people who are running the restaurants, who are pretending to be Italians, a lot of them are Jewish.

Renov: And when you bring in your insult comic and his sexy wife [Jimmy Barrett and his wife Bobbie] . . .

Weiner: Oh yeah.

Renov: What an opening that was! [Laughter] The Jewish world just comes flowing in, like through a hole in the dike.

Weiner: That was based, very loosely, on Jerry Lewis. It's all about the talent. To pretend that Jewish comedians are not part of television? I mean they *are* television. *The Goldbergs* was the number one TV show for the first few years of TV's existence. There's a theory that's because Jews owned all the furniture stores and sold lots of televisions. The reason why *The Goldberg*s was popular is because most of the TVs were owned by Jewish people! [Laughter]. Nat King Cole has a huge TV show but he can't stand next to Rosemary Clooney. They can't touch, and he is a sex symbol. No one could deal with that either. Peggy actually brought it up at one point that her father didn't like the way her mother liked Nat King Cole. Don's gonna get into the sponsorship thing. They're gonna be including comedians. Jerry Lewis, someone like that's going to come in. So Bobbie Barrett, Jimmy Barrett, they were the lower class version of Rachel Menken. To me.

Renov: And Faye Miller?[8]

Weiner: Faye Miller. Well she's connected to Greta Guttman from the pilot, the researcher with the German accent. There were a lot of Jews in the field of psychology who were physical and spiritual descendants of Freud. They descended on Madison Avenue through Bernays. Edward Bernays was the man who invented the term "public relations" and changed it from the term "propaganda." He was Freud's nephew.

He's the man who figured out how to get women to smoke. I think Bernays is the one who told John D. Rockefeller to give out dimes, because he had such a horrible public image, even though he was a very generous man. He looked like a skeleton, he had destroyed many lives through ruthless business and he had this criminal father on his back. People found out about his past which he tried to hide the whole time. Getting film of him handing out money was a PR move that I think originated with Bernays. And the one I know for sure that is attributed to him is in the '20s, in a Suffragette march. He had one of the women stop in the march, pull up her flapper skirt, pull a cigarette out of her garter belt, and light her cigarette as an act of political defiance. "You've come a long way, baby," the slogan for Virginia Slims, fifty years later, forty years later, began there. Women smoking became a symbol of their independence and of the power that goes with the masculinity of smoking. All this was completely engineered into this public event to promote smoking, not feminism.

Bernays is a master manipulator and image controller. I always felt that Greta, who tells Don about the death wish in the pilot which is definitely Freudian, is the descendent of Bernays. *Civilization and its Discontents* is a big part of where the pilot came from. I read it in high school. It's a great thing for a teenager to read. Freud—whatever you think about his medical contributions, he is a great writer whether you're reading about Moses or anything else. He really believes in, as one of his books is titled, "character and culture."

So I felt that Greta, this research person, is the first Jewish presence in the show providing an intellectual underpinning that only an outsider can see. And the agencies will utilize it any way they can. Don's really good about it. Don does his own research. But the clients like to hear substantiation for human behavior and that is a fantasy, right? Well, let's put it this way. You can figure out how people behave, but it does not mean that they'll continue to behave that way. I felt there was a Jewish presence from the outset so I was a little bit disturbed by the fact that I had gone out on a limb to put this accurate but heroic Jewish character in the pilot—Rachel Menken. And no one seemed to notice it, you know?

Who did I see who was Jewish growing up? Woody Allen, who was cowardly and funny as hell and somehow got the girl so there's something to admire and something to not admire. The Jewish women are treated brutally by Woody Allen, brutally. As someone with a professional mother and two older sisters, I was always sensitive to that. You know, Barbra Streisand, *Funny Girl,* that's a big positive image in the movies. *Fiddler on the Roof* was a big positive thing but for the most part on TV, there's nobody. The most Jewish person on TV was Hawkeye Pierce, I guess because he was written by Larry Gelbart and a bunch of other Jews. And when I got into TV, I'm sitting in this writer's room and finding out that *The Fresh Prince of Bel-Air* and *Mr. Cooper* and all these black shows that I'm watching are all written by Jews, not that they're only Jews, but there are a lot of Jews writing "Yo Yo Yo, what's up," you know? Okay, so we're still in this form and it's reverse reverse reverse *Amos 'n Andy* or something, I don't know, but I knew that it was bold to put Rachel Menken in there and I don't think anyone noticed.

So I thought maybe the world has changed, maybe she'll just be accepted as reality, but I am aware that we are an Other and that she's aware of it and there's nothing she says in the pilot that is not true. She's dealing with being treated as a woman, which has got to be an extra part of it. Her father shows up, and says, "It reminds me of the Czarist ministry," and she says, "I don't know what you're talking about." And the big debate about whether he would have an accent and the fact that they weren't German Jews, that they were Russian Jews . . . That's already all new for American entertainment, believe it or not. I wanted them to be Rothman. I wanted them to be the Guggenheims. I wanted them to be, you know, from the German Jewish elite, but it was not the experience that I ended up wanting to reflect. And I love the idea that they had that department store that was like everything else in New York, on the verge of decay, and that she could say to the men in the room, "I want customers like you." Because there is a parallel universe, the world of Jewish advertisers, as Pete says. Pete Campbell, who has the best politics of anyone in the show—I mean, over the life of the show you do realize that, he's on the right side of everything. He is a true liberal. He is not a racist, he's not even a sexist really. He likes Kennedy right away. He's on the moral side of almost all the social issues. He really is. When he hears Harry Crane say something bad about Kennedy after he gets assassinated or when Martin Luther King is assassinated, and granted, Pete is responding to his own family, he's outraged. He's a true Roosevelt liberal. I don't think he wants Jews in his neighborhood, but he does not think they should be lynched.

So the world building was to reflect New York and to throw it into the mainstream American public. Despite the overconfidence of certain people raised in safe environments. If you're raised in Manhattan and you don't celebrate any of the holidays and you're completely assimilated in every way, you're still kind of shocked if someone says, "What does Rosh Hashanah mean to you?" Like everybody in New York knows it's gonna be quiet on Rosh Hashanah. You know? In *The Lost Weekend*, now granted, written by Billy Wilder, Ray Milland can't pawn his typewriter because it's a Jewish holiday. And he goes to the bar and the guy says, "We close on Rosh Hashanah. We close on their holiday, they close on St. Patty's." Right? Everybody in New York knows that. They might not remember until they get there, but they're like, "Oh yeah, it's that thing when they're gonna be closed." So regarding the world building, including Jews in this way is not because I'm Jewish necessarily.

Don Draper has the same problem as Rachel Menken. In fact he has a worse problem because he doesn't even have any money like Rachel does. Right? But maybe his problem's not as bad because he's a man. All of a sudden, you're in the existential reality of humanity and all of the trappings that we have don't matter.

It may just be my own perception having, as they say, grown up in these two worlds. I came out and said I was Jewish by putting that woman in that pilot. That in itself I felt was new. I'm not saying that anyone doubted that Mel Brooks was Jewish, okay. Or Woody Allen. But I came out and said it and declared it as positive. And had some pride about it and tried not to be defensive about it and said, "This is going to help me tell this particular story." And it's for everybody. Because I am, at least in my mind, in both worlds, in all worlds, having sat and listened everywhere. You are Jewish, it's an ethnic thing. Some people think it's a racial thing, whatever you want to assign to it. It's not the thing you run out and yell about it, not my generation. The last time I remember anything of Jewish pride was Israel winning a war which went against the stereotype, the vision of the Jew who is cowardly, avoids military service, has no nationalism, all these other things. So that was one thing that was happening in the early '70s when I was growing up. And the other thing was Mark Spitz, a Jewish sex symbol. These are the things that were sort of in the back of my mind and I didn't really see myself associated with any of that. I'm not, you know, talking about Israel all the time. I'm not a segregationist or any of these things. So for me, growing up in this assimilated world where it's, "Hey, we know what you are but keep your mouth shut. Aren't you lucky you're a preppy." That's what your parents always wanted you to be, that was their idea of social mobility, opportunity. That's the tradition, you know? My father was always talking about, you know, Freud, Marx, Einstein, like that's us! This is something to be proud of. And these scientists.

It's not like there's no one to look up to but I made a decision that I was going to be kind of defiant about that. It's not only not my generation but it was not the manner of the people that had trained me either in college, or in the professional world. Even though, my third or fourth show, I watched Bob Ellison who was Irish Catholic sit down after the table read with the Greenblatt's and we got all the deli going around and I thought, "Oh my god, I am in a Talmudic tradition." Going over this script and punching up these jokes, the profanity and the disrespect for authority and all that. I am in a tradition and it's Jewish. I couldn't believe it. I'm acting like I'm typical in some way but I was raised in a very assimilated environment. My father was Ronald Reagan's doctor. Did not share politics with them. Nancy Reagan always sent them a big Christmas wreath. And I was just thinking: she was in show business all of her life. She really thinks that my mother wants a Christmas wreath? It's just not possible. We were not Christmas tree Jews. But nothing is codified. You know how it is. Everybody who's more Jewish than you is crazy, everybody's who's less Jewish than you is Christian.

Renov: So then, a couple of seasons in, you introduce a character who is the son of a Holocaust survivor.

Weiner: Right, right.

Renov: This is a time when, other than *The Diary of Anne Frank*, a film George Stevens makes in 1959, Americans are not very aware of the Holocaust.

Weiner: *Night*, Elie Wiesel's book had come out.

Renov: Yeah but it's slim pickins at that point.

Weiner: Yeah, but see that's where I get back, just to go full circle, to comedy, our jazz.

I was going to tell about advertising moving into the modern era, or the postmodern era or whatever you want to call it. There were always jokes in advertising. "Who's on First" is a joke on advertising, do you know what I mean? There, all of the linguistic bullshit that goes along with the sales pitch. I don't think it's an exaggeration to say that, in American culture, seventy percent of the humor is a takeoff on advertising in some way. It's a fake ad, it's an authoritative voice, it's a joke about people selling things, it's literally a takeoff on an ad half the time. How many sketches on *Saturday Night Live* are based on advertising? It's in *Mad Magazine* and in the movies. A lot of jokes are about this disconnection between the salesmanship, the perception of that person and the reality. So Jews, Italians, these white minorities, and then black people become part of this story. Eventually black comedians become essential to the message. Bill Cosby is one of the great stars of advertising. Now that story won't be told the same way but that man is the achievement of this whole drive that I'm talking about for midcentury America which is "I am not black, I am not white, I am superstar." And, "You know me. You know me, because I'm telling the truth." And this is the big joke. It looks like this, but it's really like this. We're trying to sell you something. This whole tone, this whole demeanor is Jewish. Or at least Outsider.

So, I was telling the story of ethnic people coming in and crafting that message which became the sales technique for everybody. So, "That's some spicy meatball"... I don't know but I'm fairly sure was written by a Jewish person with an Italian stereotype. Stan Freberg is the beginning of it on some level. *Mad Magazine*, Jerry Lewis. All of this comes into advertising in the mid-sixties and so why wouldn't Ginsberg? Roger says it: everybody's got one. Eventually the creative department's going to be fifty percent Jewish people. Maybe more, even in these super white shoe places. They want that quote unquote "Jewish sense of humor." They don't call it that anymore, they call it counter-culture, they call it anti-authoritarian, they call it sick comedy—Lenny Bruce, Mort Sahl, Woody Allen. Nichols and May. Nichols and May are the perfect example of the assimilated Jewish voice. The mother is talking to the son, it's never said what it is. But it is that voice. And that is advertising. Advertising co-opts that immediately and it's a place for creative people to survive and it goes all over the place in entertainment. So Ginsberg was part of that and a chance for me to say, "Well they're gonna have someone like that in the firm." And so you start thinking, "Well, who is this young hip person?" He could either be someone who just got out of Columbia and is from Westchester or the Bronx. This is not Pete Campbell's generation. It's the next generation. These are not the cardigan sweaters. These are the army fatigue jackets, these are the dope smoking comedians, comedy writers.

I don't think I've ever said this in public before, but I got to tell him before the show ended, so I feel comfortable with it and he approved. Art Spiegelman, you know, *Maus*. I read that before I made the show, during my years after film school before I had a job. And I am fascinated with the transition from that horror into American life. There are all these studies now about genetic traits being passed on, right? That you can actually be changed by inheriting the struggle. And I love the idea that Ginsberg was mentally not well put together because he was born in a camp and had been raised by someone in deep grief and deep denial and that he would have a good sense of humor. It's a cliché but his genius was on the verge of mental illness. He was socially inappropriate because he's basically an animal, right? Raised by a survivor and that those would be his strengths also in his work, you know? And just a chance to remind everybody that, okay, we've got the *Fiddler on the Roof* generation. We have the Russian Revolution generation of Jews and Poles and then we have this chunk of people who came here after the war that we as a country felt collective guilt about, Jewish and non-Jewish. And they found a way into it, and they were definitely represented immediately in entertainment. I picked him because I wanted to remind people, when we're doing the show, once they were on board with the show, what the continuum was like, that the Holocaust was that recent. Very important. The same way I told them when Ida Blankenship died, that she was born in a barn and died in a skyscraper. You had to know that there was someone who was a young, scrappy American citizen working on Madison Avenue in an almost white collar job who could have been born in a concentration camp, survivors, you know? Don's looking at pictures of them, first season, like, "Wow, that's Buchenwald. That's weird that that happened to those people. Sure glad we rescued them. Those poor people, I hope they like it in Israel. Oh, they're coming here?" And then there's Ginsberg. So, that's where that came from. And yeah, he was nuts because that's not a message. That's about a guy who's nuts. And if you don't think that being in that environment could make you crazy . . . I mean, it doesn't make everyone unstable, but he certainly had a good reason to be.

Renov: Yeah, sure, the suicide rate was very high for survivors.

Weiner: And by the way, that's part of *Maus* too with the mother. And Spiegelman, he got it. I don't know if you recognized it but when he saw Ginsberg's father . . . That's another moment where I'm declaring myself, the father's blessing. This is not my romantic attachment to Judaism. Ginsberg and his father—two incredibly secular people with no traditional family. It's been destroyed by a cataclysmic world event. There's nothing like a family there. Ginsberg denies he has a family. He says he's a Martian later. But he denies he has a family and he says no one's gonna care. And he gets home and there's his father who is a dad. And he whips this prayer out at the last minute because it's a habit, it's almost a superstition. It reminds me of kids, like, you know, wiping it off the way that your kids do when you smooch 'em. I love that about it. I love that that was underneath it, that this guy could express his affection with that tradition. And of course there was great debate whenever you bring up anything religious. You're always sorry.

Renov: Did you get feedback? Did you get mail? Did you get phone calls?

Weiner: I didn't get a lot of mail from it. It was much more when we were making it that everybody weighed in on it. "That's not how we do it." "I never heard of that." "I don't think you do that at home, that's done in the temple." There are no two Jews who think that there's the same way to slice bread, you know, and no two Catholics who will . . . Everybody's had a different way that they got communion, even though it is literally dogmatic. So, I just relied on my experts and on personal experience. And you know what? I've seen this growing up, being at a friend's house Friday night. The dad just did this. So why doesn't Ginsberg's father do it? It's not allowed? It's only for rabbis? It's only for the cantor? It's only done in the temple? I don't believe it. When we were doing the *shiva* scene, our assistant editor Michelle Lerner's father, a rabbi, gave us notes. And of course you can research all this stuff and make sure it's right. It is not prescribed anywhere to cover the mirrors. That is not a religious rule. It's a superstition and it probably predates Judaism. So there's shit like that that I want in there, that people say, "I don't think that's right," "They're not bringing cake, they're not bringing cake, not on Friday night. They would bring savory things." I'm like, "Shut up! Shut the fuck up!" Right? And I have a rabbi there when we're doing the *ma'ariv* service for the *shiva* and I know that, at least for him, it's right. And I still have people coming out of the woodwork telling me, "That's not right," "Why was he doing that?" What are you gonna do? That's what I'm talking about living with something that's real. What is it, two Jews, three opinions?

I have to say, also, in defense, my parents had all of this pride. I was bar mitzvahed, my sisters were not bat mitzvahed. I've sort of been hard on this assimilation aspect but there was so much pride. But along with this pride is the threat. And they were raised with that threat, even though neither of them are products of the Holocaust. My father's family is from Poland around the turn of the century and then my mother's family is from the Russian Revolution. But the idea of telling people that you're Jewish is scary. You shouldn't do it. You should keep your head down. Why does everybody need to know that? My children are so comfortable with it and they're so integrated. There's some multiculturalism to it too. They're kind of proud of it. They've got their thing and black people have their thing. We take to them to St. Peter's Basilica and one of them puts his arm around the other and says, "This is their Temple." It's just a different world view. "What are you doing for Christmas?" the supermarket checker asks and they say, "We don't celebrate Christmas." And I'm thinking that my mother right now would just pinch me, "Shut up!" And that was earned. They'd been slapped in the face a lot, believe it or not. Symbolically.

Renov: Back in the '80s I had Barney Rosenzweig come to a TV class that I was teaching at USC.

Weiner: Right, and he did *Cagney & Lacey*?

Renov: *Cagney & Lacey*. And it was at the height of *Cagney & Lacey* and he said to the class that he felt that he was one of the luckiest men alive because he felt like he had his finger on the pulse and could have an impact on the public conversation. Because at the time there were just three networks. What do you think about the power of show runners? What do you think about people like yourself who, for a moment, have the public's attention? You've received as many awards as anyone.

Weiner: That's very nice. But the audience is so fragmented, you're having an impact in a certain world, maybe you're having an impact in the part of the world that can actually change things sometimes. Part of studying advertising was realizing, "Well, why do they have these ads for things like Intel in the middle of the golf game, when you can't buy Intel." And someone explains to you that ad is for six people in the world. There are six men, billionaires, decision makers who might be listening to Texaco Opera or watching the golf game on Sunday afternoon. There are people who are more important than other people in terms of what the world ends up like. This is something we're really coming to accept right now.

Renov: You mean the one per centers?

Weiner: One per cent? It's less than that. Maybe it's always been that way but it's really, really in our face right now. I think the interesting thing is that there aren't that many people who have the job, in entertainment, who actually have something to say.

So even if they hide behind the fact that they're just being entertaining, you know, it's not your job to be political. I don't think Dickens thinks he's shining a light on poverty, believe it or not. He could've become Rousseau if he wanted to. He is telling a story that he thinks his audience will relate to and he's taking it for granted that he's elevating this as a topic. That's the radical move, not "we must abolish the workhouses now that you've read this book."

The social impact I was very interested in, probably secretly, maybe not so secretly, was on a generation that didn't understand the sacrifices made for them, especially feminism. Feminism, when the show went on the air, was a dirty word. We went on the air at the height of the *Girls Gone Wild* thing. Which is like, "I'm a feminist because I fuck anybody I want," and it's still that, by the way. It shows up in *Girls*. I'm not gonna say that it's Lena Dunham's politics, but that's what that character is. Those characters' politics are so confused and their self-esteem gets confused with their sexuality, with their politics and all kinds of things. The beautiful girl is still having the easiest life and I think that may be part of what Lena Dunham's saying. But I would say that feminism was dead and embarrassing and Susan Faludi had written *Backlash*[9] and Barbara Ehrenreich had written her book and I thought, "You're out of your mind. You're out of your mind if you don't think it's better now and you are backsliding. It's getting worse and worse and worse." So that was an agenda that I had. I had an agenda to say, "Do you know what it was like for gay people. Do you know what it was like for Jewish people. It's actually better now." But it's still bad. This shit all went underground. Men's objectification of women has been legislated against completely, but it's there. Because it's biological.

So I think the show runner's job is to entertain people and it'd be great if you had something to say and if it was personal in some way. But I'm gonna cop out a little bit on the politics and say that I believe in the politics of the personal and that Peggy Olsen realizing that she is getting less because she's a woman is a big story. Bobbie Barrett tells her what the advantages are of trying to be a man or of being a woman. Peggy didn't even notice it. She didn't even know. She's trying to do her job. "What do you mean they don't want me? I had the best idea." *That*. When Abe comes and tells her that she's a symbol, she's says "What? No I'm not." "So you work for Goldwater?" "Yeah!" For an advertising person? They'll work anywhere, they don't have a moral center about work. They're getting paid by the people who do the job. But, you know, a lot of right wing people just loved the show. And they don't seem to know my politics, which means I've succeeded.

Also, you know what, I don't really have any politics when it comes to character. I don't judge anything. You know, there's some quote attributed to Elie Wiesel, I don't know if it's true, but he said he couldn't write about Hitler because he would have forgiven him. There is a thing when you get into the head of your character where you're just asking, "What do they want?"

Notes

1. Rachel Menken, played by Maggie Siff, is the daughter of a first-generation Jewish immigrant whose slightly down-market department store is in need of the services of Don Draper's ad agency. Draper is both attracted and disturbed by Rachel Menken's intelligence and forceful personality.
2. "Mad Men" was produced by Lionsgate for AMC, a basic cable network.
3. In the 1940s, Abraham Maslow, an influential psychologist, described a pyramid of basic and growth needs that fuel and motivate human existence.
4. *The Lonely Crowd* (1950) was a landmark sociological study of American character conducted by David Riesman, Nathan Glazer, and Reuel Denney.
5. Hancock Park is a formerly all-white enclave favored by the first wave of Los Angeles business and community leaders in the 1910s and 1920s.
6. An insert shot breaks the continuity of a long take to isolate a detail of the larger scene. In this case, Weiner is referring to a medium close up of Don Draper's hand reaching into his desk drawer to remove one of several perfectly laundered white shirts.
7. Don shows up for a prayer service, a part of the *shiva* ritual, the traditional seven-day period of mourning for family members during which the community offers nurture and support.
8. Faye Miller is a brainy and beautiful research psychologist in whom Don Draper shows interest in an early season.
9. Susan Faludi's *Backlash: The Undeclared War Against American Women* was first published in 1991.

Works Cited

30 Rock. Created by Tina Fey, performances by Tina Fey, Alec Baldwin, and Tracy Morgan. Broadway Video, Little Stranger, and NBC Studios, 2006–13.

The Amos 'n Andy Show. Created by Charles J. Correll and Freeman F. Gosden, performances by Alvin Childress, Spencer Williams and Tim Moore. CBS Television Network, 1951–53.

Cagney & Lacey. Created by Barbara Avedon and Barbara Corday, performances by Tyne Daly, Al Waxman and Martin Kove. CBS, Filmways Pictures, and Orion Television, 1981–88.

Cleopatra. Directed by Joseph L. Mankiewicz, performances by Elizabeth Taylor, Richard Burton, and Rex Harrison. 20th Centry Fox, MCL Films S. A., and Walwa Films, 1963.

The Diary of Anne Frank. Directed by George Stevens, performances by Millie Perkins, Shelley Winters and Joseph Schildkraut. 20th Century Fox Film and George Stevens Productions, 1959.

Dostoevsky, Fyodor. *Crime and Punishment.* Russian Messenger, 1866.

Eliot, T. S. *The Waste Land.* Liveright, 1922.

Faludi, Susan. *Backlash: The Undeclared War against American Women.* Crown, 1991.

Fiddler on the Roof. Directed by Norman Jewison, performances by Topol, Norma Crane, and Leonard Frey. Mirisch Production Company and Cartier Productions, 1971.

Flaubert, Gustave. *Madame Bovary.* Revue de Paris (serial), 1856; Lévy Frères (2 vols.), 1857.

The Fresh Prince of Bel-Air. Created by Andy Borowitz and Susan Borowitz, performances by Will Smith, James Avery, and Alfonso Ribeiro. NBC Productions, Quincy Jones Entertainment and Quincy Jones-David Salzman Entertainment, 1990–96.

Freud, Sigmund. *Civilization and its Discontents.* Internationaler Psychoanalytischer Verlag Wien, 1930.

Friends. Created by David Crane and Marta Kauffman. Warner Bros. Television and Bright/Kauffman/Crane Productions, 1994–2004.

Funny Girl. Directed by William Wyler, performances by Barbra Streisand, Omar Sharif, and Kay Medford. Columbia Pictures and Rastar Productions, 1968.

Girls. Created by Lena Dunham, performances by Lena Hunham, Allison Williams, and Jemima Kirke. HBO, 2012–.

Girls Gone Wild. Directed by Victoria Lea Rudd. Feel Good Films, 2013–.

The Goldbergs. Created by Gertrude Berg. NBC, 1949–56.

Hangin' with Mr. Cooper. Created by Jeff Franklin, performances by Mark Curry, Holly Robinson Peete, and Sandra Quarterman. Bickley-Warren Productions, Jeff Franklin Productions, and Lorimar Television, 1992–97.

Happy Days. Created by Garry Marshall, performances by Ron Howard, Henry Winkler, and Marion Ross. Henderson Productions, Miller-Milkis Productions, and Miller-Milkis-Boyett Productions, 1974–84.

Homer. *The Odyssey.*

Joyce, James. *Ulysses.* Beach, 1922.

The Lost Weekend. Directed by Billy Wilder, performances by Ray Milland, Jane Wyman, and Phillip Terry. Paramount Pictures, 1945.

Lukacs, Georg. "Narrate or Describe." *Writer and Critic and Other Essays.* Merlin, 1978, pp. 110–48.

Mad Men. Created by Matthew Weiner, performances by Jon Hamm, Elisabeth Moss, and Vincent Kartheiser. Lionsgate Television, Weiner Bros., and AMC, 2007–15.

Maslow, Abraham H. "A Theory of Human Motivation." *Psychological Review,* vol. 50, 1943, pp. 370–96.

Riesman, David, Nathan Glazer, and Reuel Denney. *The Lonely Crowd.* Yale Univ., 1950.

Roseanne. Created by Matt Williams, performances by Roseanne Barr, John Goodman, and Laurie Metcalf. Wind Dancer Productions, Carsey-Werner Company, and Paramount Television, 1988–97.

Saturday Night Live. Created by Lorne Michaels. NBC Studios, NBC Universal Television, and Broadway Video, 1975–.

Seinfeld. Created by Larry David and Jerry Seinfeld, performances by Jerry Seinfeld et al. West-Shapiro and Castle Rock Entertainment, 1989–98.

The Simpsons. Created by James L. Brooks, Matt Groening and Sam Simon, performances by Dan Castellaneta, Nancy Cartwright, and Julie Kavner. Gracie Films, 20th Century Fox Television, and Curiosity Company, 1989–.

The Sopranos. Created by David Chase, performances by James Gandolfini, Lorraine Bracco, and Edie Falco. HBO, Brillstein Entertainment Partners, and Park Entertainment, 1999–2007.

Spiegelman, Art. *Maus.* Pantheon, 1991. Serialized in *Raw,* 1980–91.

Stella Dallas. Directed by King Vidor, performances by Barbara Stanwyck, John Boles, and Anne Shirley. Samuel Goldwyn Company, 1937.

The Story of O. Directed by Just Jaeckin, performances by Corinne Cléry, Udo Kier, and Anthony Steel. A. D. Creation, Somerville House, and Terra-Filmkunst, 1975.

Tolstoy, Leo. *Anna Karenina. Russian Messenger,* 1875–77.

———. *Death of Ivan Ilyich.* 1886.

———. *Sevastopol Sketches (Sebastopol Stories).* 1855.

———. *War and Peace. Russian Messenger,* 1865–67.

Wiesel, Elie. *Night.* Central Union of Polish Jews in Argentina, 1956.

About the Contributors

LISA ANSELL is Associate Director of the Casden Institute for the Study of the Jewish Role in American Life at the University of Southern California. She received her BA in French and Near East Studies from UCLA and her MA in Middle East Studies from Harvard University. She was the Chair of the World Language Department of New Community Jewish High School for five years before coming to USC in August, 2007. She currently teaches Hebrew language courses at the Hebrew Union College-Jewish Institute of Religion.

LAWRENCE BARON held the Abraham Nasatir Chair in Modern Jewish History at San Diego State University between 1988 and 2012. He was appointed the Ida King Distinguished Visiting Scholar of Holocaust and Genocide Studies by Stockton University for the fall semester of 2015. He has authored *Projecting the Holocaust into the Present* (Rowman & Littlefield, 2005) and edited *The Modern Jewish Experience in World Cinema* (Brandeis Univ., 2011).

VINCENT BROOK has a PhD in film and television from the University of California, Los Angeles. He teaches at UCLA, California State University, Los Angeles, and Loyola Marymount University. He has authored or edited seven other books dealing with media subjects, many from a Jewish perspective, including *Something Ain't Kosher Here: The Rise of the "Jewish" Sitcom* (Rutgers Univ., 2003), *Driven to Darkness: Jewish Émigré Directors and the Rise of Film Noir* (Rutgers Univ., 2006) and *Woody on Rye: Jewishness in the Films and Plays of Woody Allen* (Brandeis Univ., 2014, co-editor).

SHAINA HAMMERMAN holds a PhD in Jewish History and Culture from the Graduate Theological Union in Berkeley. Her forthcoming book, *Black Hat, Silver Screen: The Hasid in Film*, will be published by Indiana University Press in 2017. Her original research and cultural criticism have appeared in both peer-reviewed journals and popular publications. Her next book project is about American television and the limits of diversity.

DAVID ISAACS has worked as a TV and film writer/producer for over forty years. Along with his writing partner Ken Levine he has written multiple episodes and served as producer or creative consultant for series such as *M*A*S*H**, *Cheers*, *Wings*, *Frasier* and *Becker*, and has been nominated for six Emmys with one win for co-producing the first season of *Cheers*. He is a professor of Screen and TV Writing and Vice Chair of the Writing Division of the USC School of Cinematic Arts.

ROSS MELNICK is an associate professor of film and media studies at University of California, Santa Barbara. His most recent book is *American Showman: Samuel "Roxy" Rothafel and the Birth of the Entertainment Industry* (Columbia Univ., 2012). His work has appeared in *Cinema Journal*; *Film History*; *Historical Journal of Film, Radio and Television*; *The Moving Image*; and other journals and edited collections. He is also the co-founder of the exhibition history website "Cinema Treasures."

JOSHUA LOUIS MOSS is an assistant professor of screenwriting and media studies at California State University, Chico. He holds a PhD and an MA in critical studies from the University of Southern California's School of Cinematic Arts and a BFA in film and television production from New York University's Tisch School of the Arts. His upcoming book *Why Harry Met Sally: Subversive Jewishness, Anglo-Christian Power, and the Rhetoric of Modern Love* will be published by University of Texas Press in early 2017.

MICHAEL RENOV is the Haskell Wexler Endowed Chair in Documentary and Vice Dean for Academic Affairs at the USC School of Cinematic Arts. He is the author of *Hollywood's Wartime Woman: Representation and Ideology* (Umi Research, 1988), and *The Subject of Documentary* (Univ. of Minnesota, 2004), editor of *Theorizing Documentary* (Routledge, 2012), and co-editor of *Resolutions: Contemporary Video Practices* (Univ. of Minnesota, 1995), *Collecting Visible Evidence* (Univ. of Minnesota, 1999), *The SAGE Handbook of Film Studies* (SAGE, 2008) and *Cinema's Alchemist: The Films of Peter Forgacs* (Univ. of Minnesota, 2011). In 1993 Renov co-founded Visible Evidence, a series of international and highly interdisciplinary documentary studies conferences that have, to date, been held on five continents.

HOWARD A. RODMAN wrote the films *Joe Gould's Secret*, *Savage Grace*, *August*, and the novel *Destiny Express*. He is president of the Writers Guild of America West; professor (and former chair) of screenwriting at USC's School of Cinematic Arts; an artistic director of the Sundance Screenwriting Labs; and a member of the National Film Preservation Board. In 2013 he was named a Chevalier de l'Ordre des Arts et des Lettres by the government of France.

JOEL ROSENBERG is Director of the Program in Judaic Studies at Tufts University and a faculty member in the Tufts Program in International Letters and Visual Studies. His publications include *King and Kin: Political Allegory in the Hebrew Bible* (Indiana Univ., 1986), translations of *Kol Haneshamah* (Reconstructionist prayer books), a commentary on Genesis for *The Harper Collins Study Bible*, the essay "Jewish Experience on Film: An American Overview" for the 1996 edition of the *American Jewish Year Book*, and he has recently completed a book titled *The Era of Catastrophe: A Judeo-Cinematic Trajectory—Five Studies in Mass Media and Mass Destruction* (forthcoming).

STEVEN J. ROSS is Professor of History at the University of Southern California, and Myron and Marian Director of the Casden Institute for the Study of the Jewish Role in American Life. He is the author of *Working-Class Hollywood: Silent Film and the Shaping of Class in America* (Princeton: Princeton Univ., 1998), *Movies and American Society* (Oxford: Blackwell, 2002), and *Hollywood Left and Right: How Movie Stars Shaped American Politics* (Oxford: Oxford Univ., 2013), which received a Film Scholars Award from the Academy of Motion Picture Arts and Sciences. The *New York Times Book Review* selected *Hollywood Left and Right* as one of its "Recommended Summer Readings" for 2012. He is currently writing *Hitler in Los Angeles: How Jews and Their Spies Foiled Nazi Plots against Hollywood and America* (for Bloomsbury Press). Ross's Op-Ed pieces have appeared in the *Los Angeles Times, Wall Street Journal, Washington Post, Politico.com*, and the *Huffington Post*.

JEFFREY SHANDLER is Professor and Chair of Jewish Studies at Rutgers University. His books include *While America Watches: Televising the Holocaust* (Oxford Univ., 1999), *Adventures in Yiddishland: Postvernacular Language and Culture* (Univ. of California, 2005), *Jews, God, and Videotape: Religion and Media in America* (New York Univ., 2009), and *Shtetl: A Vernacular Intellectual History* (Rutgers Univ., 2014). Shandler has served as president of the Association for Jewish Studies and is a fellow of the American Academy for Jewish Research.

The USC Casden Institute for the Study of the Jewish Role in American Life

The American Jewish community has played a vital role in shaping the politics, culture, commerce and multiethnic character of Southern California and the American West. Beginning in the mid-nineteenth century, when entrepreneurs like Isaias Hellman, Levi Strauss and Adolph Sutro first ventured out West, American Jews became a major force in the establishment and development of the budding Western territories. Since 1970, the number of Jews in the West has more than tripled. This dramatic demographic shift has made California—specifically, Los Angeles—home to the second largest Jewish population in the United States. Paralleling this shifting pattern of migration, Jewish voices in the West are today among the most prominent anywhere in the United States. Largely migrating from Eastern Europe, the Middle East and the East Coast of the United States, Jews have invigorated the West, where they exert a considerable presence in every sector of the economy—most notably in the media and the arts. With the emergence of Los Angeles as a world capital in entertainment and communications, the Jewish perspective and experience in the region are being amplified further. From artists and activists to scholars and professionals, Jews are significantly influencing the shape of things to come in the West and across the United States. In recognition of these important demographic and societal changes, in 1998 the University of Southern California established a scholarly institute dedicated to studying contemporary Jewish life in America with special emphasis on the western United States. The Casden Institute explores issues related to the interface between the Jewish community and the broader, multifaceted cultures that form the nation—issues of relationship as much as of Jewishness itself. It is also enhancing the educational experience for students at USC and elsewhere by exposing them to the problems—and promise—of life in Los Angeles' ethnically, socially, culturally and economically diverse community. Scholars, students and community leaders examine the ongoing contributions of American Jews in the arts, business, media, literature, education, politics, law and social relations, as well as the relationships between Jewish Americans and other groups, including African Americans,

Latinos, Asian Americans and Arab Americans. The Casden Institute's scholarly orientation and contemporary focus, combined with its location on the West Coast, set it apart from—and makes it an important complement to—the many excellent Jewish Studies programs across the nation that center on Judaism from an historical or religious perspective.

For more information about the USC Casden Institute,
visit www.usc.edu/casdeninstitute, e-mail casden@usc.edu,
or call (213) 740-3405.

www.ingramcontent.com/pod-product-compliance
Lightning Source LLC
Chambersburg PA
CBHW060953230426
43665CB00015B/2177